THE LION OF ROUND TOP

The Life and Military Service of Brigadier General Strong Vincent in the American Civil War

H. G. MYERS

CASEMATE
Philadelphia & Oxford

Published in the United States of America and Great Britain in 2022 by
CASEMATE PUBLISHERS
1950 Lawrence Road, Havertown, PA 19083, USA
and
The Old Music Hall, 106–108 Cowley Road, Oxford OX4 1JE, UK

Hardcover Edition: ISBN 978-1-63624-111-1
Digital Edition: ISBN 978-1-63624-112-8

A CIP record for this book is available from the British Library

Printed and bound in the United States by Integrated Books International

For a complete list of Casemate titles, please contact:

CASEMATE PUBLISHERS (US)
Telephone (610) 853-9131
Fax (610) 853-9146
Email: casemate@casematepublishers.com
www.casematepublishers.com

CASEMATE PUBLISHERS (UK)
Telephone (01865) 241249
Email: casemate-uk@casematepublishers.co.uk
www.casematepublishers.co.uk

Front Cover Image: Strong Vincent provided by the Liljenquist Family Collection of Civil War Photographs at the Library of Congress of the United States.

This book is dedicated to the memories of those gone before who fostered my love of history:

Charles Raymond Struble (1920–2006)
Richard Roy Myers, Jr. (1949–2007)
Richard Roy Myers, Sr. (1922–2010)
Christine Jane (Kibby) Myers (1923–2014)
Mildred Louise (Nehls) Struble (1920–2018)
and to a beloved friend and mentor,
Dr. Mark J. DelMaramo (1959–2017)
who helped inspire me to tackle a book at all.

Contents

List of Illustrations

Foreword

This book is going to be controversial. And that's a good thing.

The past is not a fixed point; it keeps changing. Or, more accurately, what happened remains the same, but our understanding of it—that thing we call history—keeps changing. At least, it should. The book you hold is going to make you reconsider something you were pretty sure was true. And that is where the "good thing" part of it comes in. Consider how many times you have been surprised to learn that something you viewed as fixed and permanent turned out not to be either of those things. That boss you thought was fair turns out not to be. That person you thought was honest turns out to be a fraud. That team you were sure was destined to lose wins it all. No matter how sure you are about something, there is always a chance that you were wrong.

And so it is with history. We think we understand it, but sometimes what we think we know turns out to be wrong. History is written by people, and even with the best of intentions people make mistakes. We assume that we can trust eyewitness accounts, though police officers will tell you that eyewitnesses are notoriously unreliable. In my Research Methods class, I used to give students multiple eyewitness accounts of famous historical events like the Boston Massacre or the battle of the Alamo, and then ask them to explain what happened. They were shocked to discover how often witnesses contradicted one another, or even contradicted themselves when the same witness gave different accounts to different people at different times. Stories change and grow as witnesses change or add things based on what they have heard other people say, or what their memory incorporates into the story. We do not always remember what happened. What we remember *becomes* what happened.

We need to bear in mind that almost everyone wants other people to think well of them. There is always that temptation to make yourself the hero, to emphasize your role even at the expense of someone else, to make your friends look better and your rivals look worse—or perhaps the witness just got it wrong. Maybe there is no malice intended at all, only an honest mistake, nothing more sinister than the desire to appear admirable. And over time you may even come to believe the story yourself. And if you become important—a leading general, a decorated hero, a president, a governor, an important writer—then your story becomes important to you, because it may be the foundation of your fame. And that fame, in turn, enables you to propagate the myth.

However, there are usually other witnesses to these momentous events, and they may disagree with what we have come to believe. If they are not leading generals, however, or decorated heroes, or presidents, or governors, or important writers, then their stories may not get as much attention. They may tell that story over and over at reunions, and meetings, in speeches and in articles, in journals and in newspapers. But these are not "important" people, so their story does not get as much attention. They were witnesses, though, and their stories should matter too. And in this book, they do.

We think we know a lot about the American Civil War. We know who the heroes were, and the villains. We know what happened at significant places on important days. We know this because it is the story we grew up with, the story we have heard over and over. We have seen the history books, although they may in fact be simply repeating the same old stories over and over, with no real attempt to find out if they are true. We have read novels and seen films that reinforce our acceptance of the legend, without questioning what those novels and films are based on. We do not ask whether they are in fact the truth, or simply the same old story told in the same old way. And there is a reluctance to abandon heroes, even if it only means replacing them with new heroes. That is why this book will be controversial.

What happened on July 2, 1863, on a hill we call Little Round Top in a town named Gettysburg is one of the most-repeated stories of the Civil War, a shining moment in the greatest battle in that greatest of

American conflicts. It features intense drama, taut action, suspense, tragedy, triumph, and heroism. In this book, Hans Guthrie Myers will show you that some of what you thought you knew about that day, and that place, is wrong. He will not significantly diminish the luster of heroes, but he will add a new one to the pantheon. Even so, it will change the narrative. Be open to new consideration of what you thought you knew. This is how we learn the truth. This is how history gets written.

Dr. Frank P. Varney

Author of *General Grant and the Rewriting of History: How the Destruction of William S. Rosecrans Influenced Our Understanding of the Civil War* and *General Grant and the Verdict of History: Memoir, Memory, and the Civil War*

Acknowledgements

Writing a book is no mean feat—particularly when that book has been in gestation for nine years. This project began during a visit to Gettysburg in 2013. Growing up in Erie, Pennsylvania, I had always known the name "Strong Vincent." I knew that his character appeared briefly in the 1993 film *Gettysburg,* knew he was the namesake of a local high school, and that a family friend had spoken at the rededication of the 83rd Pennsylvania's monument at Gettysburg as a representative of Strong Vincent High School. But that was where my knowledge ended.

I must thank, along the way, those who have aided me in producing first the short paper, then the longer conference paper, then the undergraduate research capstone, then the master's thesis, and now—finally—this book. And there is no better place to begin the thanks than with the woman whose connection with Strong Vincent and the 83rd Pennsylvania was one of my first touchstones to their story, Dana Massing, who represented her school at the centennial rededication of the monument in Gettysburg in the 1980s.

At the Erie County (PA) Historical Society's Hagen History Center, I must thank former Executive Director George Deutsch, Reference Assistant Pauline Stanton, former Director of Library and Archives Annita Andrick, and her successor, Theresa Gamble. There is no better place to start a passion project than the reading rooms of the local historical society—and the seeds planted by their collection on General Vincent blossomed into this book.

I must also thank Darlene Hunt of the Fort LeBoeuf Historical Society of Waterford, Pennsylvania, for her knowledge of Waterford history and the families of Judge John Vincent, Captain Martin Strong, and Amos Judson, among others.

Additionally, I must thank the library and interpretive staff of Plimoth Plantation, part of the Plimoth Patuxet Museum in Massachusetts, for their assistance in attempting to locate records and papers relating to the Strong family in 17th-century Massachusetts.

My next show of gratitude must be given to David D. Miller III, Associate Curator of Armed Forces History at the Smithsonian Institution's National Museum of American History in Washington, D.C., for bringing to my attention that General Vincent's sword is on display in the museum's exhibit, "The Price of Freedom: Americans at War." The opportunity to stand before the sword—to see a tangible, physical object associated with Vincent—galvanized my determination to do honor to his legacy.

At the Pennsylvania State Archives in Harrisburg, my gratitude is directed to Rich Saylor and to his colleagues for fielding a battery of emails across nearly seven years relating to records of the 83rd Pennsylvania, and to General Vincent in particular.

Additionally, I must thank a trio of phenomenal National Park Service historians, without whose assistance this work would not be possible: John Heiser at the Gettysburg National Military Park Library and Research Center; Robert E. L. Krick at Richmond National Battlefield Park; and John Hennessy at Fredericksburg and Spotsylvania National Military Park.

Turning north to Maine, I must thank Matthew Bishop of the Bangor Museum in Maine for his assistance in locating records relating to Joshua Lawrence Chamberlain and to the 20th Maine in particular. My thanks are also due to Marieke Van Der Steenhoven, the Special Collections and Archives Assistant at Bowdoin College in Brunswick, Maine, who was integral in understanding the dispensation and spread of the vast sums of Chamberlain's personal correspondence.

Heading far to the west, my thanks go out to the Special Collections staff at the California State University Northridge Library for the access and use of the Captain John M. Sell Civil War Collection.

Thanks must also be offered to the late James and Myra Wright of Canfield, Ohio. Mr. and Mrs. Wright were pioneers of research into General Vincent's life and were strong, fierce advocates of his legacy; for being the driving engines behind the creation of the statue honoring General Vincent in Erie, Pennsylvania, and for amassing a collection of records relating to his tragically short life.

I must also thank Robert T. Guerrein, the historiographer and historian of the Cathedral of St. Paul (Episcopal) in Erie, Pennsylvania, which was the Vincent family church following their relocation from Waterford to Erie.

Next, my thanks must be offered to Ted O'Reilly of the Manuscript Department of the Library of the New-York Historical Society in New York City for his efforts to help me locate the papers in their holdings relating to the court martial of Lieutenant Colonel Caspar Trepp and the personal papers of Vincent's division commander, James Barnes.

I also must thank the six individuals who have—in one form or another—been forced to listen to my ramblings about Strong Vincent for the better part of a decade: my mother, Valerie R. Myers; my undergraduate advisor and mentor at Thiel College, Dr. James C. Koshan; the former director of the Langenheim Memorial Library at Thiel College, Allen S. Morrill; and the three members of my thesis committee at the University of Indianapolis, Dr. A. James Fuller, Dr. Lawrence Sondhaus, and Dr. Ted Frantz.

I owe a great deal of thanks to a myriad of proofreaders throughout the history of this project. Whether they read the full manuscript or just a portion of it, I am deeply in their debt. I will list them here in no particular order: Benjamin Snow, Jennifer Lippert, Sean Oros, Sarah McConnell, Colton Amolsch, Christina Huselton, Cole AllSmith, Isabella Bungo, Makenna Sanders, Amanda Dixon-Hendricks, and Kierra Anderson.

I owe an enormous debt of gratitude to Dr. Frank P. Varney, author of the two-volume reexamination of Ulysses S. Grant's memoirs, *General Grant and the Rewriting of History* and *General Grant and the Verdict of History*, whose work inspired my own efforts to correct the historical record regarding Joshua Chamberlain and Strong Vincent, both for his pioneering research and for generously agreeing to write a foreword to this volume.

Last, but certainly not least, I must thank David Farnsworth, Ruth Sheppard, Megan Yates, Hannah McAdams, Felicity Goldsack, Daniel Yesilonis, Helen Boyd, and all the folks at Casemate Publishers who have shepherded me through the process of turning this manuscript into the book you now hold in your hands.

To everyone I have named, and to my friends and family for whom there is, sadly, not space in these pages and without whom I would be nothing, I extend the deepest thanks of all.

Hans G. Myers
Erie, Pennsylvania

A Note on the Text

In the interests of clarity for the reader, in the following pages I use the traditional Roman numeral styles of reference for Federal Army corps (e.g. I Corps, II Corps, etc.) and the plain English for Confederate army corps (First Corps, Second Corps, etc.) so that a simple glance may be enough for the reader to ascertain which side a particular corps belongs to. I have also chosen to employ the name "Federal" as opposed to "Union" to refer to troops of the United States Army for the purposes of delineation between the war aim of the preservation of the Union and the armies of the United States government. For each chapter of this work, I have chosen for an epigraph lyrics from songs contemporaneous to the era and applicable to the subject matter of the various chapters (exempting the introduction and the appendix), in the name of thematic consistency, and to provide readers with a taste of the culture of the nation as directly related to the ongoing Civil War.

In the Army of the Union, if they post us in the van,
We'll clear the way before, if the bravest soldiers can;
We will drive the rebel forces from their strongholds to the sea,
And will live and die together, in the army of the free.

The army of the free, the army of the free,
We will live and die together, in the army of the free.

We may rust beneath inaction, we may sink beneath disease,
The summer sun may scorch us, or the winter's blasts may freeze,
But whatever may befall us, we will let the rebels see,
That unconquered, we shall still remain the army of the free.

We are proud of our Division, 'mid a half a million souls,
And only resting on our arms till the war-cry onward rolls;
When our gallant General Porter calls, why ready we shall be,
To follow him forever, with the army of the free.

Though we live in winter quarters now, we're waiting but the hour,
When Porter's brave Division shall go forth in all its power,
And when on the field of battle, fighting we shall be,
We'll swear that no disgrace shall stain the army of the free.

Then hurrah for our Division, may it soon be called to go,
To strengthen our brave brothers who have marched to meet the foe;
God bless it, for we know right well, wherever it may be,
'Twill try to add new lustre to the army of the free.

Porter's Division Song (The Army of the Free)
Frank H. Norton, c. 1862[1]

Introduction: The Vanishing of Vincent

> "If I can show that the retention by the Union army of this key to the battlefield on July 2, 1863, is due to Strong Vincent and his gallant brigade, aided at the supreme moment by O'Rorke and his regiment, I shall feel that Vincent, O'Rorke, and the men of their commands who gave up their lives in that supreme effort did not die in vain."
>
> FIRST LIEUTENANT OLIVER WILLCOX NORTON,
> 83RD PENNSYLVANIA VOLUNTEER INFANTRY[1]

It is a story everyone knows—or thinks they know. Under the sweltering heat of a summer sun in 1863, amid wave after wave of Confederate troops, the 20th Maine under Colonel Joshua Lawrence Chamberlain stood alone. Astronomically outnumbered, his thin blue line stood among the trees and boulders of the rocky heights of Little Round Top, stubbornly holding its ground "to the last." When the ammunition expired, Chamberlain, in a show of brilliance, ordered his men to fix bayonets and counter-charge. The audacity of the maneuver disoriented the Confederates, who broke and retreated. The genius of Joshua Chamberlain and the grit and determination of the 20th Maine saved the Federal Army of the Potomac on the second day at Gettysburg.

But this story is a modern invention, first introduced to popular culture in a magazine article in 1913 before mutating to become the bedrock of books, documentaries, and films. As Joshua Chamberlain has become synonymous with Gettysburg, the true history of the battle that scorching July day has been obscured. Without a doubt, the men of the 20th Maine fought bravely and redoubtably on the craggy slopes of Little Round Top. And without a doubt, Chamberlain's unorthodox bayonet charge was an act of ingenuity and heroism. But for over a century, far too much attention has been paid to Chamberlain and his regiment. They did not—as some historians have claimed—stand alone on Little Round Top. They did not single-handedly win the battle for the Federal left. And, above all else, they have taken far too much attention away from the other men of their brigade who held the same line, and from the man without whom none of them would have stood to defend the hill.

Nearly 30 years after the guns fell silent in Gettysburg, Pennsylvania, in the fall of 1889, the society column of the *Pittsburgh Dispatch* carried for its readers the revelation that a prominent widow was staying at the Hotel Duquesne on her way home from the battlefield. Her late husband was immortalized in the public consciousness as heroic, gallant, and brave by newspaper articles and columns, which were still fixated on the three-day battle at Gettysburg 26 years earlier, describing it with the zeal and fascination befitting the largest battle ever fought in the Americas. The spot where the man had fallen, mortally wounded, was a highlight of tours led by veteran, historian, and battlefield preservationist John Bachelder for luminaries and dignitaries including President and First Lady Rutherford, and Lucy Hayes. The man was the namesake of a Grand Army of the Republic Post, was the man the first monument on the battlefield outside of the national cemetery had been placed for, and now stood in bronze atop a magnificent granite monument on the slopes of the rocky hill which he had given his life to defend. Yet over 130 years after the *Pittsburgh Dispatch* informed its readers that "Mrs. Strong Vincent" was staying at the Hotel Duquesne, the name of her husband has been nearly lost to history.[2]

Brigadier General Strong Vincent commanded the Third Brigade, First Division, V Army Corps on July 2, 1863, when it climbed the rocky slopes of the hill today known as Little Round Top to prevent the envelopment of the Federal left flank and to protect the integrity of the famous "fishhook" line employed by Major General George Meade throughout the battle. Yet his reputation and his legacy have been diminished, especially over the past century, to benefit his subordinate, then-Colonel Joshua Lawrence Chamberlain. Over the past 50 years, Chamberlain's supremacy has exploded to nigh-unassailable heights: his popularity booming from Michael Shaara's 1974 novel *The Killer*

Angels, Ken Burns's 1990 documentary series *The Civil War*, and Ted Turner and Ronald Maxwell's 1993 film *Gettysburg*. Joshua Lawrence Chamberlain has become the almost uncontested hero of not just Gettysburg, but the American Civil War. His mustachioed stare looks out at us from dozens upon dozens of book covers, scores of heroic paintings, and from products ranging from coffee mugs to beers, throw pillows to pens, notecards to t-shirts.[3]

What caused the subordinate to eclipse the commander? While the easy answer to this question is that Vincent died and Chamberlain lived, there is more to it than that. Though it is relevant to keep in mind that the historical record of Chamberlain's service—particularly at Gettysburg—is worthy of closer scrutiny by the larger historical community, the following is not an examination of Chamberlain's post-war self-promotion, which is discussed at further length in the appendix. Instead, working with the assumption that Joshua Chamberlain does not deserve the full credit for the defense of Little Round Top, the following seeks to answer the question of just who the man was who ordered Chamberlain to hold his ground "at all hazards" on that July afternoon in 1863. While there is a mountain of literature on Chamberlain, including numerous published collections of his letters, uncounted biographies, and published memoirs, there is comparatively little on Strong Vincent.

One relatively recent self-published biography of Vincent has been out of print since its initial run in 1997, and a short pamphlet-form biography was prepared for the dedication of a monument to Vincent in his hometown of Erie, Pennsylvania, during the city's bicentennial. Beyond these two works, no historian has attempted to examine the life of the 26-year-old man who has been relegated to a supporting role in the story of Gettysburg. But often in volumes about the American Civil War, or even more specifically about the battle of Gettysburg, Strong Vincent is simply absent. When he does appear, it is usually only a brief mention in the familiar story of Chamberlain and the 20th Maine. He then vanishes back into the ether that has concealed him from modern eyes.[4]

Who was Strong Vincent? This project began, in some ways, during my visit to Gettysburg in May 2013, just prior to the sesquicentennial of the battle. As I stood on the crest of Little Round Top, I wondered just who the man who ordered Joshua Chamberlain and the 20th Maine to hold the left end of the Federal line really was. The more I researched, the more letters and articles, papers, and reports that I read, the more I realized that Strong Vincent is far more important than a bit player in the life of Joshua Lawrence Chamberlain. This privileged, educated young officer was a prism through which the American Civil War could be viewed with regards to a personal story of duty, patriotism, and sacrifice.

In the following pages, evidence will be presented that, despite his privileged background, Vincent consistently chose to act against his personal best interests in order to support the war aims of the Federal government throughout his service in the American Civil War: something that cannot be said for Joshua Chamberlain.

Following a detailed examination of the sources, it appears to me to be without question that Brigadier General Strong Vincent has been critically discounted and undersold by generations of historians.

Vincent was a more dynamic—and arguably a more important—figure for historians than Joshua Lawrence Chamberlain. He demonstrates the ideals of patriotic service to his nation without the attendant grumbling and self-importance of men such as Chamberlain, who once complained that commanding a brigade without the extra pay and allowances of a general's star was "an 'injustice' that 'quite cancelled the complement' of having been given responsibility for the brigade." Vincent more than anyone else was responsible for the preservation of the Federal left flank at Gettysburg. His military record and service illustrate his devotion to cause and comrades far above and beyond the call of duty: a man who believed wholly and utterly in the cause in which he was engaged; a man who deserves far greater credit than he has received, for the defense of Little Round Top on July 2, 1863. His death on the battlefield should have made him a martyr to his country, with a name as easily recalled as that of John Reynolds or Elmer Ellsworth. Instead, his story has been largely forgotten—even in his own hometown of Erie, Pennsylvania, where his only memorials are a school that has borne his name since 1930, and a statue that is quite literally overshadowed by other monuments on the city's bayfront.

Having been forgotten and neglected for far too long, it is time for Vincent to take his place in the history of the Civil War, and especially its most famous battle.[5]

In the following pages, I have reconstructed the life of Brigadier General Strong Vincent and placed him back into the context of the American Civil War. Using the 83rd Pennsylvania, his regiment, as a proxy where issues of uncertainty regarding Vincent's actions and exploits arise, and pulling back for, at times, broader perspectives on where the war is at certain moments in order to provide context are, I hope, crutches that the reader will allow me.

CHAPTER I

The Strongs and the Vincents: Early Life, Education, and Courtship

"Ho! the car Emancipation
Rides majestic thro' our nation,
Bearing on its train the story,
Liberty! a nation's glory.
Roll it along, thro' the nation,
Freedom's car, Emancipation!"

"Get Off the Track!" A Song for Emancipation,
Jesse Hutchinson, 1844[1]

The name "Strong Vincent" was arrived at by the baby's parents as a means to join together the surnames of their families: two of the most prominent and influential families in northwestern Pennsylvania, with lineage stretching back far into the 17th-century colonial period. It could be argued that Strong Vincent's ancestors were representative of the genesis of the United States, and that the zeal with which he would fight for the twin causes of Union and liberty stemmed from his ancestry, a family heritage of religious tolerance, moral rectitude, the importance of education, and the traditional "Protestant work ethic" that so typified the stereotypical "Yankee" of the early republic. His paternal ancestors, then with the name Van Sant, had come to what is today the United States as French Huguenots fleeing religious persecution following the revocation of the Edict of Nantes in 1685. His matrilineal stock was in the North American colonies before the arrival of the Van Sants in 1685: Elder John Strong arrived in the colony of Plymouth, not yet a part of Massachusetts Bay, in 1635, before settling in the colony of

Connecticut. There, he served as supervisor of East Windsor for some years before retiring to Northampton, Massachusetts, before his death. By the time that Bethuel Boyd Vincent married Sarah Ann Strong on June 24, 1834, their families had both become among the most prominent and prosperous in northwestern Pennsylvania.[2]

Bethuel Boyd Vincent was the son of a respected and admired local judge, John P. Vincent, and earned his fortune in careers as a surveyor, civil engineer, and merchant throughout northwest Pennsylvania. Around the time of his marriage, Bethuel Vincent was a partner in an iron forging firm and machine shop—Vincent, Himrod & Company—and shortly thereafter in a banking house, Vincent, Bailey & Company. When his son was born, Bethuel was serving as the treasurer and clerk of the newly incorporated borough of Waterford, Pennsylvania. Bethuel's bride, Sarah Ann Strong, was renowned for her beauty. Local lore and family tradition holds that the Marquis de La Fayette, on his tour of the United States in 1825, was so moved by her beauty that he dismounted his horse at her father's toll gate and crossed the farmyard in order to kiss her cheek. Her father, Captain Martin Strong, had been among the first settlers of Erie when he arrived and staked out a claim in July 1795. He eventually owned 800 acres, operated a tavern, inn, and toll gate, and financed the construction of the first Presbyterian church in Erie County from his own pocket for $800. With the marriage of Bethuel and Sarah in 1834, two of the most prominent families in Erie County were joined, and the birth of their first son on June 17, 1837, saw them honor their heritage by naming the boy Strong, for his mother's family.[3]

Strong Vincent was born in the house of Judge Vincent, his paternal grandfather, at the corner of First and Cherry Streets in Waterford, just down the street from his parents' home at the corner of First and High Streets. Waterford, the former site of the French Fort de la Rivière au Bœuf (frequently shortened to "Fort Le Boeuf"), where George Washington had once arrived with orders from the governor of the colony of Virginia to request the French leave Virginia's lands,* was the center of Bethuel Vincent's commercial activities at the time of the birth of

* Thus precipitating the French and Indian/Seven Years War.

his first son. The household into which Strong Vincent was born was one that, if not embodying liberal ideals of equality, was closely affiliated with them through Bethuel's business partner, William Himrod. Vincent and Himrod had been friends and business partners for some years, and while Bethuel Vincent's views on slavery are not clearly known beyond his membership in the Republican Party (he acted as a Pennsylvania delegate to its 1860 nominating convention), William Himrod was a vocal and strident abolitionist.

Himrod was a founding member of the first anti-slavery society in Erie County in 1836. He was known locally to be a conductor on the Underground Railroad, arranging for the passage of escaped slaves across Lake Erie and into the Canadian territory that today is the province of Ontario. In 1828 and 1829, Himrod had purchased a wide expanse of land bounded by Sassafras, Cherry and Sixth streets on Erie's west side right up to the bluffs overlooking the city's Presque Isle Bay. Christening the neighborhood "New Jerusalem," Himrod made the lots available to African-Americans, poor whites, and Jews at steeply discounted prices. He founded and endowed the French Street School for Colored Children and The Himrod Mission—the first educational institutions to cater to African-Americans in Erie County—in 1824 and 1839 respectively. One can only speculate the influence played by William Himrod's vocal and quite public abolitionism in the formation of the character of his business partner's son, Strong.[4]

Bethuel Vincent moved his family from Waterford to Erie, Pennsylvania, in April 1843, to be closer to the forge that he operated with Himrod. At this time, the Vincent family had grown to include three children: Strong and his sisters, Blanche and Belle. They all moved into Captain Martin Strong's two-story frame townhouse on the northeast corner of State and Eleventh Streets in Erie, just down the block from the foundry, located on State Street between Eleventh and Twelfth. Vincent, Himrod & Company was among the first forging firms in western Pennsylvania to operate a blast furnace, and the firm quickly established other satellite foundries and operations around the region. Their "Clay Furnace," named for Henry Clay, was the first in western Pennsylvania to be fueled by bituminous coke, and helped to spawn the town of

Hermitage in Mercer County, Pennsylvania. Their Sharpsville Furnace helped establish the town of Sharpsville, also in Mercer County. The Presque Isle Factory and an iron ore mining and processing facility on Presque Isle led to expanded industrial development in Erie itself. Young Strong, shortly after turning six in the summer of 1843, was enrolled at the Erie Academy and began instruction in the typical collegiate preparatory educational curriculum of the mid-nineteenth century: reading, writing, and arithmetic, growing to include the classics, Latin, Greek, and philosophy as he grew older.[5]

Writing many years later, the family's second son, Boyd, would recall his childhood at the house on State and Eleventh Streets, where he was born in 1845, as consisting of "Bible-reading, family prayer, study of Sunday-school lessons, strict Sunday observance, carefully regulated amusements." In spite of the wealth and largesse of the family provided by Vincent, Himrod & Company's success, the children were not allowed to grow indolent or lazy. "Each boy had to take his share, too, of the daily 'chores' about the house, caring for the horses and cows, building fires, carrying coal and ashes and blacking all the shoes every Saturday night." Indeed, Boyd recalled his father's frequent exhortations that there were to be "no lazy boys about me. Don't stand back and wait for the other fellow. Jump in and put your own hand to it."[6]

Bethuel Vincent was a six-foot-tall, 225-pound industrialist with a bald pate, mutton-chop sideburns, and small, gold-rimmed spectacles. His household was not one in which idleness was tolerated in any capacity. Boyd recalled his father's "Old Testament" sternness, but also reflected that "no man ever loved his children more tenderly." By the time the family moved again—to a small brick house on the south side of Ninth Street near Peach Street—the total number of Vincent children had doubled with the birth of Boyd, Rose, and Kate. Belle, sadly, had died at nearly the age of two. Within a year, however, in 1850, the family moved again, this time to a large brick mansion on the northwest corner of Peach and Ninth Streets, where their next door neighbors were the Reeds, the "first family" of Erie. William Reed was the great-grandson of Colonel Seth Reed, Erie's first settler, and his children—still living at home—were Sarah A. Reed and William Ward Reed, the highly noted local philanthropist and the bridge-building railroad engineer respectively. Boyd, writing later in life, would remember an "intimate friendship" between the Vincents and the Reeds.

That same year, Bethuel Vincent was elected Burgess of Erie. He was to be the last man to hold the position before the incorporation of the city and the establishment of the office of mayor.[7]

In 1851, the family welcomed another son, Reed, named for the recently deceased elder William Reed. At about the same time, Strong Vincent, now a strapping boy of 14, proclaimed to his father that he had had enough schooling to get through life, and he required no more. A short biography of Vincent by one of his friends and later classmates, William Swan, provided Bethuel's response to this assertion: "Very well, my son, but nobody can be idle about me. If you leave school, you must go into the foundry." Bethuel Vincent's disdain for idleness and laziness thus sent his firstborn to tend the furnaces. In the brief biographical notice of his son written for his family history, all Bethuel Vincent noted about this period was that Strong "learned trade of iron moulder, '50 to '52." The inconsistency with the year—Strong would have been 13 in 1850—is likely explained simply by Bethuel Vincent, years later, listing the incorrect date in his family history papers. The biography by Swan, Vincent's future friend, classmate, and colleague, assured its readers that Strong, "too proud to yield," obliged his father's demand and performed "almost a man's work" for six months as a foundry employee in his father's firm. At the end of those six months, Strong, who had always possessed a remarkable memory for facts and figures, was sent to work as a clerk in the counting room of the firm ("Clerk in Foundry office, '52 to '54," as Bethuel noted it). By the time he was 17 years old, Strong Vincent was serving as the chief clerk of the accounting office for Vincent, Himrod & Company, and was also working as an overseer on the foundry floor.[8]

At some point prior to the fall of 1854, Strong Vincent again approached his father and proposed that he return to school in an effort to obtain "a scientific education" in order to "become a more successful worker of iron," as Swan phrases it. Strong's younger brother Boyd, writing years later, recalled of their father: "Feeling the lack of liberal education in his own case, no sacrifice on his part was too great in order to give his children the best education the country could offer." The arrangements were quickly handled, and Strong Vincent was enrolled at the scientific school of Trinity College in Hartford, Connecticut, to receive the education he desired.[9]

Roughly six miles to the west of Trinity College's Summit Street campus is the town of Farmington, Connecticut. When Strong Vincent arrived at Trinity College, Miss Porter's School, a private preparatory school for young women located in Farmington, was celebrating its 11th anniversary, and already beginning to attract national attention for the liberal beliefs of its founder regarding female education. Dismissing the acceptable norms of the day, school founder Sarah Porter's curriculum for young ladies included chemistry, astronomy, botany, physiology, Latin, German, arithmetic, history, geography, trigonometry, and other fields in which females in the mid-19th century were absolutely the minority.[10]

Due to a lack of extant personal correspondence, the details of how Strong Vincent met Elizabeth Carter are now lost, but however it happened, their courtship began at this time, while she served as a teacher at Miss Porter's School in the mid-1850s. The young collegian would travel out to Farmington on weekends to take scenic walks through the Connecticut countryside with Elizabeth, or she would travel into Hartford to promenade the streets with him. On one such occasion, in 1856, "a guard or watchman" in Farmington made a comment overheard by the young couple impugning the honor of Elizabeth. According to Roy Stonesifer, "Vincent struck him and knocked him out." One of Vincent's contemporaries at Trinity College, Dr. John McCook, would later tell the story to his son, who would present it at a lecture at Trinity in 1940, quoting his father as stating that Vincent "responded to the affront with the same gallantry and vigor he was later to display in the Civil War," and implying there were multiple blows to the unfortunate guard or watchman. This affair resulted in Strong Vincent being required to leave Trinity College. Whether he was expressly expelled or simply pressured to withdraw, the "escapade at Farmington," as a friend termed it, resulted in Vincent's enrollment at Harvard College in the fall of 1856.[11]

Bethuel Vincent may or may not have had a hand in his son's transfer to Harvard. Recalling Boyd Vincent's comment that "no sacrifice was too great" for his father to ensure the best education possible for his children, however, it seems likely that Bethuel played some role in the transition. Vincent's Harvard classmate—and one of four major sources on his life—William Swan proclaimed that Vincent attracted attention across the Cambridge campus because of his "well-formed and powerful frame" and "striking and handsome" facial features. Swan claimed Vincent "looked many years older than he really was, and … his mind corresponded to his body. One would have said, on hearing him converse, that he was twenty-five years old," as opposed to the 19 he actually was when he arrived at Harvard.[12]

With his classmates recalling most fondly his physicality and conviviality, it should come as no surprise that Vincent was not the strongest academically in his class at Harvard. In the 19th century, grades at Harvard were determined based upon a series of oral examinations—or recitations—to ensure that students were following and completing their lessons. "He was not a hard student," Swan admits. "If the old recitation list were to be consulted, the marks against Vincent's name would hardly predict such a life of credit to himself and his College." When Vincent graduated from Harvard in the spring of 1859, his recitation grades placed him as the 51st of 92 students.[13]

His academic record further revealed a streak of "immoral" behavior; the only area in which Vincent reached the head of his class was in the ranking of demerits. He was privately reprimanded by Harvard faculty no fewer than 14 times for "absence from prayers," or for "smoking in the yard."[14]

By the time Vincent graduated from Harvard in the spring of 1859, he had given up on the idea of a scientific education and set his sights beyond the family ironmongery business. He had decided that "[a] learned profession was more to his taste," and he determined to become a lawyer. Upon graduation, Vincent returned to Erie to read law under the supervision of William S. Lane. Another prominent citizen of the city, Lane had served two terms as president of the City's Common Council (on which Bethuel Vincent had also served), was a member of the board of directors of the Sunbury and Erie Railroad Company (which, in 1861, became the Philadelphia and Erie Railroad) and of

Strong Vincent as a young man, circa 1860, photographed in Erie. (*Courtesy of the Theodore Karle Civil War Collection, Erie County Historical Society/Hagen History Center, Erie, Pennsylvania*)

the Philadelphia and Reading Railroad, and served as the president of the local bar association at the time when Strong Vincent entered his law office. Lane's legal partner, William Galbraith, had just been named Deputy Attorney General of Erie County* by President James Buchanan. Having such a mentor was an auspicious sign for the young graduate's future career, promising important connections and possibilities.[15]

Following the examples of his father, Himrod, and Lane, the young lawyer became involved in the civic life of his hometown. His Harvard classmate, William Swan (who would remain a life-long friend of Vincent

* The position of Deputy Attorney General at the county level is today known as District Attorney.

and his family, and who served alongside Vincent in the Army of the Potomac)* recalled that by 1860, when Vincent was admitted to the Pennsylvania bar, he "was taking an influential part in the public affairs of the city and county, and stood high in the estimation of his fellow-citizens." His civic activities included membership in the new Republican Party in Erie County, where he took "especial interest" in the election of 1860, serving as one of several local speakers who stumped for Abraham Lincoln for president of the United States. When Erie County cast its total of 8,978 votes for president on November 6, 1860, 6,160 of them were for Lincoln, ensuring he carried the county with a healthy 69 percent of votes cast.

On December 12, 1860, a little over a month after the election, Strong Vincent was admitted to the bar, and was almost immediately made a partner of Lane and Galbraith's firm.[16]

Five days later, on December 17, 1860, the secession convention called by the South Carolina state legislature was gaveled into session in the Baptist church of Columbia, South Carolina. Three days after that, on December 20, 1860, members unanimously voted to secede from the United States of America. Strong Vincent's life would soon change dramatically, as would the lives of millions of young men across the nation.[17]

* Brevet Colonel William W. Swan was an officer on the headquarters staff of Major General Romeyn B. Ayres, who commanded the Second Division, V Corps, for most of the war.

CHAPTER 2

Lieutenant Vincent of The Erie Regiment: January to August 1861

"I stray by the brookside alone, Where oft we have wander'd before,
And weep for my lov'd one, my own, My Willie has gone to the war!
Willie has gone to the war, Willie, Willie my lov'd one my own;
Willie has gone to the war, Willie, Willie my lov'd one is gone!"

Willie Has Gone to War, Stephen Collins Foster and George Cooper, 1862[1]

The so-called "Secession Winter" of 1860–61 saw seven states secede from the United States. They organized themselves into the Confederate States of America for the express purposes of protecting the Southern "peculiar institution" of slavery in the wake of the election of Abraham Lincoln. The nascent Confederacy came into being on February 8, 1861. The next day, it elected for its president Jefferson Davis of Mississippi. Four more states would follow them into secession within a few months.[2]

In the early months of 1861, war was in the offing, and Strong Vincent stood ready for it. Upon returning from Harvard in 1859, Vincent had joined the Wayne Guards, the Erie militia company that had organized that year and that was overseen by the sheriff of the county, Captain John W. McLane, a veteran of the Mexican–American War. As events continued apace through February and March 1861, Captain McLane had his militiamen drilling and preparing for the coming conflict.[3]

The war began with the firing on and surrender of Fort Sumter: a 34-hour artillery duel between Confederate shore batteries and the Federal fort beginning on April 12, 1861. On April 15, Abraham Lincoln issued a call for 75,000 volunteers to "suppress said combinations [the Confederacy], and to cause the laws to be duly executed." Just below Lincoln's proclamation in the columns of *The Erie Weekly Gazette* on April 18, 1861, John McLane issued a call to arms, summoning the men of Erie County to rally to their flag and their country. McLane had been commissioned a colonel in the Pennsylvania State Militia by Governor Andrew Curtin, and his call of muster was set for April 21. In response to his summons, 1,200 young men descended upon Erie to enlist in McLane's regiment. Among them were two young men who would, in later years, become two more of the four principal sources for any examination of Strong Vincent's military career. Amos M. Judson, a Yale graduate, lawyer, and editor of the *Waterford Enquirer* was among the enthusiastic volunteers of what became Company E of McLane's regiment; while Oliver Willcox Norton, the son of a Presbyterian minister and himself a schoolmaster in Springfield Township, was among the scrum of enlistees that became

Colonel John W. McLane, commander of the Erie Regiment and of the 83rd Pennsylvania, in uniform as a colonel of the United States Army, circa 1861. (*Courtesy of the Captain John M. Sell Civil War Collection, California State University Northridge Library*)

Company G of the same regiment. Judson would go onto publish the official regimental history in 1865, and Norton spent the last 30 years of his life doggedly defending the reputation of Strong Vincent.[4]

Vincent was named as second lieutenant of Company A by Colonel McLane, serving under company commander Captain Thomas Austin, the owner of a watch and jewelry store in Erie. The regiment set itself up in "Camp Wayne," a vacant lot on Sixth Street at the intersection of what had been known since Erie's founding as Parade Street due to its footing at the bayfront on the site of the 18th-century French Fort De La Presqu' Ile. There, they began to drill and train for war. The men received their "Union Blue" uniforms at Camp Wayne, as within days of its swearing into state service on April 27, the citizens of Erie County raised $17,000 to equip the regiment. Orders from Governor Curtin directed the regiment to Camp Wilkins in Pittsburgh to be sworn into Federal service—but Strong Vincent had one final piece of business to attend to before heading off to war.[5]

Vincent had never ceased his communications with Elizabeth Carter, who still worked as a teacher at Miss Porter's School. Now, in mid-April, 1861, he sent her a telegram informing her of his decision to join the fight—and requesting that they be married as quickly as possible. Elizabeth agreed, and Vincent took leave of the Erie Regiment to rush to Jersey City, New Jersey, where they wed at the Dutch Reformed Church on April 25. The newlyweds, unwilling to be separated quite yet, traveled together to Pittsburgh, where the new Mrs. Vincent resided in a hotel near Camp Wilkins. News of their wedding ran in the May 1, 1861, edition of *The Erie Weekly Gazette*, whose staff reported happily, "Our young friend having previously enlisted, is now 'off to the wars' ... We trust he may safely return to his fair bride after filling the demands of his country upon his services, and thereafter enjoy long continued and uninterrupted domestic felicity."[6]

The "Erie Regiment" departed for Pittsburgh on May 1, 1861, and even the miserable weather could not dampen the men's enthusiasm. Amos Judson would recall that their departure occurred "in the midst of a drenching rain," as "headed by our band, we marched up State street to the depot where we took the cars for Pittsburg amidst the roar of artillery, the waving of handkerchiefs and the tears and prayers of our friends for a safe return." That same day, Colonel McLane presided over the election of officers, which saw Strong Vincent elevated to first lieutenant of Company A. McLane also selected Vincent to serve as the regimental adjutant—perhaps because of his family's good name, perhaps because of his competence in his short tenure as second lieutenant, but no rationale for McLane's decision has survived. It is likely that Vincent's time in the Wayne Guards from 1859 to 1861 had played a role in McLane's thought process: Vincent was very likely to have known to the colonel before his official enlistment.

Regardless, the young lawyer-turned-soldier was already on the rise in the army dedicated to crushing the rebellion by the beginning of May 1861. The new adjutant met the regiment at the depot on the morning of May 2, having arrived in Pittsburgh before them, and joined the columns as the regiment "marched through several of the principal streets, our band playing and our banners flying … the novelty of the scene, together with our picturesque uniforms and the music of our band attracted crowds of lookers-on who followed us in admiration to our place of rendezvous." Settling in at Camp Wilkins, which had been established at the Pittsburgh fairgrounds on Penn Street (now Penn Avenue), the soldiers began to take advantage of day passes to experience the largest city that many of them had ever seen.[7]

The Erie Regiment's stay at Camp Wilkins proved to be short-lived. The impromptu camp on the fairgrounds had been named as the rallying point for all the volunteer regiments being raised in western Pennsylvania, and swiftly became crowded. Colonel McLane had been named commandant of the camp by Governor Curtin, and McLane took Lieutenant Vincent with him on his staff, making Vincent the adjutant of Camp Wilkins in addition to the Erie Regiment. The men at the camp were subjected to 12-hour days of drills, inspections, parades, and learning the ins and outs of military formation. A newspaperman from Erie, visiting Camp Wilkins in late May, proudly proclaimed that, "If any of the boasting Rebels down South imagine that one of their traitor crew can whip three Northern men, they will experience a terrible disappointment when the Erie boys happen along."[8]

In early June, after six weeks at Camp Wilkins, the Erie Regiment was withdrawn to the new Camp Wright on the banks of the Allegheny River, where muskets were finally distributed and where they would continue their training.[9]

To the soldiers growing restless on the banks of the Allegheny, Vincent was not making a particularly good impression. Oliver Norton wrote later in life of his first memory of the Lieutenant:

> My first recollection of him is his appearance as adjutant in forming the line of the regiment for its first dress parade. As I stood, a private in the ranks, and heard his command on the right, "To the rear open order, March!" and saw the line officers step to the front in an irregular line and heard him correct their faults, then saw him march to the center, halt, turn on his heel, face the colonel ... salute with his sword and report, "Sir, the parade is formed," I confess my first impression of him was not favorable. I thought him a dude and an upstart.[10]

To compound the frustration of the soldiers, the regiment received orders to march no fewer than four times during the month of

Private Oliver Willcox Norton in a tintype photograph in the uniform of the "Girard Guards" militia company, circa 1861. (*Courtesy of the Theodore Karle Civil War Collection, Erie County Historical Society/Hagen History Center, Erie, Pennsylvania*)

June—to Washington, Chambersburg, Harrisburg, and Harper's Ferry respectively—yet each time, the orders were almost immediately countermanded. "It began to grow apparent to every one," wrote Judson, "that we were never destined to see any active service." Further increasing the frustration of the men was the stark fact that they had not been paid once—even after two months of enlistment—and had never been sworn into Federal service. The discontentment of the soldiers grew so apparent with "the rare spectacle, so seldom witnessed now-a-days, of a regiment spoiling for a fight," that Colonel McLane saw fit to summon the regiment into the drill square one July morning. The temperature was already in excess of 100-degrees Fahrenheit, but McLane delivered a speech to the men regarding his continued determination to serve the state even if he must "make a free and voluntary gift of his services to her," and then put his regiment through "three hours of the most animated and perspiring drill that we have ever had."[11]

It was not only the men who were growing discontented. Even the energetic and martial Colonel McLane was chafing at being stuck at Pittsburgh. He traveled to the War Department in Washington and demanded that Secretary of War Simon Cameron tell him when his troops would be sworn into Federal service. The Army of Northeastern Virginia, under the command of Major General Irvin McDowell, was gathering at the capital—preparing to march "on to Richmond," as newspaper headlines declared across the nation—and McLane worried that he and his men would miss the opportunity to participate in the crushing of the Rebellion. President Lincoln's May 3 proclamation calling for 42,000 men to serve three-year terms of service had overshadowed the summons of the 90-days men; McLane was informed that his regiment would be federalized if, and only if, the men would, on the spot, sign three-year enlistment papers. Returning to Camp Wright, McLane presented the proposal to his men, but most of them scoffed at the three-year terms of service. The war would, they all knew, be over before the end of the year. Why should they enlist for three? The regiment voted to remain together as one unit to serve its 90-day term of service, and thus foiled Governor Curtin's planned federalization of the regiment.[12]

Amos M. Judson, in the uniform of a lieutenant of the 83rd Pennsylvania in March 1862. (*Courtesy of the Theodore Karle Civil War Collection, Erie County Historical Society/ Hagen History Center, Erie, Pennsylvania*)

With the refusal of the regiment to split into two factions—those who would enlist for three-year terms and those who would not—the unit was released from camp, and returned to Erie on July 20, 1861, where they were welcomed home with a picnic in the city's Central Park.* Colonel McLane made a brief speech informing his men that they were to serve the rest of their terms of service—until August 1—on furlough at their homes. The men indulged the hospitality of the city, enjoying the great picnic prepared for them. Judson later recalled their welcome home in his regimental history. "Although we had seen no active service and had not returned covered with the laurels of war, … the people of Erie received us with all the honors that are usually awarded to the heroes of a hundred battlefields."[13]

---

* Today known as "Perry Square" for Commodore Oliver Hazard Perry, who raised his Lake Erie fleet in the city in 1813 prior to his victory over the British in the battle of Lake Erie.

The very next day, after member of the Erie Regiment picnicked in the park and were turned loose to spend the rest of their enlistments on furlough, the Confederates routed McDowell's Army of Northeastern Virginia at the battle of Bull Run. As the stunned and terrified army straggled back into Washington City under a driving rain on July 22, panic seized the capital that the victorious Confederates were about to fall upon the city. Even President Lincoln was compelled to admit to a congressman that the situation was "damned bad." John McLane received a telegram from the War Department on July 24 naming him a colonel in the United States volunteers and commanding him to raise a new regiment. The war would not pass Erie by after all.[14]

CHAPTER 3

The 83rd Pennsylvania: August 1861 to March 1862

"The army is gath'ring from near and from far,
The trumpet is sounding the call for the war;
McClellan's our leader, he's gallant and strong,
We'll gird on our armor and be marching along!"

MARCHING ALONG: THE POPULAR ARMY SONG AND CHORUS,
WILLIAM B. BRADBURY AND M. A. KIDDER, 1862[1]

"RECRUITS WANTED! U.S. VOLUNTEERS!" The proclamations were plastered across Erie's two newspapers and notice boards across three counties in the last days of July 1861. Colonel McLane's new summons for a regiment of 1,000 men was hindered by recruiting activity in Erie on behalf of the regular army, the U.S. Navy, and the "Perry Artillery," a local company that had been accepted into Federal service as part of the Independent Battery "B" of the Pennsylvania Light Artillery.

As was customary across the nation, McLane promised captaincy to any man who could bring a fully formed company to Erie for service in the regiment. The first to arrive were the "Finney Guards" of Crawford County, led by Captain DeWitt McCoy on August 3. Strong Vincent had re-enlisted on three-year papers almost as soon as McLane's call for volunteers for the new regiment had come off the printing presses. "Surely the right will prevail," he wrote to "Lizzie," as he affectionately called his wife. "If I live, we will rejoice over our country's success. If I fall, remember you have given your husband as a sacrifice to the most righteous cause that ever widowed a woman." Vincent joined McLane in helping to raise men to meet the regiment's enlistment quota and spoke

Strong Vincent in uniform as a lieutenant in the Erie Regiment, sometime between April and August of 1861. (*Courtesy of the Theodore Karle Civil War Collection, Erie County Historical Society/Hagen History Center, Erie, Pennsylvania.*)

at recruiting meetings across the county. Unfortunately, these speeches do not appear to have survived.[2]

The largest and grandest of these recruiting meetings took place in Farrar Hall, a 1,500-seat theater on West Park Place in Erie, where stars such as Edwin Booth and Laura Keene typically graced the stage. On the night of August 24, 1861, the hall was instead dominated by Colonel McLane and leading citizens of Erie County, including Strong Vincent, Deputy Attorney General for Erie County Galbraith, W. S. Lane, and seasonal Erie County resident Dan Rice, the noted circus impresario and clown whose stage persona served as the basis for later depictions of "Uncle Sam."[3]

The regiment began to stream into Camp McLane at the old fair-grounds on Buffalo Road about two miles east of Erie. Some 300 of McLane's recruits were "veterans" of the Erie Regiment of the spring, and these formed a solid center of the new regiment that was already drilled and disciplined. In the tradition of volunteer infantry throughout the history of the United States up to that point, Colonel McLane held elections for the positions of colonel and major of the regiment at Camp McLane in early September 1861. McLane was neatly confirmed as colonel, while the position of lieutenant colonel was left vacant, anticipating an appointment by Governor Curtin. Strong Vincent was elected to be major of the new regiment.

There is very little evidence to suggest why Lieutenant Vincent of Company A, Erie Regiment was selected for this prestigious position. For the veterans from the original formation, it may have been in testament to his competency as the adjutant of Camps Wright and Wilkins, as well as his service as regimental adjutant; for the new arrivals, it is more than likely his surname was the basis of his support. Strong's father was well known and highly regarded throughout the region as an employer and philanthropist; his grandfather, Judge John Vincent, had been a widely respected and admired jurist. Most importantly, for whatever reason the senior officer held, Vincent remained a favorite of Colonel McLane. On September 8, the last of the 10 companies of the regiment arrived at Camp McLane, and, that afternoon, the regiment was sworn into Federal service as the 83rd Regiment of Pennsylvania Volunteer Infantry.[4]

Owing to Vincent's previous experience as regimental and camp adjutant, Colonel McLane sent the major to Washington ahead of the men to arrange their bivouac, and to requisition tents, weapons, uniforms, and the other accoutrements of soldiery. Vincent was to ensure that everything was prepared for the regiment to integrate itself swiftly and easily into the Federal Army, which was becoming a growing presence around Washington City. Its new commander, Major General George B. McClellan, had found little to celebrate when he took command in the aftermath of First Bull Run: "I found no army to command; a mere collection of regiments cowering on the banks of the Potomac, some perfectly raw, others dispirited by their recent defeat." McClellan, who had won fame with a series of minor strategic victories in the mountains of western Virginia in the early months of the war, reorganized the shattered remnants of McDowell's army in the aftermath of Bull Run, creating the

Army of the Potomac. He created a provost marshal's office to enforce military discipline, banned alcohol from military camps, established a satellite network of training camps around Washington for the tsunami of new troops pouring into the capital, and established review boards to review the qualifications of officers. The latter cashiered a total of 310 incompetents unable to pass the boards, a sort of precursor to the civil service reform of the 1880s that, in this case, brought the ideals of a meritocracy to the officer corps.[5]

Despite his successes, McClellan's pomposity and ego—which would make him anathema to many of the Washington politicos—were already beginning to rear their heads. Commenting on his position in the waning days of July 1861, McClellan informed his wife, in an exchange that has now become infamous, that:

> I find myself in a new and strange position here—Presdt, Cabinet, Genl Scott & all deferring to me—by some strange operation of magic I seem to have become *the* power of the land ... I almost think that if I were to win some small success now I could become Dictator or anything else that might please me – but nothing of that kind would please me—*therefore* I won't be Dictator. Admirable self-denial![6]

Major Strong Vincent arrived in the midst of McClellan's frenetic army-building in Washington in mid-September 1861. Entrusted with organizing the regiment's bivouac and supplies, his first stop would have been the War Department, a two-story brick building with large Ionic columns facing Pennsylvania Avenue, directly northwest of the Executive Mansion across from Lafayette Square. From there, he would have been directed to McClellan's headquarters at the home of Captain Charles Wilkes on Jackson Square, where the commanding general "attended to the smallest of details, conferred with generals, and then rode forth to inspect camps and to watch the training each day." Whether Vincent met McClellan on this occasion is uncertain, but what is clear is that this was the first point of connection between "Little Mac" and the 83rd Pennsylvania, a relationship that would engender much fondness for the young general in the hearts of the boys from northwest Pennsylvania. Despite the arrogance that would make him so many enemies in Washington and elsewhere, McClellan was, and would remain, beloved by the soldiers of his army.[7]

On September 19, as darkness was falling over the capital, the 83rd Pennsylvania arrived at the Washington railroad depot. Staggering from their railcars, the men were directed by Vincent into "Soldiers' Rest," a massive hall erected behind the railroad station, which served as a commissary for up to 2,000 newly arrived soldiers at a time. Once the men were fed, Vincent organized them into column-of-fours along with the wagonloads of supplies he had secured, and led them through the darkened streets of Washington City to the site McClellan's staff had selected for the regiment's bivouac: Meridian Hill, which lay on the fringes of the city, but still within the bounds of the District of Columbia. Judson would recall that, "here, beneath the clear rays of a midnight moon, with the great dome of the Capitol looming up grandly in the distance, we spread our tents upon the ground and made our first bivouack." After two days of non-stop rail journey with seldom more than a couple of hours rest at stations, most of the men simply threw their blankets or the cloth of their tents down and went to sleep without bothering to erect a shelter.[8]

On the soldiers' first full day in Washington City—September 20, 1861—the supplies Major Vincent had secured were distributed from their wagons. Uniforms were donned, cartridge boxes and canteens affixed to belts with brass "U.S." buckles, haversacks slung over shoulders, and Harper's Ferry-made muskets with socket bayonets were issued. Colonel McLane also held a second election for regimental officers. One Captain Fleming, the regular army officer that McLane had believed Governor Curtin would assign to the regiment, had never arrived to take the position of lieutenant colonel. In this new election, Major Vincent was, by a vote of the men of the new 83rd Pennsylvania, made lieutenant colonel of the regiment, while Dr. Louis Naghel took Vincent's place as major. Once again, there is no documentary evidence to suggest why the soldiers of the regiment selected Vincent for this position; however, it may be inferred that they noted Vincent's competent performance in organizing their supply chain, bivouac, and other successful preparations for the regiment's arrival in Washington City in just a few days. "We lay at Meridian Hill a week," wrote Judson, "and during that time the men were uniformed and were armed with the old Harper's Ferry muskets.

These were exchanged for the new Springfield muskets a few weeks after." The regiment would remain on Meridian Hill until October 1, keeping up "our regular exercises in company drill." Oliver Norton wrote home to his sister that "My soldiering now is not play, it is work."[9]

The regiment was assigned to the brigade of Brigadier General Daniel Butterfield on October 1, in the division commanded by Brigadier General Fitz John Porter, and moved from Meridian Hill to Arlington Heights, Virginia, and then to Hall's Hill—four miles west—to join its new command.

Private Norton was excited by the location. "As far as I can see in every direction, the white tents of our enemy dot every hilltop. The rebel camps are within two miles of us, their pickets and ours shooting each other every night." The drilling that the men of Butterfield's brigade endured was almost incessant: six days a week for nearly 10 hours a day, everything from company to regimental marching, firing, bayonetting, and forming defensive positions. The month of October went by as the manual of arms was drilled into the men of the brigade, and the men of the regiment found themselves on picket and guard duty with real stakes for the first time. "We are in Secessia and the meanest part of it, too," Norton wrote to friends from Hall's Farm. "We are very severely drilled and are improving fast," he informed them in the same letter, bragging that "I was on [picket] last night, and in four hours I think I challenged over fifty men."[10]

The 83rd's new division commander, Fitz John Porter, was the only Army man in a family of Navy men. His father was Captain John Porter, and his uncle had been Commodore David Porter, the charismatic, if somewhat mercurial, commander of the USS *Essex* during the War of 1812.* General Porter's cousins were also all Navy men: Commodore William D. Porter, Admiral David Dixon Porter, and, by adoption, David Glasgow Farragut. Opting to attend West

* For more on the astonishing and somewhat eccentric career of Commodore David Porter, George C. Daughan's *The Shining Sea: David Porter and the Epic Voyage of the U.S.S.* Essex *during the War of 1812* (New York: Basic Books, 2013) is highly recommended.

Point, young Fitz Porter graduated eighth in the class of 1845. He was breveted first to captain at Molino del Rey and then to major at the battle of Chapultepec during the Mexican–American War, then became an instructor at West Point, served in the Utah War against the Mormons in 1857 and 1858, and aided in the withdrawal of Federal forces from Texas during the Secession Winter. Most importantly, Fitz John Porter was close friends with George B. McClellan, ensuring that, so long as "Little Mac's" star was on the ascent, so too would be that of Fitz John Porter.[11]

Their brigade commander, Daniel Butterfield, had graduated from Union College in Schenectady, New York, at the age of 18. Son of a co-founder of the American Express Company, Butterfield had served as the colonel of the 12th New York State Militia when the unit had been among the first Federal troops to reach Washington City following the surrender of Fort Sumter. By the book, rigid, and serious, Butterfield was a disciplinarian of a brigade commander—and would, in short order, literally write the book on soldiering: *Camp and Outpost Duty for Infantry*. He possessed a fondness for music and would make a hobby throughout the war of authoring bugle calls for his men.[12]

At Hall's Hill, Butterfield's brigade lay in camp in a line. At the right flank lay the 17th New York—the "Westchester Chasseurs," as they were dubbed, due to the regiment's high proportion of well-heeled Westchester County sons of New York gentry. Led by Colonel Henry S. Lansing, the 17th New York, like Butterfield's 12th New York, had been raised on two-year papers as opposed to the traditional three-year papers of most regiments of the army. In its line of camp, the 83rd Pennsylvania came next, then the 12th New York, and on the left stood the 16th Michigan. "Stockton's Independent Regiment," as the group of men from Michigan had first been known, began its life in Detroit, unaffiliated with the state recruitment scheme due to an ongoing feud between its colonel, Thomas Baylis Whitmarsh Stockton, and Michigan Governor Austin Blair. Fifty-six years old in 1861, gruff, grizzled, and proud, Stockton was the uncle, by marriage, of Confederate General James Longstreet, and had served, off and on, for three decades with the regular army by the time the Civil War erupted.[13]

At the end of October, General McClellan reviewed Porter's division, and the 83rd Pennsylvania occupied the right of line, the traditional place of honor in a military review. "Our regiment was very highly complimented by the General, as one of the best, if not the best, on the field," Norton wrote enthusiastically to a friend at home. Amos Judson, standing near McLane in the line, recorded the interaction: "Gen. McClellan, on passing along the lines with his staff, rode up to Col. McLane and said, 'Colonel, I congratulate you on having one of the very best regiments in the army!'" Two days later, on October 28, 1861, the last regiment of Butterfield's brigade arrived in camp after nightfall, emerging out of the Virginia darkness. "Among the invisible things were where we were going to get supper, where we were going to sleep, and what covered the expanse of darkness beyond," wrote the new arrivals' regimental historian—and the fourth of the major sources on Vincent's military career—Eugene Arus Nash.[14]

It was the 44th New York Regiment, dubbed "Ellsworth's Avengers" by the Empire State in tribute to Colonel Elmer Ellsworth, a New Yorker who had been killed on May 24, 1861, while removing a massive Confederate banner from the Marshall House Inn of Alexandria, Virginia. Every town and ward across New York State had been encouraged to submit men to the regiment: all to be no shorter than five foot, eight inches, of good physical build, and strong moral character. Led by Colonel Stephen W. Stryker, the 1,000 men of Ellsworth's Avengers represented all of New York State, not simply Buffalo, Albany, or New York City alone (though those three municipalities had contributed more men than were necessary for the creation of the regiment). The regiment had arrived at Hall's Hill practically fresh off the train that had borne them to Washington, with no campsite, no established mess system, and no idea of what to do upon arrival to the brigade.[15]

Luckily for Ellsworth's Avengers, the 83rd Pennsylvania was there to help. Calling the regiment "[a] good Samaritan, numerous, generous, and hospitable," Nash wrote that on the first night, the Pennsylvanians "not only furnished the supper, but pitched our tents ready for sleeping." The two regiments were swiftly joined in friendship that night as "the field and staff officers of the 83d Pa. entertained the field and staff officers of the Forty-Fourth N.Y., and the several companies of the 83d Pa. entertained the corresponding companies of the Forty-Fourth N.Y." It was, Nash notes, "the beginning of an abiding friendship between the two regiments."[16]

Ever after, the men of the 83rd Pennsylvania and the 44th New York would be as close as it was possible to be. The two regiments would follow one after another in the line of march, fight side-by-side on every battlefield, and bivouac beside one another for the duration of the war. So inseparable were they that the pair of regiments began to be wryly referred to as "The Butterfield Twins," or "Butterfield's Twins," by other members of the Army of the Potomac.[17]

Yet there was still playful competition between the two regiments. One veteran recalled that "[a] generous rivalry sprang up, each regiment striving to outdo the other in drill, discipline, and all the manifold duties of a soldier's life. Although under different officers, the two organizations were like one great regiment." This camaraderie in the early days at Hall's Hill in the fall of 1861 no doubt led to Vincent becoming friendly with his counterpart in the 44th New York, Lieutenant Colonel James Clay Rice, a lawyer from New York City. Rice was already a combat veteran by the time he arrived at Hall's Hill: he had originally been a lieutenant in the 39th New York and had fought at the first battle of Bull Run before being commissioned as lieutenant colonel of the 44th New York. He was a Yale graduate, and had spent the antebellum years before entering the bar as a teacher and newspaperman in Mississippi. The 32-year-old Rice and 24-year-old Vincent often took their meals together at one or another's tent, and wiled away their hours of rest holding forth on politics, law, and the progress of the war.[18]

On the same day that the 44th New York would arrive in camp, the 83rd Pennsylvania buried its first member to die in the war. Writing home to his parents in Erie, First Lieutenant John M. Sell—who had previously been a bookseller in Erie—reported that, "We buried our first soldier yesterday, a Mr. Carr of the Tionesta Rangers, his disease was 'bloody flux,' the result of the disentery [sic]. The funeral caused many solemn faces, probably they were thinking they too might be as many miles from friends and home!" Lieutenant Sell's words were more prescient than he knew; J. H. Kerr was simply the first of many losses the 83rd Pennsylvania would suffer through the next years.[19]

Vincent was adjusting well to military life. He convened an "officer's school" to train the line officers of the regiment, and according to the recollection of Private Norton, he apparently made quite a successful schoolmaster. "What he did not know about tactics and army regulations he learned, and forced the junior officers to learn and practice." Vincent also cut quite a figure when the regiment was on parade: "Vincent was of medium stature, but well formed. He was a fine horseman, and when mounted looked much larger than when on foot." With his chestnut-brown mutton-chops and intense blue eyes, Lieutenant Colonel Vincent was certainly a striking young man in uniform. But he not only looked the part; he played his role as an officer quite well, winning praise for his competent work.[20]

In November, rain was a constant companion of the troops. During one downpour, Porter's division—now consisting of 11,000 men—was paraded before not only McClellan and his staff but also President Lincoln, Secretary of State William H. Seward, and Secretary of War Simon Cameron, as part of a drill competition held by the commanding general. The nearly 70,000-strong Army of the Potomac marched together for the first time that rainy November day on the muddy streets, and put on "an imposing ceremony" that "afforded an opportunity to observe the magnitude of a large army when marshalled in one body." One soldier of the 83rd Pennsylvania wrote home to the *Crawford Journal* of Meadville, Pennsylvania, with an account of the exercise: "It rained during the entire review, yet we went through it all as soldiers only know how to do and came to our quarters at night covered with mud and feeling somewhat damp." Private Norton, ever the faithful correspondent, discussed the review in a letter home, crowing on their triumph, "Our regiment has earned the reputation of being the best in General Porter's division ... Last Friday the trial came off. The weather was rainy and every way unfavorable ... General McClellan said he was highly gratified with the discipline of the troops. He never saw better movements in his life."[21]

Brigadier General Butterfield, no doubt also highly gratified, issued a commendatory order to his brigade. "The General commanding feels called upon to congratulate and commend the Eighty-Third for the very general spirit of attention to duty that seems to pervade the regiment. Their attention to drill is especially recommended as a worthy example to the rest of the brigade." Their performance so impressed McClellan that he authorized Porter to reclassify the 83rd as a Zouave regiment—a high compliment from the "Young Napoleon." Specializing in light infantry tactics, including open-order formations, prone firing positions, and rapid movement, Zouave units were particularly famous for their bright, garishly colored uniforms (the 83rd Pennsylvania's included shades of orange and green with Union Blue) and fez caps. When it came to romantic notions of war in the 19th century, the Zouave was eclipsed perhaps only by the cavalier. The men of the 83rd were soon besieged in their camp by French tailors and clerks taking measurements and filling out forms to order, direct from Paris, 1,000 uniforms of the *Chasseur de Vincennes* for the men of the 83rd, along with accompanying French-style tents, picks, hatchets, shovels, mallets, nightcaps, blankets, knapsacks, bugles, brushes, and much more. The new uniforms were delivered in early December, and rapidly proved their impracticability to Colonel McLane. The jackets were too tight, causing the men to overheat; the baggy trousers snarled in the underbrush on picket duty; and the feathered shakos were an absurd nuisance. Colonel McLane swiftly ordered that the Zouave uniforms were to go into storage, and no part of them was to be worn without his express approval.[22]

Lieutenant Colonel Vincent, in an effort to combat drunkenness in camp, cracked down on the regimental sutler in late November, ordering him to close up shop by 5pm. While this fostered a little discontent among the men, it did nothing to lessen Vincent's reputation among his fellow officers. Vincent caught the eye of Brigadier General Butterfield, who named him brigade inspector, giving him charge of both camp and parade inspections of the brigade. This position carried with it the implication that Vincent was fluently conversant with army rules and regulation both on the parade ground and in camp, thus showing that the young lawyer had acclimated to his life as a soldier—that his "officer school" had paid off. He would be engaged in the work of inspector for most of their stay in winter quarters at Camp Leslie (the name given to the encampment at Hall's Hill), work that would be alleviated by the arrival in camp of his wife, Elizabeth, for a few weeks from mid-December to mid-January.[23]

The men of the 83rd Pennsylvania and 44th New York collaborated to decorate their camps for the approaching holidays. The roads among the tents were turnpiked, and companies tramped up and down every one of them to smooth them down. The men laid sidewalks along their new roads, built sprawling arches of evergreens over the main entrances to every one of their "streets," and pine and cedar trees filled the company quarters and mess tents. The headquarters were "tastefully decorated" with evergreen arches and gates, and the camp was illuminated at night. Judson quotes a Washington newspaper's breathless praise of the sight, "The camp presented an appearance the most unique and fascinating imaginable, giving the effect at a little distance, of a fairy glen, rather than the stern and almost forbidding aspect of an ordinary military encampment." Paper lanterns of red, white, and blue cast colorful shadows as metal stars hung from the branches of the decorative pines and cedars and evergreen arches to catch and reflect the patriotic lights.[24]

The most breathtaking sight, however, was the regimental headquarters of the 83rd, where the men had erected "a huge tent, T shaped—one wing a dancing hall, floored and carpeted with canvass [sic]; the other with a table set and loaded with delicacies." This unconventional headquarters was "profusely decorated with branches and sprigs of cedar. Chandeliers of bayonets, forming sockets for as many candles, each circle apparently hoops of different sizes captured from some lady's dress and handsomely wound with tissue paper, were unapproachable in their effect." At the head of the dance floor potion of the tent, the flags of the brigade's regiments were displayed.[25]

With the band of the 44th New York set up in a corner of the headquarters ballroom, the two regiments hosted a New Year's Festival. The affair—which was the source of the coverage by a Washington newspaper—was a gala ball with guests of honor including senators and members of Congress for each state represented in the brigade, Secretary of State Seward—who had a nephew who was a private in the 44th New York—and his wife, and Major General George B. McClellan and his wife, Ellen. McClellan gave a brief speech in which he toasted their hosts, the men of the 83rd and 44th, as "being the equal of any regular in the army."[26]

Present that evening with her husband was Elizabeth Vincent. Since the dissolution of the Erie Regiment in July, Elizabeth had moved in with Strong's family at their mansion at Ninth and Peach Streets in Erie, and now she had the company of her husband in winter quarters for a New Year's Festival that Amos Judson likened to a scene from Spenser's *Faerie Queen*. Elizabeth's close friend and former employer, Sarah Porter, wrote to a mutual friend after receiving a glowing letter from Elizabeth, "I am most thankful that she had those weeks in the camp. They were comparatively quiet, and she thoroughly enjoyed them."[27]

There was little to be done throughout the winter, as ice and snow cancelled drill and made battle impossible. "The only comfort the soldiers could find," wrote Judson, "was in hugging the firesides within their tents, smoking their pipes, and playing at their favorite games of euchre, cribbage, and old sledge." To his sister, Oliver Norton commented on their daily routine. "In the daytime we sit round the tents, reading, telling stories, grumbling about the rations, discussing the prospects of marching, cursing the English about the Mason and Slidell affair,* expressing a willingness to devote our lives to humbling that proud nation, and talking of this, that and the other." For some of the time, at least, Elizabeth remained in Virginia to keep her husband company. It would not be until March that Major General McClellan would begin activating plans to move the army towards Richmond.[28]

During the long layup in winter quarters, Oliver Norton was made the regimental bugler for the 83rd, even as discontentment was swelling from the continued inaction of the army. Fights broke out among the ranks, and swiftly thereafter came sickness: of the 161,524 soldiers of the Army of the Potomac, 18,177 were on the sick list in February 1862, 76 of them from the 83rd Pennsylvania, which led

* In November, 1861, the USS *San Jacinto* had intercepted the RMS *Trent*, a British Royal Mail vessel, and had forcibly removed from it two Confederate diplomats, James Murray Mason and John Slidell. The situation caused widespread outrage in Britain, and brought the United States and Great Britain perilously close to war until President Lincoln ordered Mason and Slidell released on December 26.

Butterfield's brigade in its number of men "absent, hospital." By the end of the month, four soldiers had died of illnesses contracted in camp, and eight more were discharged due to disease. Irritability flared among the ranks, particularly when news arrived in mid-February that Brigadier General Ulysses S. Grant had seized Forts Henry and Donelson on the Tennessee and Cumberland Rivers in Tennessee during a winter campaign.[29]

It was not only in the ranks of the Army of the Potomac that discontentment at its inaction simmered; the honeymoon between Lincoln and McClellan had come to an end. "If General McClellan does not want to use the army, I should like to borrow it for a while," Lincoln flatly informed Brigadier Generals Irvin McDowell and William Franklin in a meeting that winter. At another point, Lincoln despaired to Quartermaster General Montgomery C. Meigs that McClellan's illness and hesitation were the tip of an iceberg of innumerable problems, proclaiming that, "the bottom is out of the tub." McClellan did not harbor a much more favorable view of the president. "I can't tell you how disgusted I am becoming with these wretched politicians," McClellan had raged in a letter to his wife from October. He proceeded to condemn Lincoln as "nothing more than a well meaning baboon." One from November was even less charitable: "I went to the White House shortly after tea where I found 'the original gorilla,' about as intelligent as ever. What a specimen to be at the head of our affairs now!"[30]

To further disrupt the calculus of the movement of the Army of the Potomac, Lincoln's Secretary of War, Simon Cameron—noted for his famously flagrant corruption, to the extent that he was famously panned by radical Republican Congressman Thaddeus Stevens with the colorful opprobrium that he would steal anything, but that Stevens, upon reflection, "[did] not think he would steal a red hot stove,"—resigned in January, and was replaced by the temperamental Ohio-born lawyer Edwin M. Stanton, who had been a close friend of McClellan's for months and who shared his contempt for Lincoln. Yet Lincoln and Stanton swiftly became friendly, and McClellan was left out in the cold by his one-time confidant. Fed up with McClellan's recalcitrance to even discuss a plan, Lincoln issued General War Order No. 1 on January 27, 1862:

> *Ordered*, That the 22d day of February, 1862, be the day for a general movement of the land and naval forces of the United States against the insurgent forces; that especially the army at and about Fortress Monroe. the Army of the Potomac, the Army of Western Virginia, the army near Munfordville, Ky., the army and flotilla at Cairo, and a naval force in the Gulf of Mexico be ready to move on that day.[31]

Tensions came to a head at a meeting in the morning of March 7, 1862, at the Executive Mansion, where Lincoln was briefed by McClellan on his grand plan to carry the Army of the Potomac to land at Urbanna on the James Peninsula and strike at Richmond overland, avoiding entirely the need to assault Joseph E. Johnston's Confederate Army at Manassas Junction. Only McClellan left a record of the private meeting; the egotistical general wrote that Lincoln raised the prospect of Washington being left nearly defenseless by McClellan's plan to leave behind only a token force to defend the capital. Lincoln further enraged McClellan by stating that he had heard from some who alleged the plan had "the traitorous intention ofleaving Washington unprotected." McClellan swore to present the plan to a council of his generals for approval, remove himself from the room, and instruct them to bring their commentary on the plan to Lincoln. The president would be given the endorsement of the plan by the general officers of the Army of the Potomac that afternoon. Lincoln grudgingly gave his assent, though he ordered the army must be in motion by March 18 and that the army be formed into four corps. In the ensuing reorganization, Butterfield's Brigade became the Third Brigade of the First Division, III Corps, under Brigadier General Samuel P. Heintzelman.[32]

In their camp at Hall's Hill, Lieutenant Colonel Strong Vincent and Captain Hugh S. Campbell of the 83rd Pennsylvania, intrigued by a sutler's proclamation that he was selling bullet-proof vests of "a very tough kind of steel" which "weigh[ed] four pounds," strapped one of the vests to a sack of straw and took turns shooting it. The steel vests "turned the balls efectnaly [sic]," according to Private John Rice of Company E, 83rd Pennsylvania, who described the incident in a letter home to his family. Rice did not, however, think he would be purchasing one of the vests: "They only cost $5.50 … I quess [sic] they are a pretty good thing but I dont [sic] think they will stand a 64 pounder." Rice would be killed four months later on July 1, 1862, during the battle of Malvern Hill.[33]

Shortly before embarking upon his plan to assault Richmond, reports reached McClellan that Johnston's Confederate Army was withdrawing from Manassas and Centerville. "The retirement of the enemy towards Richmond had been expected as the natural consequence of the movement to the Peninsula," McClellan later wrote, "but their adoption of this course … was unfortunate in that the then almost impassable roads between our positions and theirs deprived us of the opportunity for inflicting damage usually afforded by the withdrawal of a large army in the face of a powerful adversary." In the ranks, movement of any sort led to enthusiasm. "The 'grand army' has at last moved," crowed Oliver Norton in a letter to his cousin. The "McClellan anaconda," as Amos Judson put it, "began to uncoil [itself] and move slowly along in the direction of Manassas."[34]

The 83rd marched in anticipation of battle, yet found only abandoned works of comically weak strength at Manassas. Regardless, Judson wrote, "to us it was a victory, and it had been gained without a blow." McClellan would write of "naturally very strong" defenses at Manassas and Centreville, proclaiming "that an assault of the enemy's positions in front of Washington, with the new troops composing the Army of the Potomac, during the winter of 1861–2, would have resulted in defeat and demoralization was too probable." Most contemporaries did not judge Johnston's defenses so kindly as did McClellan, with the *New York Tribune* concluding that "the fortifications are a damnable humbug and McClellan has been completely fooled." Withdrawing back to Washington, McClellan doubled down upon his planned route to victory: transporting his massive army downriver and through Chesapeake Bay to land on the Virginia Peninsula between the James and York Rivers, making a drive for Richmond from the south and east.[35]

On the morning of March 22, 1862, the men of Butterfield's brigade boarded their transports to be ferried down the Potomac. The "grand army" was truly on the move.

CHAPTER 4

The Swamps of the Chickahominy: Late March to September 1862

"Then McClellan followed soon, both with spade and balloon,
To try the Peninsular approaches,
But one and all agreed that his best rate of speed
Was no faster than the slowest of 'slow coaches.'
Instead of easy ground, at Williamsburg, he found,
A Longstreet indeed, and nothing shorter,
And it put him in the dumps, that spades wasn't trumps,
And the Hills he couldn't level 'as he orter.'"

Richmond is a Hard Road, John Reuben Thompson, 1863[1]

George McClellan's Peninsula Campaign should have been an easy victory. His "more than 100,000 men, nearly 15,000 horses and mules, 1,224 wagons and ambulances, 44 artillery batteries, and enormous stockpiles of equipment, pontoons, ammunition, forage, and foodstuffs" dwarfed the Confederate opposition between his army and Richmond, a token force of 11,500 men manning the Warwick River line under Major General John Bankhead Magruder. Prior to moving in force on Richmond, McClellan needed to sweep aside both Magruder's main body in the Warwick River line and the rebel forward position at Big Bethel.[2]

While voyaging down the Potomac River to Old Point Comfort and the beginnings of the Peninsula Campaign, the men of the 83rd Pennsylvania passed beneath Mount Vernon, the plantation of George Washington, perched on the bluffs overlooking the river. "In passing Mt. Vernon the bells tolled and all eyes were turned toward the last resting place of the Father of our Country. Many reflections were awakened in viewing this time honored spot." Butterfield's brigade traveled down the Potomac on March 22, arriving off Fortress Monroe on March 23 and disembarking their transports on March 24. As the brigade entered camp along the Yorktown Road, some of them thought back to Mount Vernon a few days before: "[Washington's] native State of Virginia, the mother of Presidents, was in revolt against the flag he first unfurled to the breeze and against the government that his valor and statesmanship helped to establish."[3]

The Virginia Peninsula itself threatened to derail McClellan's plans almost immediately. McClellan's plan had been created in Washington without proper reconnaissance of the ground he intended to march across. Historian Chester Hearn notes: "Nothing on the lower Peninsula resembled the open, pristine, and well-drained road to Richmond as stated by McClellan. To most observers the roads were the worst they had ever seen, especially after a rainfall." Rather than encountering a macadamized road to Richmond, McClellan and his troops found themselves mired in the swamps, briars, brakes, and fens of Virginia. The 83rd Pennsylvania's camp on the Yorktown Road was in a swamp. Amos Judson wrote of the experience, "while there we had the pleasure of being drowned out, once or twice, by heavy showers of rain."[4]

An earlier effort to force the Peninsular approach to Richmond in June 1861 had led to a Confederate victory in the battle of Big Bethel, in which Magruder repulsed Major General Benjamin F. Butler's forces. The rebel position was strong. Earthworks dominated the road, and rumor had a force of 2,000 Confederates manning the fortifications. Porter's division was given orders to advance on Big Bethel, Virginia, on March 27, 1862, as a reconnaissance in force. The 83rd Pennsylvania led the division in the line of march, throwing out skirmishers and flankers as it marched the "perfectly level and sandy" road to Big Bethel from Hampton, and prepared for battle. At about noon on March 30, the 83rd Pennsylvania reached the edge of the swamp at the fringes of the Big Bethel defenses.[5]

Writing to his sister, Oliver Norton described the Confederates' defensive positions at Big Bethel. "There are a line of earthworks in the edge of a pine woods. In front of these is a large level field or two or three hundred acres, and in front of the field an extensive swamp full of wet holes, thickets, briars, and vines. The road leads through the middle of this swamp to the field."[6]

Colonel McLane rode the length of his regiment, ordering his men to stick to their colors and form into line of battle. Commanded down into the swamp on the left of the road, the regiment advanced. "We had just entered [the swamp] and were forcing our way through when we heard the crack of rifles in the woods ahead," Norton wrote in his account of the reconnaissance at Big Bethel. "Into the woods we went, pell mell, on a double quick, o'er brush, o'er brier, o'er bog, o'er brake," wrote Amos Judson. "All was now bustle and excitement in the Eighty-Third." Norton, with perhaps a note of humor, wrote to his sister that, "you ought to have seen us go through those thickets then. Pell-mell we went, over bogs and through vines and places I never would have thought a man could get through under ordinary circumstances." The regiment crashed out of the swamp and to the edge of the field in front of the Confederate entrenchments, where Colonel McLane and Lieutenant Colonel Vincent—having left their horses back with the artillery—"hurried to and fro, with revolvers in their hands" guiding the men back into line of battle in preparation for the assault. The regiment paused for only a moment. "With sabres drawn and bayonets fixed, with our hearts in our throats and with the King of Terrors staring us in the face, we commended ourselves to the God of Battles and rushed forward." Color Sergeant James C. McKinley shoved the foot of the flagstaff into the rampart as the men of Pennsylvania went over the top of the Confederate entrenchments, and found them empty.[7]

The burst of rifle fire that the men of the 83rd had heard as they struggled through the swamp were the only shots fired for Big Bethel: potshots fired by the squad of Confederate cavalry that had been at the earthworks to see when Federal forces would appear, and that had swiftly withdrawn back to Yorktown. It had been a bloodless conquest—except for the scratches the soldiers had received scrambling through thornbushes and brambles.[8]

Major General McClellan arrived at Fortress Monroe on April 2. The Army of the Potomac's general advance towards the Warwick River line began on April 4, 1862, with "Porter's Division, with Averell's cavalry" at the head of the great marching army's right column, aimed squarely at Yorktown. Confederate deserters had reached McClellan's lines, and the news that Magruder could field no more than 8,000 men to resist the Army of the Potomac's currently deployed 66,700 greatly buoyed McClellan's expectations. "Everything has worked well today," the commanding general cheered to his wife. On April 5, the advanced pickets of the right wing of McClellan's Army of the Potomac reached Yorktown.[9]

Confederate Major General John Bankhead Magruder had always possessed a flair for the dramatic. Famously fond of amateur theatricals, Magruder mounted perhaps the greatest in American history before Yorktown in the spring of 1862. Marching some of his men in an almost endless circle from Yorktown to the James River and back again behind the cover of trees, Magruder gave the illusion that the nine-mile long defensive works from the York River to the James were bristling with Confederate troops. One regiment, the 14th Louisiana, marched from the York to the James and back six times, tramping back and forth for 24 hours. Magruder hid drum and bugle corps behind trees, keeping up an endless barrage of bugle calls and drum taps. He engaged officers to shout marching orders to phantom regiments, and had regiments march back and forth between different defensive positions.[10]

Magruder's ruse worked.

McClellan himself advanced to the front by Yorktown and made a personal reconnaissance of the Confederate lines. He wrote: "It was now, of course, out of my power to turn Yorktown by West Point; I had, therefore, no choice left but to attack it directly in front, as best I could, with the force at my command … [Reconnaissance] convinced me that it was best to prepare for an assault by the preliminary employment of heavy guns, and some siege operations. Instant assault would have been simple folly." McClellan's left flank had also run into the defensive works along the Warwick at Lee's Mill, where its advance had been checked by a sturdier-than-expected defense.[11]

The Army of the Potomac's advance had stalled on April 5, a day after it had begun. Any desire to try and force the Warwick Line had been sapped from McClellan by the news that President Lincoln had formally detached McDowell's corps of McClellan's army to be held in Washington to defend the capital—which also arrived on April 5.[12]

"Little Mac" was indignant. A telegram he sent to Washington pleaded with Lincoln to reconsider detaching McDowell; and where once he had spoken of glorious successes, McClellan now complained of being outnumbered and outgunned:

> The Enemy are in large force along our front and, apparently, intend making a determined resistance. A reconnaissance just made by Genl. Barnard, shows that their line of works extends across the entire Peninsula from Yorktown and Warwick river. Many of these are formidable. Deserters say that they are being reinforced daily from Richmond, and from Norfolk. Under these circumstances I beg that you will reconsider the order detaching the first Corps from my Command.[13]

Lincoln's response, showing no sympathy with McClellan's protests, arrived swiftly. "You now have over one hundred thousand troops, with you … I think you better break the enemies' line from York-town to Warwick River at once. They will probably use *time* as advantageously as you can." Yet McClellan insisted that what stood before him at Yorktown was "the whole force of the enemy … probably not less than one hundred thousand men and possibly more." The major general fulminated to his wife that removing McDowell's corps from his army was "the most infamous thing that history has recorded," and Lincoln's encouragement to break Magruder's line was dismissed with a tart "I was much tempted to reply that he had better come & do it himself."[14]

While their commanding general and commander-in-chief feuded by telegram, the men of the Army of the Potomac settled into the second siege of Yorktown in American history. Butterfield's brigade was posted on the extreme right of the army, with its right flank against the shores of the York River at Wormley's Creek. To their front, a thick band of trees provided cover against their Confederate adversaries that many Federal soldiers along the line lacked. Two thousand yards past the trees, the Confederate defensive lines bristled with cannon and musket. Chosen by Major General Porter to supervise the entrenchment of the division, Lieutenant Colonel Vincent threw himself into the project with vigor. His friend, Colonel Swan, wrote that Vincent "made the siege of Yorktown a study. He knew the position and importance of every work and every gun along our lines." Despite the distance between the lines, the Siege of Yorktown was hardly quiet. Private Nash of the 44th New York recalled that "the batteries, skirmishers and sharp shooters of the two armies, were almost constantly engaged." His Pennsylvanian counterpart, Private Judson, concurred. "As soon as the enemy discovered that we were at work in the trenches, they opened fire on us from the fort and night and day threw mortar shells, many of them with such precision that they fell among the men and occasionally did some damage."[15]

In his report from serving as general of the trenches, Brigadier General Butterfield stated that he had issued a set of five instructions to "the field officers of divisions in charge of working details in the trenches." These orders were for the officers to keep detailed records of how many men were working on the trenches, who commanded them, what they were doing, what engineer supervised the work, what hours the men were working, and what they accomplished, as well as commentary regarding "the progress and condition of the work necessary, or of interest" to McClellan. Butterfield noted, somewhat sourly, that "in no case were any reports received or the order in any way complied with, except by Lieutenant-Colonel Vincent, commanding details working in trenches from your division." Once more, Vincent had attracted favorable notice from his superiors; the remainder of Butterfield's report is nothing less than a bitter rant to Major General Porter on the failure of other officers along the siege works to file the reports he had requested. Simply by obeying orders, Vincent had increased his cachet with his superior officers.[16]

Abruptly, on May 1, "the firing of the enemy had been quite brisk," and then it "increased in rapidity" on May 3. The sudden tenor of the bombardment woke many of the men of the 83rd, including Amos Judson. "The roar of their cannon was heard over fifty miles, and we could hear the reverberation of each successive explosion for a long time as it gradually died away in the distance, like the successive waves of the sea beating upon the shore." Major General Porter was certain the Confederates were abandoning Yorktown, and ordered a portion of his division to rush the Confederate works in an effort to capture any enemy soldiers loitering in their trenches.[17]

The sounds of explosions from within Yorktown—military stores being destroyed—echoed through the night of May 3–4. By sunrise, the United States flag had been planted atop the Confederate works by the 22nd Massachusetts and the 62nd Pennsylvania. Porter had been just a day away from completing the full siege lines when Magruder's Confederates abandoned the city.[18]

In his report on the siege of Yorktown, General Porter concludes by stating, "I desire to present the names of the following regiments, which, under their respective commanders, were continually in the trenches, and most faithfully and cheerfully, under all circumstances, frequently most trying, performed their laborious and dangerous duties" during the month-long siege of Yorktown. A short way down the list, Porter includes "Eighty-third Pennsylvania, Colonel McLane and Lieutenant-Colonel Vincent."[19]

McClellan's army began to try and outflank the Confederates. Brigadier Generals Joseph Hooker and William F. Smith's divisions pursued Magruder overland, while Brigadier General William B. Franklin's division was sent up river to try and pen Magruder's forces on the peninsula. Hooker and Smith's advances stalled and snarled at Williamsburg on May 5, and Franklin's landing force was pinned on the beach on May 7. Still determined to try and trap the Confederates, McClellan sent more men up the Pamunkey River. Porter's division were among those in the latter group. As part of this plan, Strong Vincent and the 83rd Pennsylvania landed at Eltham's Landing, Virginia, on May 9.[20]

A day after their arrival, Lieutenant Colonel Vincent was selected by Brigadier General Porter to undertake a reconnaissance up the Pamunkey River towards Richmond. "The precise object of this expedition we never fully comprehended," Amos Judson wrote after the war, "but we were given to understand that it was to capture some guerillas, or night marauders, who had lately been in the habit of coming down the York River Railroad and plundering some plantations on the Pamunky[sic]." After nightfall on May 10, Vincent commanded five companies of the 83rd Pennsylvania as they crossed the York River to West Point at the mouth of the Pamunkey. They began, led by "a contraband guide previously engaged for this purpose," to head inland for roughly five miles.

The plantation on which they stopped was a thousand acres and inhabited by over a hundred enslaved African-Americans. Its "little metropolis of Doric mansions reposed upon the romantic shores of the river in all the simplicity of that severe and primitive style of architecture," Judson noted sardonically of slave shacks set against the columned mansions of the slaveowners. As the men of the 83rd under Vincent began to cross the plantation's fields, the guard dogs—"those faithful guardians of Southern homes (and of their negroes, too)"—began to bark. This roused from sleep the enslaved persons of the plantation, who emerged from their shacks to see shadowy forms holding muskets glinting in the moonlight.[21]

Panicked, they took flight. In the darkness, the 83rd was none the wiser who had emerged, and, as Judson wrote, "the moment our men saw those dusky forms flitting hither and thither, in panic and affright, they knew that the enemy was routed, horse, foot, and dragoon; and, with the enthusiasm with which we always pursue a flying foe, they charged forward, with a yell and a double quick." Unfortunately, as the "half dead with fright" enslaved persons sprinted away from the shrieking furies that pursued them, they ran for the banks of the Pamunkey, which the plantation overlooked on steep bluffs. In the darkness and in terror, the enslaved persons charged over the precipice. Lieutenant Colonel Vincent and his men charged after them, "down the banks of the Pamunkey, tobacco-growing stream rushed assailant and assailed, pursuer and pursued, soldier and nigger, all rolling and tumbling together in a heap." Only after all parties involved had crashed down to the riverbank below did Lieutenant Colonel Vincent manage to exhort the enslaved persons to surrender. "But our men, with repeated demands to halt and surrender, again dashed forward, seized the enemy by the throats and claimed them as prisoners of war. Nor was it until they had come to this hand to hand encounter and secured the prize of victory, and the sooty countenances of the affrighted foe had begun to gleam … that the truth broke upon them." The guerillas the soldiers had thought they had found turned out to be terrified African-Americans: enslaved men, women and children who had mistaken them for the very guerillas that Vincent sought.[22]

Once the situation had become apparent to Vincent, the lieutenant colonel and his men began to speak with the enslaved persons of the plantation. They were given "a repast consisting of hog-meat, hoe-cake and buttermilk" while the enslaved people told Vincent all they knew of Confederate movements and forces in the area. The owner of the plantation had fled, having "business of an important nature to transact in a neighboring state," as soon as McClellan had landed upon the Peninsula. His overseer had followed swiftly, leaving the plantation, as Judson wryly noted, "without maturing the necessary preparations with which to withstand an assault or repel an invasion."[23]

The men of the 83rd had not found or fought any Confederate guerillas, but the enslaved persons of this unnamed plantation provided Vincent and his men with a heavy supply of food and forage, as well as information regarding the disposition of Confederate forces near West Point. With the blessings of their hosts, the men of the 83rd slept until shortly before dawn, and then returned to the river, crossing back to Eltham's Landing.[24]

The reconnaissance up the Pamunkey may not have ferreted out the Confederate guerillas that Lieutenant Colonel Vincent had sought, but it was an important event nonetheless. Strong Vincent had never before encountered enslaved persons or slavery in the context of plantation life. He had no doubt encountered some house slaves during the 83rd's long sojourn in Washington City, but here, along the bluffs overlooking the Pamunkey, Strong Vincent first came face-to-face with slavery as the majority of the South's four million enslaved African-Americans lived it. The evidence of the savage brutality of the master and his overseer would have surrounded the Pennsylvanians on that night along the shores of the Pamunkey. While the lack of documentation makes it difficult to confirm, it is reasonable to speculate that, raised in the circumstances which he was, with the noted abolitionist William Himrod in close proximity for most of his life and a devout father who abhorred personal laziness and idleness, Vincent more than likely would have seen the evidence of slavery's barbarity and been repulsed by it. He had no qualms, at least, about opposing the expansion of slavery, as an enthusiastic supporter of Lincoln's 1860 presidential campaign. But whether or not Vincent can be argued to be an abolitionist is only speculation. It is, however, speculation based on a fragment of extant documentation. While Vincent left no record of his direct thoughts of the incidents of May 10–11, 1862, his increasing hostility towards the Confederacy as the war progressed, revealed in extracts from personal letters quoted by Colonel Swan, may potentially be traced to this encounter. It may be argued that Vincent anticipated the gradual shift towards a "hard war" mentality by nearly a year, telling Elizabeth after the expedition up the Pamunkey that "We must desolate the country as we pass through it, and not leave the trace of doubtful friend or foe behind us … make them believe … that the life of every man, yea, of every weak woman or helpless child in the South is of no value whatever compared with the integrity of the Union."[25]

The advance along the Peninsula towards Richmond continued. By May 16, the men of the 83rd Pennsylvania were encamped at White House, Virginia, pitching French-style tents on "seven thousand acres of very productive land on the Pamunkey river, late the property of the rebel General Lee." The White House plantation was, technically, the property of Lee's son, William Henry Fitzhugh Lee, and had been bequeathed to him by his grandfather, George Washington Parke Custis, the step-grandson of George Washington. The plantation was the ancestral estate of the Custis family; it was at White House where George Washington had met Martha Dandridge Custis, and it was where he had come to court her in the days before their marriage. Now, the grounds teemed with soldiers of Washington's United States Army. Norton, a fiery abolitionist, was enamored with the "several hundred slaves" on the White House grounds. "They were a happy set of darkies when they learned that they were free," Norton wrote to his sister. "They were most of them born on the place. I saw one old Uncle Tom, over sixty years old, who had never been five miles from the place in his life." Much less charitable, however, was Norton's view of the local whites: "The white inhabitants of the country are a miserable set. Every house exhibits the white flag as our troops pass. They are mean enough to take advantage of such protection and refuse a drink of water to our troops almost suffocated with heat."[26]

The front lawn of the White House plantation became McClellan's headquarters, and the river beneath the plantation teemed with gunboats, transports, barges, cargo scows, and sundry ships making up the Army of the Potomac's massive support flotilla. Francis Keeler, a soldier in the 16th Michigan of Butterfield's brigade, wrote to his beloved at home that, "the masts of the vessels in the river as seen from our camp look very strange in a clover field, and are the only indication of navigable water so near by." The Army of the Potomac was preparing to move out, to take up a line upon the banks of the Chickahominy River, as Confederate forces under General Joseph E. Johnston had retreated across the river on May 15.[27]

McClellan's army was 23 miles from Richmond in a straight shot along the York River Railroad to the Confederate capital. He planned to advance on the city and besiege it, as he had Yorktown. Using the railroad, he could haul his massive cannons to the very gates of Richmond; other avenues, such as the James River, were closed to him by the Confederates' tenacious defense of Drewry's Bluff. Reorganizing the Army of the Potomac once more, McClellan transformed its three corps into five corps. Fitz John Porter and William B. Franklin—close friends and followers of the commanding general—were named to command the new V and VI Corps.[28]

Still, however, McClellan hesitated. Reports from Pinkerton agents serving as McClellan's intelligence service had grossly inflated the number of Confederate troops defending Richmond, to the tune of an army 150,000 strong and armed with 400 to 500 artillery pieces. Johnston's army, in fact, numbered no more than 56,600 men, with 144 cannons in 36 batteries—barely a third of what McClellan claimed. That did not stop McClellan from writing from the Peninsula that "the enemy were concentrating all their available force to fight this army in front of Richmond," and that "I cannot bring into actual battle against the enemy more than eighty thousand men at the utmost, and with them I must attack in position, probably entrenched, a much larger force, perhaps double my numbers."[29]

As the Army of the Potomac crept to the Chickahominy, the 83rd Pennsylvania, now part of the division commanded by Brigadier General George W. Morell as part of Porter's new V Corps, found itself encamped at the Cold Harbor tavern crossroads and Gaines Farm, two locations which would, by the end of the war, be associated with battle and bloodshed. On May 27, Morell's division was ordered to Hanover Court House in an attempt to interdict an attack by Confederate forces on the Federal overland supply lines to Washington. Excitement rippled through the ranks as the soldiers were told to ensure they carried full loads of ammunition. Eugene Nash of the 44th New York wrote, "the order had a telling look. Sixty rounds of ammunition meant something." Oliver Norton was similarly enthusiastic in a letter written in camp at Cold Harbor. "No going back. 'On to Richmond' is the watchword in earnest now." In his diary, Colonel Stockton of the 16th Michigan pronounced, "we go to fight to victory or death, God watch and protect me for my beloved wife's sake."[30]

Marching in a pitiless rain that mired the Virginia roads, Morell's division trooped towards Hanover Court House. Colonel Hiram Berdan's 1st United States Sharpshooters, outfitted not in the usual Union Blue but in uniforms of dark forest green, led the division in line of march. Berdan's expert marksmen were the elite of the Federal forces, and they had been attached to Morell's division for the effort to block the Confederate flanking attack. One soldier in the division groused that the road to Hanover Court House "was eighteen miles in length, and about one foot in depth" in the gooey morass of mud. As the division reached the crossroads of the Ashcake Road and Hanover Court House Road near Peake's Crossing and the Pole Green Church, a brief skirmish erupted between Confederate pickets—Colonel James Lane's 28th North Carolina—and Morell's advanced guard of the 25th New York and William Emory's cavalry. Berdan's sharpshooters joined the fray as they came up, and the Confederates retired towards Hanover Court House. Morell detailed a section of Martin's battery and the 44th New York Volunteers, and the 2nd Maine, as well as the recently ambushed 25th New York, to hold the crossroads in the event the division would need to fall back under fire.[31]

Brigadier General Porter expected to find the main force of the enemy at Hanover Court House. Therefore, the rest of the division continued along the road towards the village itself. Morell's main body, however, had marched right past the main action of the day; 4,000 Confederate soldiers under Brigadier General Lawrence O'Bryan Branch were standing guard on the Virginia Central Railroad at Peake's Crossing, just a short distance down the Ashcake Road from where Colonel Stephen Stryker and the 44th New York had been deployed as a rear-guard.[32]

Branch saw an opportunity to try to trap some of the Federal forces, even as his pickets led the main body of the force away. He sent forward two regiments—the 37th and 18th North Carolina—to cut off the Federal avenue of retreat. Instead, they found the 44th New York, 25th New York, 2nd Maine, and Martin's artillery guarding the crossroads. Branch quickly sized up the Federal force: "I galloped forward … and was informed by Colonel [Charles C.] Lee that the force of the enemy consisted of two regiments of infantry and some artillery." Believing that he outnumbered the Federal troops, Branch ordered every one of his regiments to assault the position. The 44th New York shifted its position as its skirmishers snarled with Branch's advance. "The regiment was advancing by the flank in an open field near the highway, a sudden and murderous fire at short range was opened by the enemy, concealed in the woods toward which it was advancing."[33]

The fighting became hot. The gunners of Martin's artillery were driven from their pieces for cover, and the noise of the fracas in the rear reached Porter and Morell, still on the road to Hanover Court House with the rest of the division. "The rear brigade (the second) … were opposite the large white house (Winston's), and the Third Brigade … in advance of them when the order came to return to the assistance of their comrades. The Second Brigade immediately faced to the rear, and was led by Colonel McQuade at a rapid pace directly through the fields towards the point where the firing was heaviest." Brigadier General John Martindale, who had chosen to remain with the men of his command in the 25th New York and 2nd Maine, led the defense of the crossroads and wrote of the intensity of the fighting: "The battle had now lasted quite an hour, and although the center of my line was broken under a cross-fire which was entirely destructive and insupportable, still the Second Maine on the right, I believe every man, and the largest body of the Forty-fourth New York, with their lieutenant-colonel and major, on the left, maintained their ground without flinching."[34]

Colonel Charles Roberts of the 2nd Maine recalled the "galling fire" of Branch's Confederates as the battle for the crossroads raged. "My ammunition being nearly exhausted, many of my men having fired away their 60 rounds, I anxiously looked for re-enforcements," Roberts wrote in his official report of the battle. He did not have long to wait; the Second Brigade emerged from the forest and formed into line of battle to counter-attack Branch's men. The 83rd Pennsylvania, the only regiment besides the 44th New York of Butterfield's brigade that would see battle at Hanover Court House, had opted to race down the tracks of the Virginia Central rather than march along the road. Colonel McLane, at the head of his men, proclaimed that "Now is the time to prove yourselves soldiers!" before leading a ferocious charge out of the woods into the field in front of their comrades from New York as, "at the very moment we debouched from the woods, [the firing] entirely ceased." The 83rd charged after Branch's retreating Confederates and primarily, in the words of Brigadier General Morell, "aided materially in securing prisoners." While they had missed the major fighting at the crossroads, the skirmish with the 28th North Carolina on the Hanover Court House Road had resulted in "two killed and thirteen wounded." Norton recorded that Sergeant Hulbert and Frank McBride of his company had both been wounded in the foot: "Sergeant H. loses his foot and Frank his toes, the only casualties in our company."[35]

"Porter's action of yesterday was truly a glorious victory—too much credit cannot be given to his magnificent Division & its accomplished leader. The rout of the rebels was complete—not a defeat but a complete rout." George McClellan's celebratory telegraph was sent to Washington from Hanover Court House itself, where the commanding general had arrived to inspect the battlefield and congratulate the men who had held off Branch's attack. Of course, in true McClellan style, the major general used the telegraph to demand reinforcements: "It is the policy & duty of the Govt to send me by water all the well drilled troops available." To his wife, McClellan made no reference to being outmanned: "I am on Fitz field of battle. His success of yesterday was a glorious victory. The old rascal has done all that I could ask. The rebels are completely routed. It is a fair presage of the great victory which awaits us at Richmond."[36]

Still, McClellan made no move to advance from his line along the Chickahominy River. On May 30, a soldier of the 44th New York was killed by "one of those terrific storms of thunder, lightning and rain so peculiar to the 'sunny South.'" The storm continued unabated—a "perfect deluge"—and flooded the Chickahominy. Taking advantage of the flooding, on May 31 and June 1 Confederate General Joseph E. Johnston attacked the left flank of McClellan's army in what would become known as the battle of Fair Oaks. On the right flank of McClellan's army, Vincent and the 83rd Pennsylvania could do nothing but listen to the sounds of battle. Perhaps the most consequential outcome of the stalemate battle of Fair Oaks was that Johnston was wounded—ironically right after chiding a member of his staff for ducking Federal fire—and was replaced by Jefferson Davis with Robert E. Lee.[37]

While Lee consolidated control of his new army, General McClellan did nothing but sit and wait for the hammer-strike to fall. Sitting in its camps beside the flooded swamps of the Chickahominy, the Army of the Potomac began to be plagued by an illness the likes of which it had never encountered before. The swamps were riddled with mosquitos and stagnant water, and the heat of the sweltering Virginia summers—coupled with the unknown quality of local wells—led to soldiers drinking the brackish and mired water of the Chickahominy. The infamous "Chickahominy Fever" began to cut through the Army of the Potomac. To this day, it is unknown precisely what the disease was, although medical historians have made guesses ranging from malaria, typhus, yellow fever, and typhoid to dengue fever. Whatever it was, the disease ravaged the Federal troops encamped along the river. By June 20, five days before Robert E. Lee would seize the initiative and attack McClellan at Oak Grove, 11,000 men—nearly a tenth of the Army of the Potomac—were absent due to illness.* Among those who had come down with the infamous and mysterious illness was Lieutenant Colonel Strong Vincent, who had been sent to recuperate at a hospital at V Corps headquarters behind the lines on June 26, 1862.[38]

---

* For more information on the impact of such fevers on the war, see Andrew McIlwaine Bell, *Mosquito Soldiers: Malaria, Yellow Fever, and the Course of the American Civil War* (Baton Rouge: Louisiana State University Press, 2010).

The next day, June 27, 1862, the 83rd Pennsylvania were bloodied at the battle of Gaines' Mill. Of the 554 men who went into the battle, 196—including Colonel John McLane and Major Louis Naghel—were casualties before the end of the day. With Vincent absent from the regiment, field command of the 83rd fell to Captain Hugh Campbell, the commander of Company E from Waterford, Pennsylvania. At the height of the fighting, the 83rd was cut off and nearly surrounded by Confederate forces. When the 11th South Carolina demanded its surrender, Lieutenant Plympton White, who had been reading law under Lane, Galbraith, and Vincent when the war began and who had declared he would enlist for life if his country needed him, bellowed back, "Hell! The Eighty-Third Pennsylvania never surrenders!" In the ensuing breakout towards the Chickahominy, White was severely wounded and captured by the Confederates. He would later die in captivity. After the battle, Campbell was elected lieutenant colonel of the regiment on the Peninsula in light of McLane's and Naghel's deaths, and Strong Vincent was, in spite of his absence, elevated to command the regiment, with the assumption he would soon be promoted to the rank of colonel.[39]

News of the catastrophe at Gaines' Mill reached Strong Vincent in his hospital bed. His friend, Colonel Swan, noted that "the sound of cannon and musketry reached the sick man's ears" during the fighting. Learning of the extent of the slaughter—a full 35 percent of the 83rd Pennsylvania were killed, wounded, or missing—Vincent "forced those who had charge of him to let him go. He compelled the servant to bring him a horse," and left the hospital to return to his regiment to oversee its retreat across the Chickahominy. By dawn, he was at the head of the 83rd Pennsylvania, leading it down the road to evacuate the banks of the river. Vincent's father, in the genealogical notice he wrote of his eldest son, recounts that he was "delirious with Chickahominy Fever" as he presided over his regiment on the march to Savage's Station, Virginia. Colonel Swan wrote: "There is a limit to the power of strong will, of enthusiasm, even of frenzy; and for Vincent to command his regiment, or do any duty whatever, was now beyond this limit." Shortly into the march, Vincent lapsed into unconsciousness and fell from his requisitioned horse into the road. His men loaded their commander into an ambulance. He remained unconscious for the duration of the march and for several days thereafter, only regaining consciousness aboard a hospital transport halfway down the James River, en route to New York City and convalescence. In his absence, on July 4, 1862, the men of the 83rd Pennsylvania elected Strong Vincent their new colonel.[40]

Upon arrival on the hospital transport *Spaulding* in New York, thanks to the efforts of a "kind lady" nurse aboard the vessel, Vincent was met at the wharf by his wife. His father arrived the next morning. Elizabeth and Bethuel Vincent had sprinted from Erie to meet Strong and were at his bedside during a three-week convalescence in Jersey City, New Jersey, staying with Elizabeth's sister while they tended to him.[41]

In a long letter written over several days, Elizabeth Vincent discussed her husband's condition with her close friend and former employer, Sarah Porter. Writing of the summons to meet her husband in New York, Elizabeth admitted that "I was in Cleveland when the first accounts came of the week's fighting. It was then that I heard of the Colonel's death and Father's departure for Fortress Monroe." Her anxiety built over the weekend from that Friday due to "intelligence that he had been left and taken prisoner" on Saturday, building frantically until "came a dispatch from Fortress Monroe, telling me to meet him in New York on steamer Spaulding and signed by my husband." Racing to her sister and brother-in-law's home in Jersey City, Elizabeth was able to meet Strong at the wharf. "That afternoon he was brought to me—oh so desperately sick and weak!" But there was a new problem: while the Chickahominy Fever had faded "when he reached Jersey City" there was now "a slight trouble with the urinary organs." This infection would prove more severe than the infamous Chickahominy Fever had been for Strong Vincent.[42]

At the end of July, Vincent was loaded onto a train and returned to Erie for the duration of his convalescence, arriving home in early August 1862. *The Erie Weekly Gazette* noted that the newly-promoted colonel, upon his return to Erie, was "in feeble health," and that it wished for a speedy recovery of "the bodily vigor and consequent fitness for the chief command of the gallant boys of the 83rd."[43]

The papers had not exaggerated. Vincent's health was quite feeble. Dr. Charles Brandes, the Vincent family's physician, wrote on August 7 that

Vincent was "much reduced and is quite feeble, being able to sit up only a small portion of the time. His present disease is *blennorrhea vesicae* and of a severe character, and is a great waste upon his system." A contemporary medical reference book reveals that "Blennorrhœa of the Vesica" is what we would refer to today as a severe urinary tract infection, with symptoms described as "violent fever with thirst; frequent and urgent want to urinate, without consequent emission, or with emission of only a few drops of deep-coloured, red and turbid, or else *sanguinolent* urine; painful tenderness of the vesical region, especially when touched, with aggravation of the pains when urinating." It is possible that Vincent developed this infection while in a military hospital, but more than likely, it developed as a result of conditions along the peninsula prior to his evacuation and was simply exacerbated by the Chickahominy Fever. Laid up in bed in Erie, Vincent's recovery was slow and no doubt agonizing. Recommended prescriptions in the medical text include sulfate and phosphate treatments of the afflicted area.[44]

In her letter to Sarah Porter, Elizabeth agonized over her husband: "I certainly think I never saw such agony. His whole frame would just sway with pain, and the cold perspiration stream off him. Leeching subdued apparently the inflammation, for the hemorrhaging ceased." Worse, the delirium continued unabated—rendering the Harvard-educated lawyer "a perfect child in everything." Thankfully, wrote Elizabeth to her friend, "If it had not been for Gen'l. Porter and his faithful John,* he never would have escaped, for he was so sick, they say, that he did not care himself what became of him."[45]

Elizabeth Vincent recorded that, despite her husband's condition, he had received a hero's welcome in Erie; a crowd had awaited Vincent at the depot, which was "too much for him." But she brought Miss Porter into her confidence with regards to the dire nature of his condition: Strong Vincent had suffered from "varicose veins … developed in the scrotum" for some time, and that, "When the fever came on, by neglect during the retreat and on the steamer, these varicose veins extended up the neck of the bladder." Quoting

* John Hickey, an Irish-born immigrant to Erie County, served as Vincent's orderly during the war.

Dr. Brandes, Elizabeth states that "his whole bladder and kidneys are evidently in a terrible condition."[46]

Throughout Elizabeth Vincent's letter, it is readily apparent when she would cease writing to minister to her husband and then take up her pencil once more to resume her report to her friend. Paragraphs begin with "Fever rises in the afternoon," "The Dr. this morning goes to work," "I feel happier today," "For three days he has done nothing," and other such phrases. The entire letter speaks to a wife's desperate anxiety over a husband in the grips of an illness that has laid him low in agonizing pain. But she seemed to have concealed her anxiety and her worry from her husband: "Each day and night I thought of you, and often Strong was able to listen, I tried to talk to him quietly and sweetly of you & Farmington. If you could have seen how often the tears would come as he tried to recall some of those old loved days, you would know how we both love you."[47]

By the time that Elizabeth finally mailed her letter to Sarah Porter in late August, Strong had begun to recover. "The Dr. lets him go to the table and will have him taken out to ride, and he can talk quietly with us every day." Seeking to provide some distraction for her ill husband through the arrival of their mutual friend, she beseeched Sarah that "I cannot be denied your visit. I need it—you do not know how much." Elizabeth wrote in conclusion, "Oh this poor forlorn country—I can't write about it. Things are desperate, and I cannot but feel as Dr. Brandes says, that it is a very bad concern. I am glad that Strong is too weak to fully appreciate it. I believe it would craze him. How we have wanted mind—but we are now on the eve of something tremendous."[48]

During Vincent's absence, the 83rd Pennsylvania had fought at Malvern Hill, Second Bull Run, and, in the days after Elizabeth mailed her letter, would fight at Antietam and Shepherdstown Ford. She was more prescient than she knew. "Something tremendous" had come for the nation, for the brigade, and for the 83rd Pennsylvania. President Lincoln issued the Emancipation Proclamation, announcing the emancipation of enslaved persons in territories that were in rebellion against the United States. A new regiment had been added to Butterfield's brigade: the 20th Maine, under Colonel Adelbert Ames. And, on a sultry summer night in late July at Harrison's Landing, on the grounds of the Berkeley Plantation where President William Henry Harrison had been born, brigade bugler Oliver Norton had been summoned to Brigadier General Butterfield's tent to sound for the first time a new bugle call that the general had written: a 24-note bugle call made up of the C major triad to mark lights out in camps. That call would soon become synonymous with death.[49]

CHAPTER 5

Colonel Vincent: October 1862 to January 1863

"Yes we'll rally round the flag, boys, we'll rally once again, Shouting the battle cry of freedom,
We will rally from the hillside, we'll gather from the plain, Shouting the battle cry of freedom.
The Union forever, hurrah! boys, hurrah! Down with the traitor, up with the star;
While we rally round the flag, boys, we rally once again, Shouting the battle cry of freedom!"

The Battle Cry of Freedom, George F. Root, 1862[1]

Following the battle of Antietam, Lee's Army of Northern Virginia slipped back south of the Potomac, but McClellan's Army of the Potomac remained encamped along the banks of the Antietam until nearly the end of October 1862. McClellan grasped at any excuse not to advance his army in pursuit of Lee, at one point claiming to General-in-Chief Major General Henry W. Halleck that he possessed only a thousand horses, which were near exhaustion. "Will you pardon me for asking what the horses of your army have done since the battle of Antietam that [would] fatigue anything?" Lincoln snapped at his general via telegram on October 25.[2]

On October 7, 1862, Vincent, now recovered from his illness, left Erie to rejoin the 83rd Pennsylvania where it had been encamped since Antietam, situated by an iron works near where Antietam Creek flowed into the Potomac River. He brought with him 25 new recruits, bringing the 83rd to 363 men, its highest number since July. The new colonel began to sort out the chaos that six weeks encamped after battle had wrought in his regiment. Colonel Swan wrote of Vincent's return to the regiment: "Both commander and men were rejoiced to be together once more; though sorrow was mingled with Vincent's joy as he looked upon the thinned ranks and war-warn flags." Vincent returned in time to personally draw up the disciplinary orders for Privates Nicholas Akerly and George Fales on charges of drunken and disorderly conduct, and of striking a superior officer—Captain David Jones—for Fales. The two men both pleaded guilty, and forfeited a month's pay. Fales, for striking Captain Jones, received a public reprimand from Vincent in front of the assembled regiment.[3]

In his history of discipline in the army, historian Steven Ramold specifically cites "long stretches of mind-numbing tedium" resulting in a breakdown of general order and discipline within the military camps of the Federal armies. Stating that "individual soldiers no longer felt obligations to the nation, army, or each other" as inaction fueled tedium and pessimism, Ramold argues that incidents such as the one involving Privates Akerly and Fales were a way for citizen soldiers to assert their continued individuality and deny their status as cogs within the machinery of the army. While the specific grievance Akerly and Fales held for Captain Jones is unclear in the records, Vincent's punishment of the guilty privates demonstrated remarkable compassion for the convicted—perhaps even evidence of private agreement with the soldiers in their dispute, even if he disagreed on the manner in which Fales had finished the quarrel by striking an officer. A public demonstration before the regiment, wherein the two privates were stripped of a month's pay and Fales was reprimanded by Vincent, was among the least severe punishments that Vincent was able to apply to the offenders under the regulations of discipline in the army.[4]

The men of the 83rd were enjoying their sojourn. Amos Judson rhapsodized in his regimental history about the "halcyon days which we passed on the romantic shores of the Potomac! For nearly six weeks did we lie, in perfect repose, in the bosom of that delightful valley." Remembering the largesse of the land, with nary an enemy to be seen, Judson proclaimed that it was their just rewards "after the trials and sufferings of the terrible seven days before Richmond and the six weeks of sweltering beneath the rays of a worse than tropical sun at Harrison's Landing; after the disaster at Bull Run, and the excitements and fatigues of the campaign in Maryland, all occurring within a period of two and a half months." Sadly for Judson and his comrades, the return of their colonel signaled the beginning of the end of their interlude along the Antietam Creek.[5]

On October 26, 1862, the Army of the Potomac finally began to cross the Potomac, marching south in belated pursuit of Lee and his army. The army moved through the Loudon Valley back into Virginia. "Of all the marches we ever made, none was so pleasant and so romantic as this," Judson wrote appreciatively of the late fall beauty of the Virginia mountains and valleys bedecked in brilliant foliage.[6]

November 4 was election day; the next day, November 5, Abraham Lincoln issued General Order No. 182, removing George B. McClellan

Color Sergeant Alex Rogers of the 83rd Pennsylvania holds the regiment's original flag near Antietam Creek in the fall of 1862. The flag seen here is currently on display in the Heritage Room of the Raymond M. Blasco, MD Memorial Library in Erie, Pennsylvania. (*Courtesy of the Metropolitan Museum of Art*)

from command of the Army of the Potomac. President Lincoln replaced McClellan as army commander with Major General Ambrose Burnside. The bewhiskered Hoosier viewed the appointment as a betrayal of a long-time friend who had saved him from financial ruin, and only the threat that Burnside's refusal to accept the command would ensure it was offered to Major General Hooker, whom he detested, convinced Burnside to accept the position. He doubted his own ability, informing a fellow officer that "I don't feel equal to it," on his first morning in command of the Army of the Potomac following the delivery of the orders.[7]

McClellan was not the only officer departing the Army of the Potomac in early November. Fitz John Porter was removed from command due to allegations of misconduct and insubordination during the second battle of Bull Run. In his place, Major General Joseph Hooker was installed as commander of the V Army Corps. The staid Porter was replaced by the energetic and egotistical personality (and frequently alleged loose personal morals) of "Fighting Joe" Hooker.[8]

The news of McClellan's dismissal roiled the army. "Little Mac" was exceedingly popular with the troops, but there was an understanding of the decision among some soldiers. Speaking for many of his comrades under arms, Oliver Norton, ever the faithful correspondent to the hearth-side, wrote to his sister that: "I think the whole army thinks as much of McClellan to-day as they ever did. We ask no better leader. I believe, too, that the President had as much confidence in his loyalty and ability the day he removed him as he ever had." Lincoln, Norton insisted, had fired McClellan only due to "pressure of public opinion," and measured Burnside as "a good man in his place, but not equal to 'Little Mac.'"[9]

Halting the Army of the Potomac on the march near Warrenton, Virginia, Burnside reorganized the army into three "grand divisions," each composed of two corps. In their camps around Warrenton, a soldier of the newly-arrived 20th Maine received his first taste of the hospitality of the Confederate citizenry. One woman who had seemed to be an "amiable lady" at first brush allegedly proceeded to wish the entire army dead when he dared politely ask for a glass of milk. In these hostile environs, the army wondered what Burnside would do, even as their new chief inspired little confidence. Brigadier General George G. Meade, then commanding a division in the I Corps, brusquely wrote to his wife of

Burnside's elevation to command that: "Burnside, it is said, wept like a child, and is the most distressed man in the army, openly says he is not fit for the position, and that McClellan is the only man we have who can handle the large army collected together, one hundred and twenty thousand men." With snow flurries already filling the air and exposure from cold nights in fly-tents sending hundreds of his men onto the sick lists, Burnside might have chosen to enter winter quarters at Warrenton. But McClellan had been removed from command for inaction, and his friend resolved he would not share the same fate. The Army of the Potomac would undertake a winter campaign.[10]

Burnside's plan called for feints towards Culpeper, Virginia, while his main army would cross the Rappahannock at Fredericksburg before driving overland for Richmond. On November 14, Lincoln approved Burnside's plan, and the three grand divisions of the Army of the Potomac began to move. Hooker had been given command of the so-called "Centre Grand Division," consisting of the V and III Army Corps grouped together. Hooker's successor as V Corps commander was Brigadier General Daniel Butterfield, who was succeeded as brigade commander by Colonel Thomas Stockton of the 16th Michigan, the senior colonel of the brigade.[11]

The Army of the Potomac moved for Fredericksburg at dawn on November 15. "The army encamped along the whole line of the road, from the Potomac to the Rappahannock," Amos Judson reported of Burnside's sprawling army on the march to Fredericksburg. Approximately 135,000 Federal troops with 410 cannons in 83 batteries were descending on the town. It was brutal marching. Oliver Norton wrote in a letter to his sister of the Virginia winter:

> The fact is, winter is upon us, and winter in Virginia, though very different from northern winters, is just as fatal to the campaign as frost is to cucumbers … Long trains of wagons … must accompany each division. Batteries of artillery, too, and when a few of these have passed along a road after … rain or snow, the following teams are floundering belly deep in mud, and everything must stop.[12]

Major General Edwin Sumner's "Right Grand Division" arrived opposite Fredericksburg on the banks of the Rappahannock on November 17, with the rest of Burnside's army arriving over subsequent days. Burnside's momentum stalled as the Confederate garrison at Fredericksburg destroyed the bridges across the Rappahannock River and defended the ford at Falmouth. Burnside planned to cross the entire army at once, via pontoon bridges, to seize the city before Robert E. Lee's Army of Northern Virginia could interpose between the Army of the Potomac and Richmond. However, his pontoon bridges had been delayed, and in the time it took them to arrive, Lee and his army of 78,000 men and 240 cannon arrived to contest the crossing.[13]

Lee's defensive line snaked seven miles along high hills swept clear of trees, blocking every crossing of the Rappahannock except for Fredericksburg itself. Federal forces would be forced to march directly into the guns of Lee's army to contest the town.[14]

As the army sat upon Stafford Heights overlooking Fredericksburg, waiting for Burnside's bridges to arrive, Colonel Vincent tended to the typical duties of a regimental commander: requisitions, paperwork, and correspondence. He demanded the resignation of Lieutenant James H. Barnett "in consequence of your protracted inability for duty by reason of Sickness, and in view of the pressing necessity of the service for officers." He selected three officers—Captain DeWitt McCoy and Sergeants Robert Gilmore and William E. Haldeman—to return to western Pennsylvania to "conduct drafted men to this regiment." He placed a requisition order for 280 uniforms and Springfield .58 rifles to meet the anticipated arrival of "Two Hundred and Eighty men … to fill this regt. to the maximum." The young colonel wrote to the government of Pennsylvania to report the "elegant national flag given to this regt." was in need to replacement after being "born[e] … through half a score of battles, amid the storm and sun of the Peninsular and Maryland Campaign." Proclaiming what remained as "tattered silk and shivered lance," Vincent informed the state that "if we would have a vestige of it saved to hang in the halls of the State, it must have a successor soon."[15]

He also wrote to the surgeon general of Pennsylvania to request the assignment of a new regimental surgeon following the retirement of the original surgeon, and related to the same issue, protested the issuance of Special Order 359 from the War Department Adjutant General's Office on November 22. "I have just recd. a copy … in which it is directed that Surgeon Wm. Faulkner 83d Penna. Vols. be dropped from the rolls for absence without leave. I have the honor to call the attention of the Dept. of Special Order No. 281 H.Q. Army of the Potomac ... by which the same officer (among others) having tendered his resignation is honorably discharged from the Service."[16]

The crush of regimental business attendant upon Colonel Vincent demonstrates how officers had to constantly tend to a morass of requisitions, commissions, resignations, and miscommunications, which were a major part of the administrative life of any organization so large as the Army of the Potomac. As a lawyer, the young colonel would have been intimately familiar with the turgid and complicated sort of language in which regulations were written. But the fact that the vast bulk of the known surviving correspondence of Strong Vincent related to his relatively mundane work of equipping his soldiers, sorting out discrepancies among the officers of his regiment, requisitioning new colors for the regiment, and collecting resignations is significant; he was clearly a man who took his responsibility for the men of the 83rd Pennsylvania seriously. For every letter to his wife that has survived, there are no fewer than four pieces of official correspondence relating to the maintenance and disposition of either the 83rd Pennsylvania, or its brigade.

By November 27, the informally-recognized Thanksgiving Day, Burnside had received his pontoon bridges. Vincent shared the holiday meal with Colonel Stockton and Lieutenant Colonel Robert Richardson of the 12th New York. As the men waited for their orders to cross the river, still in their canvas tents upon the high grounds of Stafford Heights, winter arrived in full force. A frigid rain on December 5 became sleet, hail, and then snow blanketing the ground in several inches of frigid powder. On December 6, the temperature fell like a stone. A recent historian noted that "water froze five feet away from a campfire." By December 7, the temperature stood at 16 degrees, and "a captain washing his face found the water had begun to freeze before he could dry off."[17]

Burnside finally ordered the bridging operations to begin at 1am on December 11, 1862. Under the command of Brigadier General Daniel P. Woodbury of the U.S. Army Corps of Engineers, soldiers began to labor to construct three pontoon bridges over the Rappahannock. By

3am, they reported to headquarters that they had reached midstream with the bridging operation. At 5am, with the engineers just 200 feet from the opposite shore, a shout of "Fire!" echoed over the water, and a flash of musket-fire erupted from the riverside streets of Fredericksburg. The engineers hastily withdrew across their partially-completed bridges to the Federal shore. One hundred and forty-seven Federal cannons were entrenched on Stafford Heights, overlooking the town of Fredericksburg, their bronze barrels glinting in the cold December dawn. Brigadier General Henry J. Hunt, the chief of artillery of the Army of the Potomac, ordered his batteries to fire on the Confederates in the streets of the town. The thunderous roar of his cannons expanded along the line as several batteries launched shot and shell at the Confederates contesting all three bridging points along the banks of the Rappahannock.[18]

After a few minutes of heavy firing, Hunt's cannons fell silent, and the engineers emerged from the cover they had frantically sought on friendly shores to tentatively resume the work of bridging. Once more, they came under Confederate rifle fire. The defenders were the marksmen of Confederate Brigadier General William Barksdale's Mississippi brigade, and they had prepared rifle pits and cellars for the job of holding off the Federal attempts to cross the river. "Tell General Lee that if he wants a bridge full of dead Yankees I can furnish him with one," Barksdale quipped to a courier at the height of the fighting along the river. Six times the Federal engineers attempted to resume work on their pontoon bridges only to be driven off by Barksdale's Mississippians, and six times scattered batteries of Hunt's artillery fired on the Confederate positions.[19]

Incensed at the delay, Burnside ordered Hunt to "bring all your guns to bear upon the city and batter it down." As the morning haze faded, Hunt's guns exploded, launching the first major artillery bombardment of a city in the Civil War. More than 100 guns along Stafford Heights hurled forth shot and shell into the streets and buildings of Fredericksburg, no longer aiming solely at Barksdale's men.[20]

From Marye's Heights, Confederate Lieutenant General James Longstreet watched the bombardment in horror. In his postwar memoirs, Longstreet wrote that: "It seemed all the cannon within a mile of the town turned their concentrating fire of shot and shell upon the buildings of the devoted city, tearing, crushing, bursting, burning their walls with an angry desperation that must have been gratifying to spirits deep down below." Colonel Edward Porter Alexander, an artillery officer in Longstreet's corps, admired his Federal counterpart's work: "Probably 100 guns responded, and the spectacle which was now presented from the Confederate hilltops was one of the most magnificent and impressive in the whole course of the war." Alexander continued, in more detail: "The city, except its steeples, was still veiled in the mist ... Above it and in it incessantly showed the round white clouds of bursting shells, and out of its midst there soon rose three or four columns of dense black smoke ... The opposite bank of the river, for two miles to the right and left, was crowned at frequent intervals with blazing batteries."[21]

Behind and around the blazing cannon, the men of the Army of the Potomac watched the scene with awe and dread. Oliver Norton wrote to his sister that, "It would have done a person good, or at least given him an idea of war, to have walked through the town of Fredericksburg ... one hundred and fifty pieces of our artillery played on it ... there was not much left of it untouched. It was battered and burnt, the streets were filled with a confusion of all things." Eugene Nash of the 44th New York recalled "a furious cannonade upon the city which checked the firing." Lieutenant Colonel Joshua Lawrence Chamberlain of the 20th Maine, the newest members of the brigade, remembered "a terrific fire on those offensive shelters and their occupants, under which some of the houses were set afire, the smoke and flame giving a wild background to the tense and stirring scene."[22]

Miraculously—or infernally, depending upon one's point of view—Barksdale's Mississippians remained in their positions, firing on the engineers once more as they attempted to bridge the river in the aftermath of the nearly two-hour bombardment of Fredericksburg. Hunt took to Burnside a suggestion from Major Ira Spaulding of the 50th New York Engineers, who had been suffering all day attempting to complete the pontoon bridges. Using the pontoon boats, a force of Federal infantry would cross the river and secure a bridgehead in the city of Fredericksburg, driving out the Mississippians. Burnside, anxious to advance, agreed swiftly.[23]

Out of the bushes on the Federal shore charged soldiers of the 7th Michigan, members of Colonel Norman J. Hall's Third Brigade, Second Division, II Corps, hauling pontoon boats to the water's edge as Barksdale's Mississippians began firing on them. Lying flat in the bottom of the pontoons, 70 men from the Wolverine State were rowed across the river by members of the 50th New York Engineers, and charged the wharves of Fredericksburg, driving Barksdale's men back through the town to Caroline Street as the Confederates sought to contain the bridgehead. More men of the 7th Michigan were rowed across the river in short order, and they were reinforced by the 19th Massachusetts. As fighting grew fierce on Caroline Street and the roads to the waterfront, the engineers were swiftly working to finish the pontoon bridges. By 4:30pm, roughly two hours after the end of the artillery bombardment, the first of the upper pontoon bridges was complete, and the remaining regiments of Hall's brigade charged across the river to reinforce their comrades. Suffering heavy casualties, the "Harvard Regiment," the 20th Massachusetts, made its famous charge of Fauquier Street that forced Barksdale to abandon Fredericksburg to Federal forces.[24]

With Fredericksburg now occupied by Federal troops, an orgy of looting and destruction descended on the city as regiments of the Army of the Potomac began to advance. Oliver Norton described the chaos to his sister: "The streets were filled with a confusion of all things, splendid furniture and carpets, provisions, bottles, knapsacks, dead men and horses, blankets, muskets, the pomp of war and paraphernalia of peace mingled together. Men were ransacking every house, taking everything they wanted, and baking pancakes in the kitchens." Captain Ellis Spear of the 20th Maine recalled seeing the smashed remnants of a Virginia state bank, and being handed a huge roll of Virginia state bills worth 30 cents on the dollar by a looter who promised that he was paying him off before they went into battle. "The run on the bank had been a disorderly one," Spear quipped in his posthumously published memoirs, "and not made by depositors."[25]

The looting of Fredericksburg was described by John Matteson in his recent work on Fredericksburg as "a moral collapse unlike any [the Army of the Potomac] had ever known." Widespread consumption of alcohol and lingering fury at the Confederates for dragging them into ferocious urban combat unleashed one of the most memorable and chaotic scenes of the entire war. Matteson describes the chaos vividly:

> For some, the merriment was relatively innocent. Across the town, a host of fine pianos were dragged from fashionable parlors and into the streets, where soldiers pounded out tinny versions of "Yankee Doodle" and "The Star-Spangled Banner." But others were less restrained. Men and boys eager to enrich themselves with the spoils capered about, laden with silver pitchers, lamps, and spoons. Alabaster vases and splendid pieces of statuary became projectiles, vengefully hurled at mirrors and windows. Wine cellars, patiently filled over the course of decades, were raided for their riches, and what could not be consumed was added to the general smash. The streets grew littered with "every conceivable article of goods, chattels and apparel." Libraries worth thousands of dollars were thrown into the streets. Tiring of the efforts of their musical comrades, soldiers kicked the insides of the pianos to bits and set the instruments ablaze. "Everything," a major of the 108th New York lamented, "[was] turned upside down."[26]

December 12 was mostly spent in preparing for the next stage of battle, which began on December 13. Burnside's strategy called for Major General Sumner's Right Grand Division to make a demonstration against "the heights in rear of the town" while Burnside's main attack attempted to break Lee's right—Lieutenant General Thomas J. "Stonewall" Jackson's Second Corps. By 10am on December 13, the first division of Sumner's advance—that of Major General William H. French—was in line, and its lead element, Brigadier General Nathan Kimball's "Gibraltar Brigade," was prepared to step off and begin the advance on Marye's Heights. At 10:30am, the attack order was given. The Gibraltar Brigade charged forward into a blasting fire from Confederate pickets holding the millrace just outside of town. The second the Federal soldiers emerged from the cover of buildings, Confederate artillery on Marye's Heights opened fire. Beyond the millrace, 900 yards of bare, open field, virtually devoid of cover besides undulations in the ground and fences, stretched up a sloping hill to the base of Marye's Heights, where Brigadier General Thomas Cobb's Georgia brigade stood waiting in a sunken road behind a low stone wall. Kimball's Federals, men from Ohio, Indiana, New Jersey, Virginia, and Delaware, charged after the retreating Confederate pickets—directly into the range of Cobb's riflemen. Slowed by thick, slimy mud and spongy cornfield, Federal troops found themselves virtual sitting ducks; and by the time the brigade straggled back to Fredericksburg, Kimball had lost 520 men out of the approximately 2,000 he had led forward that morning.[27]

After Burnside's attempt to break Jackson's line failed, brigade by brigade, the Federal Army was thrown against Marye's Heights as the center of gravity of the battle shifted. Corporal Holman Melcher of Company B, 20th Maine, wrote to his brother that "we could see from the hill on which we were" the battle unfolding beneath them. "The volleys of musketry were truly terrific … our troops charge up close to the enemies lines and pour in their volleys." A short distance from the men of the 20th Maine, Colonel Vincent and the 83rd Pennsylvania watched the same scene of the brutality of war.[28]

Again and again, Federal troops made the charge, until Sumner's "Grand Division" was spent and Hooker's was advanced to continue feeding men into the meat grinder of Marye's Heights. Griffin's division—containing the 83rd Pennsylvania—was to hold in the town for the time being, and Stockton's brigade, including the 83rd Pennsylvania, crossed the river at around 4pm. As they crossed, Confederate artillery shots landed in the mud and semi-frozen river around them, but did not hit the bridge. The brigade was ordered to seek cover on Prince Edward Street, as the division's reserves.[29]

The men sought cover where they could, and for an hour and a half, the brigade lay in reserve as others advanced and were, in turn, repulsed. Despite being far from the focus of the battle on Marye's Heights, the brigade was still "subjected to a pelting fire of shot and shell." The men of the 20th Maine, in the midst of their first major battle, "lay flat in the mud upon our faces, to escape the shells that were screaming and crashing over our heads." Captain Ellis Spear sat on a rock in front of his men lying in the mud, and comforted a "little dog" that had come along from somewhere. "The little fellow was shivering with terror, and I took him in my arms & held him, & soothed him as well as I could … he knew more than some cows that we passed, which were feeding in spite of the uproar." As shot and shell burst around them, Lieutenant Colonel Chamberlain was transfixed by the fact that "the dead and wounded lay thick even here, and fragments of limbs were trampled underfoot." Heedless of the exploding shells, however, Colonel Vincent stood at the head of his men, "in full view of the enemy's artillery," sword in hand, and "never wavered nor once changed his position" as shrapnel wounded men around him. It was, as Judson writes, "the first … indications of that bravery for which he afterwards became distinguished … It was not rashness that inspired him, but a high and chivalrous sense of duty."[30]

According to Edward Hill, a soldier of the 16th Michigan, the sun had set at 4:42pm and the order to advance only came from Brigadier General Griffin at 6:20pm. Oliver Norton, brigade bugler, sounded the order to advance, and Strong Vincent leapt forward, wheeling to face his men. Brandishing his sword towards the Confederate positions, "obscured with clouds of smoke, through which shone the luminous light of the Federal batteries and musketry, kindling into sheets of flame as it almost united with the enemy's fire flashing from the Sunken Road" and the heights above, Vincent yelled to be heard over the noise of battle, "Forward, Eighty-Third!"[31]

The 83rd Pennsylvania was the left-most regiment of the brigade's first line, with the 20th Maine in the center and the 17th New York on the right. In a second line behind them came the 16th Michigan, 44th New York, and 12th New York. The brigade charged through the millrace to the north of the Prussia Street Bridge, avoiding the span due to how accurately Confederate artillery had swept it clear during the day. Reforming on the bank of the millrace closest to the Confederates, cohesion in the ranks dissolved. As Norton sounded the order to charge, half of the brigade heard the order, and half did not. Consequently, the leftmost regiments, the 83rd Pennsylvania and 16th Michigan, and half of both center regiments, the 20th Maine and 44th New York, advanced, while the right-most regiments and the right half of the center regiments did not. The 83rd Pennsylvania stormed ahead through the unfinished railroad cut while the 20th Maine struggled through a brickyard on the plain leading towards the Confederate positions. Spotting what they believed to be Confederates advancing, the 83rd Pennsylvania fired a volley and charged forward to seize startled prisoners, instead finding that they had fired into the rear of the 10th New Hampshire* of the IX Corps, which had managed to conceal itself from the Confederates but had been unable to retreat until darkness fell.[32]

In the darkness, the advancing men of Stockton's brigade were tripping over the dead and wounded of the previous ineffective charges, orientating themselves towards the Jennings house—a small, whitewashed building that Stockton had designated as their objective. In his report, Vincent stated that, "the storm of shot and shell and musketry that now poured into us was exceedingly destructive. The enemy's guns completely commanded this ridge and its front slope. Officers and men fell rapidly, but there was not a waver of the line." Enfilade artillery fire blasted holes in the regiments, and Confederate marksmen picked out unlucky individuals. In a slight swale of the slope, Stockton's brigade relieved the regiments which had been pinned down under heavy fire all day, sending them racing to the rear. The brigade settled in for some long-range musketry, with no orders to withdraw. Theodore Gerrish, a private in the 20th Maine, wrote that, "through the long hours of that December night, we remained prostrated upon the wet, muddy ground. There could be no sleep; the groans of the wounded, and the scattered firing kept up between the contending lines, made a strange medley for those who listened … We were wishing the hours away, and yet dreaded to have the darkness disappear."[33]

The men of Stockton's brigade were not going anywhere as dawn broke on Sunday, December 14. The Federal soldiers in the swale fired upon the Confederates, who returned fire, and a Confederate battery attempted to hone in on where they were concealed, with no real success. They mostly lay still, in the mud and blood, with corpses around, "for, the moment a head appeared above the brow of the hill, a dozen bullets came whizzing after it." There was no real fighting on Sunday, December 14, "either out of mutual respect for the day, or because the rebels had determined to act only on the defensive, and

---

* Judson identifies them as "a New Jersey regiment," but both Vincent's report and Colonel Donohoe of the 10th New Hampshire's Report identify the regiment as the 10th New Hampshire. Vincent makes no reference to firing upon them.

Burnside had concluded it was best to act on the offensive no longer." Lying in the mud and blood of the battlefield along with his men, Colonel Vincent passed what must have seemed the longest day of the entire war pinned down under Confederate fire. As darkness fell, the men of Stockton's brigade passed 24 hours on the field before the stone wall and sunken road. Orders finally came up for the brigade to retire back to Fredericksburg. As the men withdrew, the *aurora borealis* began to shine.[34]

The defeat at Fredericksburg stung the Army of the Potomac. Oliver Norton refused to discuss it in detail in a letter to his sister: "We have had a terrible fight, but you have heard of that, and I need not give particulars. I don't feel like it, for it was nothing but humiliating defeat." The brigade remained in Fredericksburg, and Colonel Stockton had become ill from exposure during the 36 hours that the brigade had been up, between waiting to advance and being pinned down on the field. Vincent, as the next most senior commissioned colonel in the brigade, temporarily ascended to command while Stockton retired to the rear, across the Rappahannock, to convalesce at a field hospital. Under Vincent's command, the brigade served as the rear-guard of the Army of the Potomac as it withdrew from Fredericksburg, returning to the swales and slopes of Marye's Heights through the night of December 15 and into the morning of the 16th. When the order came to withdraw, a bright moon shone overhead, and it was obvious to most men that standing up, even to withdraw, would be death. "But," wrote Colonel Swan, "when the order first came the young commander had observed a few little clouds over the hills." Taking note of the impending arrival of cloud cover to conceal their movements, Vincent did not order his men to withdraw immediately. Instead, he lay on his back and stared intently at the clouds approaching the moon. "When at last the moon withdrew her face, for once unwelcome, the relief that came to every soldier's mind was inseparably connected with confidence in his commander." Vincent began personally leading the brigade, company by company, back to Fredericksburg. They had all reached the river by 7am Behind them as they crossed the river, the engineers undid the bridges, withdrawing the pontoons to the shore guarded by Henry Hunt's guns on Stafford Heights.[35]

CHAPTER 6

"I Enlisted to Fight": January to April 1863

"But our country called you, darling, Angels cheer your way;
While our nation's sons are fighting, We can only pray.
Nobly strike for God and liberty, Let all nations see
How we love the starry banner, Emblem of the free.
Weeping, sad and lonely, Hopes and fears how vain! Yet pray,
When this cruel war is over, Pray that we meet again."

WEEPING, SAD AND LONELY, CHARLES CARROL SAWYER AND HENRY TUCKER, 1863[1]

Following the debacle of the battle of Fredericksburg, the Army of the Potomac settled into its winter quarters around Falmouth, across the Rappahannock River from the ruined city. They had lost 12,653 men killed, wounded, or missing, in comparison to Confederates' 5,309. Throughout the army, there was a general despondence and malaise circulating among the troops, perhaps best exemplified by Oliver Norton's scathing words in a letter to his sister, "We have got a man now who will move, no matter what reason he has for standing still. You may think I am talking bitterly. Well, I feel so. I'm sick of such useless slaughter. McClellan never made an attack and failed, and never showed such stupidity as Burnside has." The 83rd Pennsylvania and its brigade, still temporarily under Vincent's command, were encamped at Stoneman's Station, near Claiborne Run, living in rough-hewn log huts among the snow and freezing rain.[2]

In the immediate aftermath of Fredericksburg, on December 17, 1862, Brigadier General Daniel Butterfield wrote to Edwin Stanton, secretary of war, "to recommend for promotion as brigadier-generals of volunteers Capt. S. H. Weed, Fifth Artillery, and Col. Strong Vincent, Eighty-third Pennsylvania Volunteers, for gallantry and good services in the attack of December 13 and the subsequent operations to this date." It is not known whether Vincent was aware that Butterfield had presented him for promotion, but Butterfield wrote that, "Colonel Vincent has been long under my command, and has by gallantry and devotion to duty richly merited promotion." Sadly, neither Weed nor Vincent would be promoted on Butterfield's initiative, and would both sacrifice their lives for their country within days of each other.[3]

For two weeks around the New Year, Elizabeth Vincent spent the holiday with her husband in winter quarters. Oliver Norton recalled Lizzie's visit to the regiments during the winter of 1862–63 in his memoirs: "When his duties permitted, Vincent loved to ride with her through

Elizabeth Carter, seen here in the 1850s while employed as a teacher at Miss Porter's School in Farmington, Connecticut, prior to her marriage to Strong Vincent. (*Courtesy of the Theodore Karle Civil War Collection, Erie County Historical Society/Hagen History Center, Erie, Pennsylvania*)

the camps of the army and about the surrounding country. They were followed with looks of admiration wherever they appeared. Their love was ideal. She knew the risks of the service, but she always encouraged him to do his full duty." Even without his wife present in camp, however, Strong Vincent remained a striking figure in the Army of the Potomac. "Many officers will remember Vincent's quarters near Potomac Creek, after the battle of Fredericksburg," insisted Colonel Swan. "He had a way of drawing people to himself. He had much leisure, as the men of his regiment had been long in the field, and it required but little attention to keep them comfortable and in good drill and discipline … therefore he was ever ready to extend a welcome to those who came." Vincent's reputation as a host apparently spread through the Army of the Potomac and even beyond, for Swan counted among his visitors not only "officers of the highest rank," but also politicians and sporting men—without, of course, ever naming any of his old school friend's visitors. Despite only being 25 years old, Vincent "seem[ed] the compeer of men of forty" that winter, wrote Colonel Swan, further mentioning his hair now being "a little gray" as his body was becoming somewhat stout, paired with a "decisive countenance and confident address." War was aging the colonel. On January 24, 1863, he received a telegraph from Lizzie urging him to request a leave to return to Erie to discuss an "important family matter," He virtually flew home to Erie, where his wife informed him that she was pregnant. While Confederates jeered that Burnside was "Stuck in the Mud," Vincent took advantage of his 10-day leave to pose for a carte-de-visite photograph at the studio of the Dolph Brothers at Farrar Hall, where, nearly two years before, he had spoken at the enlistment meetings for the 83rd Pennsylvania.[4]

During Vincent's leave, Abraham Lincoln relieved Ambrose Burnside of command of the army following the twin debacles of Fredericksburg and the "mud march," banishing him to command the Military Department of Ohio, comprising the states of Ohio, Indiana, Illinois, and Kentucky, on the assumption that he couldn't get into too much trouble in the Midwest. Command of the Army of the Potomac devolved upon Major General Joseph Hooker, who returned the army to a corps organizational footing and named Major General George Meade

Strong Vincent as colonel of the 83rd Pennsylvania, in a photograph taken while on leave in Erie in early February of 1863. (*Courtesy of the Library of Congress of the United States*)

to command the V Corps. A gruff, grizzled, Pennsylvanian known for an easily stoked temper that was said by one fellow officer to be "a rage so magnificent that it seemed capable of moving mountains," Meade was teasingly referred to as the "goggle-eyed snapping-turtle" behind his back by his staff officers, due to his protuberant eyes and volcanic temper. Despite this, Meade was a fighting general, stubborn and tenacious as a bulldog when pushed.[5]

Colonel Vincent returned to his regiment from his leave in early February. Wielding a riding crop given to him by Elizabeth, who had asked him to carry it as a token of her, he set to work attempting to restore his regiment. He began to recall men from duty that had assigned them away from the regiment, employing any means necessary to get them back, including, in at least one case, withholding promotion until the soldier rejoined the regiment.[6]

Throughout the stay in winter quarters, Vincent dealt with a variety of issues, including the continued fracas over the 83rd's lack of a regimental surgeon. When Ezra P. Allen, surgeon of the 141st Pennsylvania, was transferred to the 83rd, Vincent was forced to write to the surgeon general of Pennsylvania to explain that he had requested the transfer of William Church, the young senior surgeon of the 141st, so that Allen, a middle-aged man who had been made assistant surgeon of the 141st and had been the physician of its men for most of their lives, could remain in that unit because he knew the men better. But this left the 83rd Pennsylvania without a surgeon when neither man moved to fill the vacancy. Other personnel issues also required Vincent's attention. He issued a terse response to Samuel Thomas, the Department Secretary of Commissions for the Commonwealth of Pennsylvania, informing him that two newly-arrived commissions were in error: "Lt. Hunter is discharged by reason of disability, the commission will be sent him. Lt. Harrington [sic] fell at Bull Run. His commission will be forwarded to his parents." He then demanded to know when Governor Andrew Curtin would "appoint and commission a number of officers who have won promotion by gallantry and attention to duty," informing Thomas that he had sent a list of just such promotions to the adjutant general of Pennsylvania "a few days since." When the situation with surgeons Church and Allen still had not been resolved, Vincent wrote to Captain Estes, the acting assistant adjutant general of the Army of the Potomac, to explain the situation, and "ask that Surgeon Church be transferred to the 83rd Penna. and Surgeon Allen assigned to the 141st Penna." Vincent requested the acceptance of the resignation of Captain Phineas Carpenter to his superiors, stating that while "Capt. Carpenter is an excellent officer … No man of this regt. ever questioned his bravery. I should be sorry to lose him." Vincent was aware Carpenter's "wife … is an invalid and dependant[sic] ever upon his return for her life."[7]

Discipline always seemed to become an issue when the regiment was encamped for an extended time, and this was to be no exception. Vincent ordered the arrest of a soldier attempting to desert in Washington City, requesting that, "you will oblige me if it can be done, by arresting this officer again and causing him to be sent direct to Acquia [sic] Creek for his reg[iment]." Once more writing to Captain Estes to note his compliance with new corps commander George Meade's orders to check the preparedness of his men, Vincent informed him that "my command is completely equipped for service, with the exception of 41 Springfield rifles required for & 10 Slings long since required," reporting that his command had at least a week's rations, anywhere from "five to ten days forage" and a total of 24 mules available for service.[8]

For much of the time the Army of the Potomac lay in winter quarters, however, Vincent was not busy with letters or reports.

"The quiet life of this winter was a taste of the life Vincent would have chosen," Colonel Swan wrote in his brief biography of his friend. "He was ambitious for distinction, and in any walk of life would have striven for the honors men pay to those who display great merit; but to him there were honors as real, if not as dazzling, to be gained in peace as in war. At the bar and in the Senate he would have sought his laurels." His background as a lawyer led to Vincent being offered the position of president of a court martial board in mid-February, for the duration of his stay in winter quarters. Vincent accepted. In this capacity, he oversaw the trials of deserters, insubordinates, thieves, and various other soldiers who had flouted military justice. Historian Ramold describes courts martial in the Federal Army in his book on military discipline as possessing a suspiciously "un-American and un-Constitutional" tinge in the eyes of the citizen soldiers of the armies, but points out that presiding officers—such as Vincent—"proved very flexible and lenient when circumstances permitted. The judges … undoubtedly had procedures and regulations to follow, but there was room for legal interpretation, clemency, and a system of review and appeal that ensured that courts-martial were anything but rigid and unmerciful." Yet when Vincent served as the presiding judge of the courts martial in February and March 1863, the Lieber Code (antecedent to the modern Uniform Code of Military Justice) had not yet been promulgated by the judge advocate general's office in Washington under General Orders 100. This meant that Vincent relied principally on his Harvard education regarding the laws of the United States, and his own self-taught knowledge of the Articles of War and extant army regulations in order to dispense verdicts and preside over trials. Yet it was not as presiding judge of the courts martial that Vincent would attain his superior officers' notice once more: it would be as a defense attorney.[9]

Lieutenant Colonel Caspar Trepp of the 1st U.S. Sharpshooters had been born in Switzerland in 1829 and was a veteran of the French Foreign Legion. He had moved to the United States by 1859, when he first appeared in a New York City directory. When the war began, Trepp, along with his friend Hiram Berdan, had organized and raised the 1st United States Sharpshooters (U.S.S.S.). An accomplished marksman intimately acquainted with the materials and methods of marksmen, Trepp principally oversaw the training of the men. By the end of 1862, Berdan and Trepp had fallen out with one another, and on February 9, 1863, Berdan accused his second-in-command of theft of regimental stationary, indicting him formally and impaneling a court martial.[10]

The formal charges against Lieutenant Colonel Trepp included Berdan's original accusation of theft, but also added charges of "misbehavior before the enemy" during Trepp's command of Fort Davidson during the Peninsular Campaign and during the battle of Hanover Court House; that Trepp was "unable by reason of fear to give the proper commands" during the battle of Hanover Court House; that he "did abandon his command and leave them without orders during the entire day" of the battle of Malvern Hill; and that he had disobeyed orders at Fredericksburg—allegedly having said: "Do you think I am going to sacrifice my life for a few of you men?" For good measure, Berdan also threw in charges of Trepp being absent without leave and violating the articles of war. Berdan listed himself as witness to every alleged crime.[11]

Trepp's trial was held on March 2, 1863, at III Corps headquarters near Falmouth, Virginia, with Colonel Samuel M. Bowman of the 84th Pennsylvania serving as president of "a General Court Martial commenced at the head quarters pursuant to General Order No. 16 dated Febry. 9th 1863" calling for Trepp to stand trial on Berdan's charges. "To all of which charges and specifications the accused Lt. Col. Trepp 1st &c. pleaded 'not guilty.'"[12]

In the files of the New-York Historical Society, there is one sheet, written in pencil, containing questions asked of Colonel Berdan during cross-examination by Trepp's defense, and the answers provided. "Did you give him instruction on being in command of that Right line?" Vincent asked Berdan, to which Berdan responded, "I am not positive!" The exclamation point is much darker than the rest of the written text of the question or answer; whoever created this sheet was pleased with Berdan's ambivalence in response to Vincent's question. The handwriting is not that of Strong Vincent, but through this solitary page an appreciation for his legal talent can be gleaned. "Was it customary to have the senior officer as in charge of the line issue no such orders?" Vincent asked, to which Berdan responded, "I supposed so but do not know." Berdan's memory seemed to be faulty that day: "Would you be able to recognize the officer you made inquiries to for me?" "I could not swear to it, it might be."[13]

Beyond that one sheet of lined paper covered in pencil writing, and a sworn statement by Trepp refuting the charge of cowardice and neglecting his command at Fort Davidson, precious few of the nearly 100 pages in the Trepp Court Martial file are actual trial transcripts. In the end, the court martial returned a verdict of "not guilty" on all charges for Lieutenant Colonel Trepp, General Orders No. 31 proclaiming that, "the proceedings of the General court martial in the case of Lt. Col. Caspar Trepp 1st U.S.S.S. are affirmed. Lt. Col Trepp is released from arrest + will return to duty with his regiment."[14]

Vincent had secured Trepp's acquittal, though he had nothing to do with Trepp's immediate countercharges against Berdan, which led to Colonel Berdan's own court martial in April. Still, the defense of the accused Trepp caught the attention of Vincent's superiors, and in late March, he was offered the position of judge advocate of the Army of the Potomac.* In 1862, the War Department and Radical Republicans in Congress had expanded the office of judge advocate general following disagreements with its occupant when the war began, Major John F. Lee. The expansion made the office consist of 10 "field judge advocates," one for each field army and military department of the Federal Army.

---

* It is not known who, precisely, made Vincent the offer. However, Major General Daniel Butterfield, as Army Chief of Staff and Vincent's former brigade and corps commander, makes the most sense out of all of Hooker's headquarters staff.

These attorneys for the United States Army reported only to the Judge Advocate General, Joseph Holt (following Lee's 1862 resignation), the secretary of war, and the president. The position of chief lawyer of the United States' Army of the Potomac would have appealed to Vincent, who was a lawyer by trade in his civilian life. This was an elite position with only nine other lawyers in the entire country as his peers; holding the office would have been an enormous boon to Vincent's career as a lawyer and firmly cemented the young officer's place in the military. Colonel Swan, in his biography of his friend, writes that, in spite of its benefits, Vincent "did not consider the position equal to that of the command of a regiment," and Vincent refused the offer. "I enlisted to fight," Swan quotes Vincent as saying when his friends in the service—more than likely Swan and fellow lawyer Colonel James C. Rice of the 44th New York—lambasted him for refusing the position. Denying a position which would have equated to a significant increase in salary and prestige, clear post-war benefits to his career, and a removal to the relative safety of army headquarters, showed that Vincent was not serving in the army out of a sense of opportunism or self-indulgence. Vincent was content to remain where he was, serving as a front-line infantry officer. He said he had enlisted to fight, and so he would.[15]

After the Trepp case, in April 1863, Vincent served as defense attorney for Lieutenant Colonel Norval E. Welch of the 16th Michigan in his court martial brought by Colonel Thomas Stockton on the charge of disobedience of orders. Welch and Stockton had been feuding for nearly a year by the time Welch's trial began on April 16. Welch clearly coveted Stockton's position as commander of the regiment, and Stockton thought Welch an arrogant blackguard Copperhead* who defied military convention, rewrote supply orders for his own benefit, and tried to usurp control of the regiment—all charges Stockton leveled. Once

* Copperhead was a colorful epithet for anti-war Democrats in the North given to them by their Republican opponents, comparing them to the venomous snake. The anti-war Democrats, however, adopted the name as a point of pride: cutting the heads of Liberty from copper pennies to wear as badges on their lapels. Many prominent Copperheads were sympathetic to the Southern cause, and were thus viewed as traitors in the North.

more, Vincent got his client acquitted on all counts, and Welch's release spelled doom for Stockton's three-decade career with the U.S. Army. Welch proceeded to purge the 16th Michigan of any officer more loyal to Stockton than himself by bringing them up for court-martial on any charge he could find.[16]

While the army lay in camp and spring began to return to the Virginia countryside, the new flag that Vincent had requested in November arrived in camp. The original flag was given as a gift to the City of Erie by the regiment, delivered by wounded comrades returning home after the arrival of their new banner.[17]

At the end of March, the seemingly endless round-robin of efforts to secure a regimental surgeon for the 83rd Pennsylvania entered a third phase, as E. P. Allen resigned from the service altogether "for the reason assigned of the approaching death of his wife." Assistant Surgeon Michael Thompson was, however, "exceedingly anxious to obtain my recommendation [sic] & that of the Medical Directors of the Div. & Corps to you for the promotion, which both myself and those officers do not deem it our duty to the regt. to give." Requesting, yet again, "the medical charge of a regt. another Surgeon & Asst.," it must have seemed to Vincent, and to Surgeon General James King in Pennsylvania, that the 83rd simply could not keep a surgeon.[18]

In another letter written by Vincent at the end of March, he requested that "Private Norton of 'K' Co. of this regt. now detailed as Bugler at Brigade Hd. Qrs. may be ordered to return to his regt. I ask this because I have had but one Bugler for months on duty with the command. He has grown authoritative & much wind broken and is no longer fit to do what he attempts." Norton, however, was not pleased by his drop in status. In a letter to his sister, he fumed that, "Colonel Vincent could not be satisfied to let me stay when I had a good berth, but insisted on my coming back. My reward for strict attention to duty is this, retrograde promotion." Norton's chief complaints, however, were that, "some one else will, ride my horse now (you know how I have always loved a horse and can guess how I shall miss him), and some one else will carry my colors … I did squirm some to find that I was only recalled because Colonel Vincent wanted a good bugler in the regiment, and cared nothing about what they had at headquarters."[19]

The men of the 83rd Pennsylvania, Vincent included, were struggling through a series of "very strong, rainy, disagreeable" days as March ended and April began. Captain John Sell complained to his parents that, "some of us men nearly drownded [sic] in our little huts and poor wall tents." No sooner had the rain gone, Sell noted, than "the sun has shone, and the wind has flew a hurricane, completely drying up all the mud & mud puddles." Following his complaints about the weather, Sell informs his parents that, "Col Vincent took his wife home on Friday last," giving Elizabeth Carter Vincent a presence in camp, surprisingly, as late as March 27, 1863. Captain Sell had also written a letter to his brother, William, on March 26, noting that, "Col Vincent + wife leave for home to-morrow, he makes a very short stay, will be home before this letter reaches you." Besides Sell's letters, no other source refers to Lizzie Vincent in camp with her husband any time but around the beginning of the year. It is possible she may have chosen to visit Vincent at camp once more following her revelation of her pregnancy, as Captain Sell would certainly have no need to lie about her presence in camp.[20]

After months of preparation, Major General Joseph Hooker finally issued orders to his corps commanders to march on April 27, 1863. His 135,000-man army would cross the river away from Fredericksburg while a token force mounted a diversion at the city. They would flank Lee and attempt to crush his Army of Northern Virginia between themselves and the Rappahannock River. If Hooker's plan worked, the war would be over before summer.[21]

CHAPTER 7

"I Wish He Were a Brigadier-General": May to June 1863

> "We are coming, Father Abraham, three hundred thousand more,
> From Mississippi's winding stream and from New England's shore,
> We leave our plows and workshops, our wives and children dear,
> With hearts too full for utterance, with but a silent tear;
> We dare not look behind us, but steadfastly before
> We are coming, Father Abraham, three hundred thousand more!"
>
> *We Are Coming, Father Abraham*, arr. S. J. Adams; lyrics by the *New York Evening Post*[1]

The Army of the Potomac began its annual march on Richmond on April 27, 1863. Strong Vincent had returned to command of the 83rd Pennsylvania, as Colonel Stockton had returned to active service after a few months' convalescence in Washington to recover from the exposure he had suffered at Fredericksburg. Hooker's initial movements were promising. The army had crossed the Rappahannock at United States Ford and Kelly's Ford by April 29, and then the Rapidan at Ely's Ford on the same day. By April 30, the V, XI, and XII Corps had arrived at Chancellor's Tavern, in the thick tangle of woods known to the locals as "the Wilderness."[2]

The Civil War was now entering its third full year. In a letter to Elizabeth written in the waning days of April 1863, Strong Vincent seemed to evoke more of Ulysses S. Grant and William Tecumseh Sherman than Joe Hooker or George McClellan when he stated that:

> We must fight them more vindictively, or we shall be foiled at every step. We must desolate the country as we pass through it, and not leave the trace of doubtful

> friend or foe behind us; make them believe that we are in earnest; terribly in earnest; that to break this band in twain is monstrous and impossible; that the life of every man, yea, of every weak woman or helpless child in the entire South is of no value whatever compared with the integrity of the Union.[3]

This was clearly a far more aggressive take on the prosecution of the war than Vincent had evinced before. The horrors of war he had experienced at Fredericksburg, where he spent an entire day lying in muck and mud and blood; and quite possibly, though there is not currently known directly corroborating evidence for this supposition, his first-hand witness to the brutal realities of slavery at the plantation on the Pamunkey River, had hardened Vincent's zealous belief in the righteousness of the twin causes of liberty and the Union. Nothing would end this war until the South was fully and completely broken, both by military force and by the destruction of the institution of slavery which sustained the Southern war effort.

Joseph Hooker set his plan into motion for the battle of Chancellorsville on May 1. The V Corps was dispatched to the north to seize Bank's Ford, and the XII Corps, advancing along the Orange Plank Road towards Fredericksburg, 10 miles distant, plowed right into Confederate Lieutenant General Thomas J. "Stonewall" Jackson's corps. Hooker's efforts to seize the initiative—to hammer Lee before Lee could figure out where he had gone—had misfired. As Major General Henry Slocum's XII Corps reeled from Jackson's surprise appearance, Meade and the V Corps were ordered to countermarch back to Chancellorsville to be brought up as reinforcement. "On our retiring," Meade wrote to his wife, "the enemy attacked [Major General George] Sykes's division of my corps and we had a smart fight till dark." As Sykes's division of the V Corps, reinforced by elements of the II Corps, held stubbornly to McGee's Hill, an order arrived from Hooker telling the Federal forces to abandon it; the Army of the Potomac was falling back into the Wilderness to adopt a defensive position.[4]

On its abortive march towards Bank's Ford on May 1, the 83rd Pennsylvania had found "a newly deserted camp with tents all standing, and in it some of the French knapsacks and muskets we lost at Gaines' Mill." Returning that night to the main line of the Army of the Potomac, through the gnarled and thick woods of the Wilderness, the 83rd Pennsylvania got lost on the road, following three companies of the 17th New York that had become separated from their regiment. "We pushed on, however, through the thick underbrush and over the ditches and fallen trees," wrote Amos Judson, "after groping and feeling our way through the woods for two miles, we came to a very deep ravine." Colonel Vincent himself galloped off for division headquarters to report his position, for the skirmishers he had thrown out had discovered that the 83rd Pennsylvania had come to a halt "but a short distance from" Confederate troops. Major General Griffin swiftly dispatched a guide for Vincent to retrieve his regiment and withdraw it back to the Chancellorsville Road.[5]

While the 83rd Pennsylvania fumbled its way through the dark woods to the Chancellorsville Road, Confederate Lieutenant Generals Robert E. Lee and "Stonewall" Jackson were meeting over a campfire to plan the next day's battle. Jackson had intelligence that Hooker's right flank, the XI Corps under Major General Oliver Otis Howard, was "in the air," without any natural means of defense. Jackson's staff had been informed of a newly constructed road through the woods that would allow Confederate troops to move to flank the XI Corps without being detected by the main Federal line. "How many men," Lee asked his subordinate, "would you take on the flanking march?" "My whole command," Jackson responded dourly. Lee gave his consent, breaking the accepted Jominian rules of warfare by dividing his already smaller army in the face of the enemy, and Jackson's corps was on the march by dawn on May 2.[6]

The XI Corps of the Army of the Potomac was, somewhat sneeringly, called "the Dutch corps" by some other soldiers within the army, as it was predominantly made up of German immigrants to the United States and led almost exclusively by German officers. Hooker had, by all accounts, erred in placing them under the command of Oliver Otis Howard, a Bible-thumping, teetotal, firebrand New England evangelical known both mockingly and admiringly as "the Christian general," whose mandatory Methodist revival-style corps worship services and Bible studies antagonized not only the "free-thinking" Germans among his ranks, but also the Lutherans and the Catholics. Further exacerbating the issue, Howard did not speak German, and most of the soldiers under his command spoke only a little English. This corps, already lacking in cohesion, received the hammer-blow of Jackson's flanking attack.[7]

On Hooker's left flank, anchored against the Rappahannock near Scott's Dam, the V Corps remained fully insulated from the chaos of Saturday, May 2, 1863. When Jackson's corps exploded out of the woods on the XI Corps' flank late in the afternoon, the V Corps was on the exact opposite end of the army and was not part of the rout that ensued. The conventional wisdom of the day was that Lee "had already been compelled to divide his army in order to hold back [Major General John] Sedgwick* and come against us. He could not afford to divide again, for, should he attempt that, certainly Hooker would attack his separate bodies and conquer him in detail." Yet that was precisely what Lee did. Jackson's flank attack put the XI Corps to rout, and the Confederate advance stalled only because of disorganization brought on by looting the captured Federal camps and the coming of nightfall. Major General Daniel E. Sickles's III Corps and Slocum's XII Corps held the line, reorganizing during the night to face Jackson's men to the west. Jackson himself was felled by friendly fire while undertaking a reconnaissance of the Federal lines, dying of his injuries on May 10.[8]

On the morning of Sunday, May 3, the V Corps was cycled to replace the shattered XI Corps on the right flank of the Army of the Potomac. While the demoralized Germans lined up near Scott's Dam, the V Corps hooked itself to the right flank of Sickles's III Corps on the Plank Road near Hunting Run, with its right flank being reinforced by the arrival of Major General John F. Reynolds's I Corps, which anchored against the Rapidan so that Hooker's line arced from Scott's Dam to the Rapidan along the Plank Road. The United States Ford was safely in the rear of their arc, providing the Army of the Potomac an escape route if the situation further deteriorated. All that day, the men of Stockton's brigade were engaged in fortifying their new position, waiting for an attack that did not come against their part of the line. All the next day, Monday, they lay in their new entrenchments waiting for an attack that did not

* Major General John Sedgwick's VI Corps had been left behind at Fredericksburg as a diversionary force to try and pin down Lee's army against the Rappahannock.

reach their part of the line. On Monday night, May 4, the Army of the Potomac began to withdraw across the Rappahannock over the United States Ford, limping back to their winter quarters. The battle of Chancellorsville had ended in yet another ignoble defeat for the Federal forces. All told, Vincent's 83rd Pennsylvania had suffered a loss of "4 wounded, all slightly, and 1 man disabled by falling, in crossing the Rapidan."[9]

The news of Hooker's withdrawal stunned the nation. Abraham Lincoln lamented the news with cries of, "My God! My God! What will the country say!" An acquaintance of Lincoln, journalist Noah Brooks, claimed that, "had a thunderbolt fallen upon the President he could not have been more overwhelmed." The I and V Corps of the Army of the Potomac had never even been engaged, and a simmering discontentment filled the soldiers of the army that they had not even been given a chance to fight the Confederates. Hooker had simply panicked and withdrawn. The reputation of "Fighting Joe" Hooker had suffered serious damage in four days in the Virginia Wilderness. Oliver Norton wrote: "To say we were surprised would give but a feeble idea to our feelings. We felt more confident than ever that we could repulse all that could be brought against us. But for some reason, satisfactory to General Hooker no doubt, we did recross the river, and night saw us in our old camps."[10]

Once more returned to their camps, the Army of the Potomac began to dwindle; the first wave of enlistments were expiring, and Stockton's brigade lost two regiments, the 12th and 17th New York, both returned home at the close of their service. This left the brigade with only four regiments: the 83rd Pennsylvania, 44th New York, 16th Michigan, and 20th Maine. On May 18, Colonel Thomas Stockton—citing ill health, but also likely due in no small part to his failed court-martial of Lieutenant Colonel Welch—resigned from the army. As senior colonel, Strong Vincent permanently ascended to command of the brigade. His promotion meant that command of the 83rd Pennsylvania would pass to its next most senior officer. As it was, Lieutenant Colonel Hugh Campbell had lost a leg at Second Bull Run in August 1862 and had resigned from the army as a result of his injury, and Major Hugh Lamont was absent from the regiment on duty at division headquarters on the staff of Brigadier General James Barnes. Command of the 83rd Pennsylvania thus devolved to Captain Orpheus Woodward, commander of Company D. The fact that a regiment was now commanded by a captain—a position normally held by a colonel—is a stark illustration of how disease, battle, desertion, and expiring enlistments had depleted the ranks.[11]

On May 20, Vincent issued General Orders Numbered 1, 2 and 3. General Order No. 1 dealt with the assigning of his headquarters staff. Two members would come from each veteran regiment of the brigade: John M. Clark and Amos Judson from the 83rd Pennsylvania, William Jewett and Minor Newell from the 16th Michigan, and Frank Kelly and Eugene Nash from the 44th New York. General Order No. 2 proclaimed that, "The Regiments of this Brigade will be prepared to break camp tomorrow at 7 A.M. The 'Color' will sound at that hour." The brigade was moving to a new campground and would be "encamped in line of battle, the 83rd Pa. Vols. on the right, 44th N.Y. Vols. on the left, the 20th Maine in th[e] right center & the 16th Michigan Vols. on the left center." Vincent ordered "a front of 400 feet and a depth of 120 paces" for each regiment, laying out how many paces behind the "Color" line that each type of tent should be placed, with kitchens 20 paces in rear of the men's tents, which were in turn 10 to 40 paces behind the line, company officers 20 paces beyond the kitchens, and field and staff officers 30 paces beyond the company officers. General Order No. 3 established a schedule for the brigade: reveille would sound at 5am, drill would commence at 6:30am lasting until 8am, with dinner call at 12pm, more drill from 4pm to 6pm, and "Extinguishing lights Taps on the drums" at 9pm Saturdays were reserved for "bathing and washing clothes," Sundays would be the exclusive purview of brigade inspection and dress parade, and brigade-wide drills would occur on Tuesdays and Thursdays. These remarkably detailed orders were not wholly unheard of within the Federal Army—other commanders frequently were this descriptive in their orders—but they demonstrate Vincent's attention to detail and the concern for the orderliness and security of the regiments under his command. By laying out everything from latrine pits to the kitchens, he was ensuring everything had its place and was in its place.[12]

By May 27, 1863, Oliver Norton had been returned to headquarters as part of Vincent's new staff, once more serving as brigade bugler and color-bearer. "My horse is fat as a cub and sleek as a mole," Norton wrote approvingly to his sister of the horse he had been so loathe to part with in early April. The headquarters flag Norton bore was "triangular, six feet on a side. The border is blue, the middle white, and the Maltese cross is red. The red cross is the badge by which our division is known. Red, white and blue crosses, First, Second and Third Divisions of V Corps." Vincent's new headquarters, on a hill overlooking the brigade's line, was in an orchard, and Oliver Norton wrote approvingly of his tent's location, "I have pitched my tent under an apple tree that shades me all day long, and a mocking-bird sings to me the sweetest song ever heard." By army regulations, Norton and the rest of Vincent's staff were to be within several feet of Vincent at all times on the march or on the battlefield, headquarters guidon aloft to the breeze, so that couriers, senior officers, or regimental commanders could easily find the brigade commander in the midst of a march or fight.[13]

Brigadier General James Barnes, the 61-year-old engineer turned commander of the First Division, V Corps, received orders from corps commander Major General George Meade on May 28, 1863. He was to "take position on the Rappahannock River, covering the fords, and making such dispositions as will enable you to check, and, if practicable, prevent the crossing of that river by any body of the enemy's troops." The men of Vincent's brigade, the third brigade of Barnes's division, were to march to guard some of the river crossings, "posting at least a regiment at each ford, with detachments watching the dams and other crossing-places between, and posting the balance of the brigade at some suitable point in the center, so that either point, if threatened, can be re-enforced." Thus dispatched, the brigade settled into its new position to guard the fords of the Rappahannock.[14]

The four regiments of Vincent's brigade were spread along the river. The 44th New York held Bank's Ford, while the 16th Michigan guarded a milldam. The 20th Maine held United States Ford, and the 83rd Pennsylvania held Richard's Ford. "The rebel pickets are on the other side of the river, and ours this side," wrote a member of the 44th New York. "They do not fire at each other. The pickets of both sides go in swimming. The rebel pickets are not permitted to converse with us. All they say is, if we don't fire, they will not." The soldier continued to describe "one of our boys, named Lynch," who swam to the Confederate bank of the river and conversed with the Confederate pickets. Writing to Barnes at headquarters on May 30, Vincent noted that, "At daylight the enemy observed our rifle pits and hurried two regiments down into their works. In an hour they were withdrawn to the reserves." Building upon this, Vincent continued, stating that, "I have sent security parties from each regt. to patrol the immediate bank of the stream from Banks' Ford, to Deep Run, observing the position, character and number of the enemy's works and pickets." Vincent concluded his letter with a request for "a sufficient number of mounted men to act as orderlies and to patrol the country between the fords."[15]

On May 29, Vincent informed Barnes, Major General Meade had patrolled his lines, and Meade specifically referenced the patrol in his report to Hooker's headquarters on May 31: "Colonel Vincent's brigade guarding from Banks' Ford to the mouth of Deep Run; one regiment and battery at Banks' Ford; two regiments and battery at United States Ford, and one regiment at Richards' Ford. This command is so near the camps of French's division, Second Corps, that it was not deemed necessary to post any portion of the reserve near it."[16]

Amos Judson recalled the lazy days along the Rappahannock. "The rebels were posted, likewise, at every ford along the river, and they and our men had nothing to do but to while away the time as easily as they could, smoke the pipe of peace, and look lazily across the river at each other." Oliver Norton informed his cousin of one picket patrol whose members were hailed with a loud, "I say, you Yanks!" from the opposite shore, inquiring why the Federal pickets hadn't fired on newly-minted Confederate Lieutenant General A. P. Hill when he had passed along their lines. "Our boys had seen a man pass along their lines, but supposed he was the officer of the guard," Norton informed his cousin. The Confederates returned the courtesy, holding their fire as Vincent and his staff rode their lines, headquarters guidon aloft in Norton's hands. Norton, however, did not trust their courtesy. "Confound 'em! I don't think it's safe to trust them. I wouldn't be afraid of their firing at me, but I'm afraid to trust their promises with a Union officer within range of their guns." Norton's worry over Vincent showed a good deal of progress from his initial opinion of the young colonel as "a dude and an upstart" in the summer of 1861. It was an improvement of opinion shared by many of the men. Judson writes that Vincent's "capacity as a commander and his bearing as a soldier had already made a favorable impression upon the officers and men of the whole brigade … He soon proved himself to be the most popular brigade commander we had yet had; and, under his leadership, the famous old Light Brigade began to recover some of its former renown for discipline and soldierly conduct."[17]

"I have the honor to report that everything is quiet along my lines," Vincent wrote to division headquarters on June 1. His letter to headquarters that day had the primary purpose of reporting a man named Einbosie,* who had a farm near Vincent's pickets along the fords and whom he suspected of being a Confederate parolee. Vincent had arrested him as a spy the previous evening. Stating that, "he denies ever having been in the rebel service, but looks like a soldier and walks and talks like one, and declares himself a 'Secesh'," Vincent described how the commander of the cavalry forces that guarded the ford before their arrival, a "Capt. Fisher," had taken dinner with Einbosie and his family one evening. "The next morning," Vincent notes clinically, "the rebel pickets at day light cried out to ours 'How did Capt. Fisher like his dinner yesterday?' and 'What does he think of the people?' No one was at the house but the man's family."[18]

On June 3, Vincent and members of his staff undertook a review of the brigade's positions along the river. As they stood sentinel over the Rapphannock, even the most committed veterans were growing weary. In a letter to his brother William, Captain John Sell wrote that "Col Vincent … were [sic] here to-day. All well. Headq'r's of brigade is 12 miles off. 83d is on the river near U.S. Ford … I hope to God … that Jeff Davis will stop his fighting."[19]

Writing on June 4, Vincent had the unfortunate duty of reporting to division headquarters that Corporal Henry L. Davenport of the 16th

---

* Possibly "Einbacie;" Vincent's handwriting is rough and clearly hurried in this report to headquarters.

Michigan had deserted the regiment, crossing the Rappahannock to the Confederates. Two Confederate deserters Vincent had questioned confirmed that Davenport "gave the entire force of the brigade, and the disposition to them, and correctly as they repeated the information." Even more worrying in Vincent's mind was "the appearance of infantry in considerable force opposite Richards Ford and Deep Run, last night, where cavalry have been stationed heretofore. A Rebel rocket signal was observed at 9:30 o'clock P.M. last night opposite U.S. Ford. The enemy's posts and pickets are evidently stronger than our own there."[20]

On June 2, 1863, the Confederate Army of Northern Virginia had completed its reorganization. Now split into three army corps rather than its former two, Lee's army—some 75,000 men—had left its camps at dawn on June 3, and had begun to snake its way to the cover of the Blue Ridge Mountains, bearing north on another invasion campaign. It cannot be said for certain, but it is likely that Vincent's report of masses of Confederate infantry in his front were indications of the beginning of the Gettysburg campaign. He reported the movement on June 4, but stated that it had been "last night," the first day of Lee's march northwards. It is probable that the rebels he saw were flanking columns thrown out from the main body of Lieutenant General A. P. Hill's Third Corps of the Army of Northern Virginia to protect it on the march towards the Shenandoah Valley, given Hill's presence along the riverbank days before and the fact that his column passed closest to the Rappahannock on its way to Culpeper Court House and the Shenandoah Valley.[21]

Word of the Confederate movements were being carried to Major General Hooker at headquarters by spies and loyalists: a large force of Lee's army was reportedly moving upriver and massing near Culpeper Court House. Hooker wired to Washington that, "as I am liable to be called on to make a movement with the utmost promptitude … I am of the opinion that it is my duty to pitch into his rear, although in doing so the head of his column may reach Warrenton before I can return." Lincoln's response revealed the president's perpetual state of worry over the defense of Washington—a paranoia that made Lincoln keep his generals interposed between Lee and the Federal capital: "If he should leave a rear force at Fredericksburg, tempting you to fall upon it, it would fight in intrenchments, and have you at disadvantage, and so, man for man, worst you at that point, while his main force would in some way be getting an advantage of you Northward." Reiterating his point, Lincoln added, "I would not take any risk of being entangled upon the river, like an ox jumped half over a fence, and liable to be torn by dogs, front and rear, without a fair chance to gore one way or kick the other."[22]

Hooker's and Lincoln's worries about what Lee was doing increased by the hour. Cavalry forces of the Army of the Potomac fanned out trying to find the Confederate forces and, on June 6, a dispatch from Brigadier General John Buford arrived at headquarters. "Yesterday cannon firing was heard towards Culpeper. I suppose it was a salute, as I was told Stuart was to have had that day as an inspection of his whole force," it read. "I can't learn that there is any infantry north of the Rapidan, but am certain there is a very heavy cavalry force on the grazing grounds in Culpeper County." Hooker swiftly responded by sending Brigadier General Alfred Pleasonton and the Cavalry Corps to roust Lieutenant General J. E. B. Stuart and his troopers from Culpeper Court House on June 7, 1863. Some 8,000 cavalry troopers supported by 3,000 infantry and 24 cannons were under Pleasonton's command, and on June 9, 1863, they found Stuart; beginning the battle of Brandy Station, the largest cavalry action not just in the American Civil War, but in the history of the American continents. Though the Confederates held the field, Brandy Station rattled Stuart; his men had nearly been fought to defeat, and only the timidity of French Federal Colonel Alfred N. Duffié had allowed Stuart's flank to hold its ground. It would be in an effort to heal the injured psyche of his men that, within two weeks of Brandy Station, Stuart would lead his men in another effort to ride around the Federal Army and commit raids across the north, abandoning Lee's advance behind the Blue Ridge. This, in contrast, gave new life to the Federal cavalry, which had shown itself to have just as much *élan* and gallantry as its Confederate counterpart.[23]

The Confederate forces were undisputedly heading north. Pleasonton's cavalry continued to skirmish with Stuart's cavaliers up and down the Blue Ridge mountains, and on June 14, the Army of the Potomac began to march north in pursuit of Lee's army. Vincent's brigade had begun moving the day before on orders to rendezvous with the rest of Barnes's division near Morrisville. By June 15, Vincent and his men had reached Manassas Junction. They lay on the old Bull Run battlefield for two days before moving again on June 17 to Gum Spring. Amos Judson vividly recalled the "long march, through clouds of dust and beneath a scorching sun … the men, sweating beneath the heat and burden of their knapsacks, fell out in crowds and could be seen lying along every little stream, where a drop of water could be found to quench their raging thirst, or a bush to shelter them from the rays of the burning sun." Ellis Spear, acting as major of the 20th Maine, confided to his diary that it was, "exceedingly hot." Later in life, he recalled with some bitterness the "malarious country" of Virginia that they marched through from the Rappahannock to the Potomac: "The heat was excessive and the roads of clay, trodden & ground by thousands of feet & hundreds of wheels, sent up clouds of dust of unpalpable fineness, & so dense as to render it impossible to see twenty feet ahead." Sergeant John Berry of the 16th Michigan wrote in his diary: "A number of men drop dead in the ranks, sun struck."[24]

Vincent's brigade was ordered to Aldie, Virginia, on June 19. Their division commander, Brigadier General James Barnes, had received orders from Meade that evening to send troops to support the Federal cavalry attempting to dislodge Confederate horse soldiers near Ashby's Gap. In the 10 days since the battle of Brandy Station, Pleasonton's cavalry troopers had been skirmishing with J. E. B. Stuart's troopers along the length of the Blue Ridge, but the Confederates had significantly lessened the efficacy of Pleasonton's cavalrymen. Stuart's men had begun dismounting and seeking cover behind the low stone fences that were ubiquitous in the Virginia countryside. From these positions, they were immune to cavalry charge, and nearly immune to firing from the Federal troopers. Barnes selected Vincent's brigade to deal with them, and on June 21, Vincent's brigade marched to Middleburg to rendezvous with Federal cavalry in Pleasonton's command. Vincent's men deployed on the left end of Brigadier General David M. Gregg's troopers on the Ashby Gap road. "The dismounted men of the enemy were in position on the south side of this road, behind a series of stone walls running at right angles with it, the cavalry in the fields, and a battery of six guns placed near the road on the left," wrote Vincent. "A belt of woods some 200 yards marked their position." These Confederates were troopers belonging to Brigadier Generals Wade Hampton and Beverly Robertson's brigades of Stuart's cavalry.[25]

At 8am, Federal artillery opened fire on the Confederate positions. It was meant to be nothing more than a holding action; the main attack was to be carried out by Brigadier General John Buford's brigade, flanking the Confederate position. But Buford's men got mired in mud and in attempting to capture Stuart's supply train along Goose Creek, and the center of gravity of the engagement shifted.[26]

Vincent ordered the 16th Michigan to advance parallel to the road towards the front of the Confederate position in order to "dislodge their carbineers." Moving through the bank of trees, the men from Michigan opened fire on the entrenched Confederates. As they did so, Gregg's artillery continued to fire, and a Federal shell impacted in a Confederate caisson, causing it to explode dramatically. The explosion of the caisson rattled the Confederates, prompting them to fall back to another stone wall. Vincent swiftly directed the 44th New York and the 20th Maine to support the 16th Michigan while he dispatched the 83rd Pennsylvania on a flanking assault for the Confederate right. The feint was successful; the men from Pennsylvania sprang from the trees in the Confederate cavalry's right-rear and fired into them. "Finding their position turned," Judson wrote, "the enemy fled in confusion, and the Sixteenth advanced on the double quick, on the right."[27]

As the Confederates reeled and Vincent nipped at their heels, Gregg's troopers surged forward to join the pursuit. "The advance of the Second Brigade was so rapid that the enemy was compelled to abandon a gun and caisson which had been disabled," wrote Gregg. "Taking up position after position … the enemy stubbornly contested our advance." As the cavalry advanced, so, too, did Vincent's men. "Moving in conjunction with the cavalry, we drove them from this position to other stone walls immediately in the rear, dislodging them at each attack, until we pushed them across Crummer's Run."[28]

The Confederates tried to hold the bridge, setting up their three remaining cannons and forming a ragged picket line on the far bank of the stream. However, Vincent's four regiments threw out their skirmishers, who swiftly forded the stream and flanked the Confederate position once more, sending them reeling again. This kept up for four miles, Vincent's infantry flanking the Confederates out of a defensive position, a general pursuit by infantry and cavalry, and repeating it all again until the Confederates sought shelter behind a low stone wall on steeply rising ground at the far end of a stone bridge across Goose Creek. Behind the wall, the three Confederate cannons began to fire once more. L. A. Hendricks, a correspondent for the *New York Herald* who was accompanying Pleasonton's men, reported on the fight: "There was hot work for a time. Our infantry and batteries advanced with the advancing cavalry, our batteries severely punishing the enemy with grape and schrapnel [sic], and our own men being exposed to the enemy's shells and occasional Austrian rifles fired from behind stone fences." After nearly two hours in stalemate by the bridge, standing in his stirrups, no doubt exhausted—just like his men—having fought all day and advanced 13 miles before the four-mile pursuit of the Confederates, Vincent brandished his sword and bellowed for his men to, "Stop that damned battery howling!"[29]

"At a bound," writes Amos Judson, "the skirmishers of the Sixteenth, followed by those of the Eighty-Third, dashed over the bridge with a general yell, and shouting 'Shoot them!' 'Take them prisoners!' rushed up the hill, drove them from behind the walls again and put them to flight, taking a number of prisoners, both officers and men." As the Confederates reeled again, Gregg's troopers stormed across the bridge. In his report on the battle, Vincent seemed to be awestruck by the cavalry's final charges after the retreating Confederates: "The charges of the cavalry, a sight I had never before witnessed, were truly inspiring, and the triumphant strains of the bands, as squadron after squadron hurled the enemy in his flight up the hills and towards the gap, gave us a feeling of regret that we, too, were not mounted and could not join the chase." It was recalled by Amos Judson as "one of the liveliest and most exciting times we had ever yet experienced: when we were carried along, as it were, by the very tempest, whirlwind, and, I might say, joy of battle into the midst of the enemy's ranks."[30]

V Corps commander Major General George Meade was jubilant at Vincent's success in the battle of Upperville, and he supposedly exclaimed to his staff that, "I wish he were a brigadier general, I'd put him in charge of a division." Vincent's brigade was relieved and retired back towards Middleburg, pitching tents in the farmyard of a Mr. Glasscock of Aldie, Virginia, where Vincent and his staff made their headquarters and had dinner. "He set before us a good supper and breakfast and appeared very anxious to receive greenbacks in payment," recalled Amos Judson, who was serving as one of Vincent's aides-de-camp. Some soldiers of the brigade indulged in sightseeing in the area. "Not far from our camp … stood the country residence of President Monroe," wrote Eugene Nash, another of Vincent's aides-de-camp. "Many of our soldiers visited the place and would have been much pleased to have met the proprietor." Monroe's home, Oak Hill, was "then owned by Major [John W.] Fairfax, who was absent in the Confederate Army."[31]

The brigade remained at Aldie until June 25, when it began to march north towards the Potomac. Heavy and torrential rains had swept out the non-stone bridge of Goose Creek, and the brigade was forced to build its own bridge for the rest of the V Corps on the march to Leesburg, then to cross the Potomac at Edwards' Ferry, eventually halting two miles from Frederick, Maryland, on June 26.[32]

June 27, 1863, saw Major General Joseph Hooker leave his army at Frederick and travel to Harper's Ferry to inspect the garrison there, and to demand they be released to serve in the Army of the Potomac. "I find 10,000 men here in condition to take the field. Here they are of no earthly account. They cannot defend a ford of the river, and as far as Harper's Ferry is concerned, there is nothing of it." Hooker followed up his first telegram from Harper's Ferry with another: "My original instructions require me to cover Harper's Ferry and Washington. I have now imposed upon me, in addition, an enemy in my front of more than my number … I am unable to comply with this condition with the means at my disposal, and earnestly request that I may at once be relieved from the position I occupy." By all accounts, it was a recklessly impulsive bluff. Hooker's threat to resign command of the Army of the Potomac was a gamble to force Lincoln and Secretary of War Stanton to release the Harper's Ferry garrison for action against Lee's Army of Northern Virginia. Hooker's luck, however, had run out.[33]

A telegram arrived at Hooker's headquarters in Frederick, to which he had returned, at 8pm on June 27. General-in-Chief Henry W. Halleck informed Hooker bluntly that: "Your application to be relieved from your present command is received. As you were appointed to this command by the President, I have no power to relieve you. Your dispatch has been duly referred for Executive action." The knives had been out for Joe Hooker since the debacle of Chancellorsville. Halleck and Secretary of War Edwin Stanton had been pressuring Lincoln to remove Hooker since early May. The president acted without hesitation, explaining his decision at a cabinet meeting on June 28: "He had, for several days as the conflict became imminent, observed in Hooker the same failings that were witnessed in McClellan .... A want of alacrity to obey, and a greedy call for more troops which could not, and ought not to be taken from other points."[34]

The question of Hooker's successor was now to be resolved. The president had met with Major General John Fulton Reynolds on June 2, and had inquired of the bearded Pennsylvanian under what conditions he would take command of the Army of the Potomac. Reynolds, long a complainer about political interference in the army from Washington, had informed Lincoln that he would accept command only on the condition of being given a "free hand" with the troops. That was, to Lincoln and Stanton, unacceptable; and so, now that the position had come open, Reynolds was passed over. Rumors swirled through the army's camps that Major General Daniel E. Sickles was under consideration for Hooker's position due to his noted closeness with the president and Mrs. Lincoln, prompting Major General Oliver O. Howard of the XI Corps to declaim, "If God gives us Sickles to lead us I shall cry with vexation & sorrow and plead to be delivered."[35]

But Howard would have no reason to cry or plead for deliverance, as Lincoln's choice for the command of the Army of the Potomac had, in fact, already been offered the job. Around 2am on June 28, Brigadier General James Hardie arrived at the V Corps camp near Frederick, Maryland, and was led to the tent of Major General George Meade. Meade would later admit he believed he was being arrested when awoken by his staff with news of a courier from the War Department.

Instead, he was presented with General Order No. 194: "By direction of the President. Maj. Gen. Joseph Hooker is relieved from command of the Army of the Potomac, and Maj. Gen. George G. Meade is appointed to the command of that army, and of the troops temporarily assigned to duty with it." He was also given a letter from General in Chief Halleck proclaiming that, "I cannot doubt that you will fully justify the confidence which the Government has reposed in you. You will not be hampered by any minute instructions from these headquarters. Your army is free to act as you may deem proper under the circumstances as they arise."[36]

It must have seemed cruelly ironic to Meade. Just two days before his appointment, he had written to his wife that, "I see you are still troubled with visions of my being placed in command. I thought that had all blown over, and I think it has, except in your imagination."[37]

News of Meade's appointment "was received with quiet but apparent satisfaction" in Vincent's brigade. According to one soldier in the brigade, "General Meade had distinguished himself by his gallantry and fidelity in a subordinate position, but placing him in command of the army was, in a measure, experimental." On June 30, Strong Vincent wrote to his wife from camp near Frederick: "We move tomorrow for the Pennsylvania border. A general battle must ensue soon. Lee's fate is sealed!"[38]

CHAPTER 8

March to Mortality: July 1, 1863

"I see another snarl of men a-digging graves, they told me
So tarnal long, so tarnal deep, they 'tended they should hold me.
Yankee Doodle keep it up, Yankee Doodle dandy,
Mind the music and the step, and with the girls be handy."

YANKEE DOODLE, ANONYMOUS NEW VERSES, 1775[1]

On June 30, 1863, two brigades of Federal cavalry under the command of Brigadier General John Buford rode into the town of Gettysburg, Pennsylvania, and discovered residents to be near manic as a result of the localized raiding of Confederate forces. In a pair of dispatches sent that night—one to Major General John F. Reynolds commanding the left wing of the Army of the Potomac, I and XI Corps, at the nearby Moritz Tavern just north of the Pennsylvania–Maryland border, and the other to Major General Alfred Pleasonton—Buford told both officers what he had found. He informed Reynolds in his first dispatch that, "I am satisfied that A. P. Hill's corps is massed just back of Cashtown, about 9 miles from this place .... Near Heidlersburg today, one of my parties captured a courier of Lee's .... He says Ewell's corps is crossing the mountains from Carlisle ... Longstreet, from all I can learn, is still behind Hill." In his second dispatch, Buford informed Pleasonton that, "A. P. Hill's corps, composed of Anderson, Heth, and Pender, is massed back of Cashtown, 9 miles from this place. His pickets, composed of infantry and artillery, are in sight of mine." Buford knew he would have a fight on his hands when dawn came.[2]

At 5am on July 1, Confederate Major General Henry Heth's division of Lieutenant General A. P. Hill's Third Corps stepped off, beginning the march along the Chambersburg Pike towards Gettysburg with Brigadier General James J. Archer's men in the lead. The sun broke above the rolling hills of south-central Pennsylvania, and at approximately 7am, pickets of the 8th Illinois Cavalry spotted the advancing Confederates as they neared the bridge across Marsh Creek. At around the same time, the Confederates spotted the Federals. Colonel Birkett D. Fry, riding at the head of his regiment, the 13th Alabama, ordered the colors unfurled and a skirmish line formed as he spotted the blue-coated soldiers in the yard of a farmhouse overlooking the bridge and road. Lieutenant Marcellus E. Jones of the 8th Illinois Cavalry knelt by a fence in the side yard of the farm, lowered a carbine across the split-rail fence, and fired. It was around 7:30am The battle of Gettysburg had begun.[3]

Foot by foot, yard by yard, mile by mile, the Confederates surged forward, stalling and pausing when they ran into Buford's vedettes along the swales and ridges leading towards Gettysburg. Firing a quick peppering of shots from their carbines, dismounted Federal cavalry troopers then hastily withdrew back to the next ridge, deliberately fouling and slowing Heth's advance. The farm of Ephraim Whisler, in whose side yard Lieutenant Jones had fired the first shot of the battle, was separated by about three miles from the town of Gettysburg itself. In those three miles, two main geographic features dominated the landscape, Herr's Ridge and McPherson's Ridge. A force of 1,600 cavalry troopers under Colonel William Gamble was set up on Herr's Ridge as a forward position. Their instructions were to fall back to McPherson's Ridge, closer to town, when the Confederates came too close. The Confederate advance reached Herr's Ridge—a distance of just under one-and-a-quarter miles from Whisler's farm—somewhere around 9am, forcing Buford's forward line on the ridge to withdraw back to McPherson's Ridge.[4]

Major General John Reynolds arrived on the field at around 10am, just as Heth was ordering his troops to advance down the eastern face of Herr's Ridge and advance on Buford's men on McPherson's Ridge. Surveying the position, Reynolds galloped back through the town to hasten his troops. By around 10:30am, the first shot fired by Federal I

Corps units, the 2nd Maine Artillery, sounded at Gettysburg, as Reynolds ordered the guns to suppress the fire of Confederate batteries in their front so that the infantry could come on-line and relieve Buford's troopers. The 56th Pennsylvania, under Colonel J. William Hofmann, was recognized by Brigadier General Lysander Cutler of the I Corps as being the regiment that fired the first Federal infantry volley of the battle. As Cutler's men fired, barely having had time to come on-line before the Confederates were upon them, Reynolds galloped to the south of the Chambersburg Pike, sending the famous Iron Brigade of hardy Midwesterners into Herbst Woods with bayonets affixed. Reynolds roared to his men, "Forward, men, forward for God's sake and drive those fellows out of those woods!" He turned his horse, twisted in the saddle to look towards the rear for reinforcements, and collapsed, dead instantly of a shot that hit him just behind the right ear.[5]

Historian Edwin Coddington, whose book on the Gettysburg campaign remains a bedrock of current scholarship, likens the battle for McPherson's Ridge to "two swinging doors hinged together on the pike." As the Iron Brigade pushed the men of Brigadier General James J. Archer out of Herbst Woods and across Willoughby Run, capturing Archer himself in the process, the Confederate brigade of Brigadier General Joseph R. Davis, nephew of the Confederate president, was sending Cutler's men reeling north of the Chambersburg Pike. A hard counter-attack by the 6th Wisconsin on Davis's advance checked the assault and netted numerous prisoners. Its commander, Lieutenant Colonel Rufus Dawes, found himself somewhat awkwardly encumbered with several swords from surrendered Confederate officers as his little regiment of around 344 men took 232 prisoners while suffering 174 casualties in seizing the railroad cut north of the Chambersburg Pike.[6]

Around noon, a lull in combat overtook the battlefield to the northwest of town as both armies hurried reinforcements to the front. The XI Corps under Major General Howard extended the Federal defensive line to the north, while Lieutenant General Richard S. Ewell's Second Corps of the Army of Northern Virginia advanced rapidly from the north to seize Oak Ridge, boxing in the Federals on their right flank, which renewed the fighting at around 2:30pm. Confederate Major General

Robert Rodes's division slammed into the front of the XI Corps near Oak Ridge, and Heth renewed his attack upon the I Corps.[7]

Shells abruptly began to scream into the rear of the XI Corps, enfilading fire from off their right flank, as Confederate Major General Jubal Early's soldiers exploded from the trees lining the Harrisburg Road with screams like furies. Just as it had at Chancellorsville, the "Dutch Corps" collapsed under the unexpected flanking assault, except for minor pockets of tenacious resistance, speeding pell-mell back through the town towards Cemetery Hill. As the evaporation of the XI Corps left the I Corps' right flank exposed, its own position was becoming untenable due to how far back the men were being pushed—now nearly to the Lutheran Theological Seminary on Seminary Ridge—and the casualties they had sustained. I Corps commander Brigadier General Abner Doubleday, temporarily ascended to command following Reynolds's death due to his being the most senior I Corps officer on the field, began to stage a fighting withdrawal through the town, but the resolve of the men broke, leading to panicked retreat in most cases. As Federals raced through the unfamiliar streets of Gettysburg, near-entire regiments were made Confederate prisoners. One officer of the XI Corps, Brigadier General Alexander Ferdinand Schimmelfennig, was forced to seek shelter in a drainage culvert on Baltimore Street to avoid capture, and spent the subsequent remainder of the three-day battle hiding in a shed on the property of Henry and Catherine Garlach. For the most part, the vast majority of both corps reached Cemetery Hill, where Major General Winfield Scott Hancock was waiting for them. Hancock had been dispatched by Meade to take command of all forces on the field, and to this end he stopped the rout, and set the men to work beginning to fortify Cemetery Hill as the central anchor for a larger defensive line.[8]

The battle of Gettysburg did not occur in a vacuum. While it may have been an inescapable center of gravity, drawing every available soldier to it like a black hole devours a star, it was not an immediate summons. Dawn on July 1 found Vincent's brigade at Union Mills, Maryland, five miles south of the Pennsylvania line, with orders only to march to Hanover, Pennsylvania—a total of about 10 miles. No doubt it was a relief to the men of the brigade; they had already marched nearly 40 miles in the past two days. Following Major General Meade's promotion to command the Army of the Potomac, command of the V Corps had devolved upon Major General George Sykes. "During the whole march the spirits of the men of the Eighty-Third had increased in confidence as they neared the boundaries of Pennsylvania," wrote Amos Judson, "and when they found that they were about to enter the threshold of their native State and fight upon her soil, their enthusiasm knew no bounds." Given the relatively short length of the day's march, the men did not get upon the road until 8am, by which time Buford's troopers were already firing at Heth's advancing Confederates before Herr's Ridge. It was a "glorious march," with clouds overhead and citizens emerging from their houses to cheer the passing Federal troops.[9]

As the brigade approached the Pennsylvania state line, Colonel Vincent ordered the color guard and fife and drums of the 83rd Pennsylvania to be ready. Vincent and his staff, astride their horses on the state line, watched the brigade pass from the side of the road. As the 83rd Pennsylvania crossed into its home state, the flag was unfurled to the breeze and the fife and drum began to play "Welcome Here Again" and "Yankee Doodle," as Vincent had ordered.[10]

The spectacle awed those who witnessed it. Judson recalled: "As the glorious old banner, shattered and rent by the shocks of a dozen battle fields, floated once more proudly upon the inspiring breezes of the old Keystone State, long and loud shouts of joy from ten thousand iron throats broke upon the air." The enthusiasm of the men was contagious, until it seemed that "every banner was flying, every fife screaming, and every drum beating" in the V Corps.[11]

On the side of the road, watching the 83rd Pennsylvania pass into the Keystone State for the first time since 1861, Vincent doffed his kepi and rhetorically asked his staff, "What death more glorious can any man desire than to die on the soil of old Pennsylvania fighting for that flag?" As he spoke, just 14 miles away, men were dying on the bloody ground surrounding the once-sleepy college town. The brigade continued its march towards Hanover, arriving in the late afternoon. From the west, they could hear the rumble of cannon fire at Gettysburg, and word of the heavy engagement was waiting for them. They rested for two hours, then began to march west towards Gettysburg.[12]

CHAPTER 9

The Lion of Round Top: July 2, 1863

"Tell me, tell me, weary soldier from the rude and stirring wars,
Was my brother in the battle where you gained those noble scars?
He was ever brave and valiant, and I know he never fled.
Was his name among the wounded, or numbered with the dead?
Was my brother in the battle when the tide of war ran high?
You would know him in a thousand by his dark and flashing eye.
Tell me, tell me, weary soldier,'will he never come 'gain?
Did he suffer 'mid the wounded or die among the slain?"

Was My Brother in the Battle?, Stephen Collins Foster, 1862[1]

As the men of Vincent's brigade marched through the darkness of the night of July 1 and morning of July 2, "women came out and sang the Star Spangled Banner and other national airs" to the passing soldiers. They tramped west towards the battlefield, where the Army of the Potomac and the Army of Northern Virginia gathered to resume the fight, halting to rest at 2am, three miles east of Gettysburg. At Vincent's order, Oliver Norton blew reveille at 3:30am, and the brigade was back on the road by 4. As the sun rose, thermometers in Gettysburg were already recording a temperature of 74 degrees Fahrenheit, promising another hot and humid day. Just as the lead regiment, the 20th Maine, came within sight of Gettysburg itself, Vincent drew his regiment off the road and into the farmyard of Isaac Deardorff, where the men stacked arms and laid down to rest while awaiting further orders.[2]

At around the same time, Lieutenant General Robert E. Lee held a council of war with his corps commanders at his field headquarters.

Lieutenant General James Longstreet, commanding Lee's First Corps, advocated disengaging at Gettysburg, moving to the south and east, cutting Meade's communication with Washington and forcing the Federals to attack the Confederates on ground of their own choosing. Lee rejected the suggestion. His assumption, based on intelligence reports, was that there were no Federal forces on the southern slopes of Cemetery Ridge, nor on the rocky hill to its south, nor among the elevated swales of land in the midst of Joseph Sherfy's peach orchard. With a map of this information in hand by 9am, Lee's battle plan became clear. The Second Corps under Lieutenant General Richard S. Ewell, on Lee's left, would assault the Federal right at Culp's Hill in a diversionary action; Lieutenant General A. P. Hill's Third Corps would hold the center and the town; and Longstreet's First Corps on the right would stage the main action of the day, a drive for the Federal left flank over two large hills that, according to Captain Samuel Johnston,* were unoccupied. For his attack, Longstreet would have two of his three divisions on the field—approximately 14,400 men.[3]

At around 11am, Lee issued orders for Longstreet's corps to move to the right flank of the army. At Longstreet's request, Lee agreed to postpone the attack until Brigadier General Evander M. Law's brigade of Alabamans arrived on the field. Law's men had begun to march at 3am to reach the battlefield, a distance of 28 miles covered in a mere 11 hours. It was, said Longstreet, "the best marching done in either army to reach the field of Gettysburg."[4]

Lee's plan was almost stunning in its simplicity. Longstreet's corps would attack the Federal left, guiding its advance by the rocky face of a small hill just above a jumble of boulders locals called "Devil's Den." The advance would be led by Major General John Bell Hood's division of Texans, Alabamans, and Georgians. Major General Lafayette McLaws's division was to target the southern slopes of Cemetery Ridge, guided by an orchard of peach trees roughly equidistant between the Federal and Confederate lines. For support, Major General Richard H. Anderson's division of A. P. Hill's Third Corps would follow McLaws in stepping

---

* Lee's staff engineer, who had undertaken the reconnaissance ride that morning.

off to build upon his division's advance and dislodge the Federal center from Cemetery Ridge.[5]

As Longstreet's two divisions began to maneuver behind Confederate lines to move into position for the assault on the Federal left, the commander of the Federal III Corps on the Federal left, Major General Daniel Sickles, was becoming paranoid. Sickles worried that the position his corps had been placed in was dangerously situated: Cemetery Ridge dropped precipitously nearly 100 feet at the III Corps' position, and was swampy and marshy. Immediately in front lay the elevated ground of the Sherfy peach orchard along the Emmitsburg Road, and Sickles found it hard to believe that Meade had not posted him and his corps at this position so that he would receive a Confederate attack on unfavorable ground as part of some convoluted scheme to remove him from command of the III Corps. Such a scheme did not exist outside the mind of Dan Sickles, but the mere idea of it was enough to galvanize the politician-turned-general to action. He would not be caught unprepared.[6]

Most of George Meade's morning on July 2 was spent in a series of arguments with Sickles about the placement of the III Corps. Finally, Meade grudgingly agreed to send Major General Henry Hunt, the Army of the Potomac's chief of artillery, to inspect the III Corps position alongside Sickles, more than likely just to appease the paranoid major general. Riding the marshy lowlands of the III Corps' position, Sickles indicated to Hunt the rising ground of the peach orchard and asked Hunt what he thought of advancing the III Corps to that position. Sketching a theoretical line to the artillery chief, Sickles ignored Hunt's hesitance, even as the artillery chief demurred and told Sickles that he would have to take up the proposed line with Meade. Sickles, though, was determined, and informed Hunt of his worry about a flank attack sweeping over his left from the large, heavily-forested hill to the south. In an effort to mollify Sickles, Hunt suggested he send a reconnaissance forward into Pitzer Woods on Seminary Ridge, directly across from his current line and his proposed peach orchard line. Sickles agreed without hesitation, dispatching Colonel Hiram Berdan's 1st and 2nd United States Sharpshooters at about noon.[7]

Approximately 100 men of Berdan's two sharpshooter regiments stealthily crossed the shallow valley separating the two ridges and entered Pitzer Woods. Led by Colonel Berdan and Lieutenant Colonel Trepp, the men had not gone far into the trees before they came across Brigadier General Cadmus Wilcox's Alabama Brigade of Anderson's Division, Hill's Third Corps, just coming on-line under the cover of the trees. Berdan's men closed with the enemy and opened fire. "We attacked them vigorously upon the flank, and from having come upon them very unexpectedly, and getting close upon them, we were enabled to do great execution, and thew them for a time into confusion." The resulting snarl of three different Confederate divisions, as Anderson's line reeled back and collided with those of both McLaws and Hood, slowed the start of Longstreet's assault. The green-clad Federal marksmen withdrew swiftly before a Confederate counter-attack could effectively be launched.[8]

Berdan's reconnaissance report reached Sickles around 2pm. It confirmed the corps commander's worst fear—an enemy force was massing in his front and working towards his left flank under the cover of trees. On his own authority, Sickles ordered his III Corps to advance to occupy the theoretical line he had described to Henry Hunt, his right flank in the air parallel to the Emmitsburg Road, left flank anchored on Devil's Den. With brass bands playing marches and flags snapping in the breeze, the III Corps marched forward—much to the amazement of every other Federal soldier watching along Cemetery Ridge. Major General Hancock, watching with his staff from the II Corps' position at the center of the line, near a copse of trees, demanded of the empty air, "What in hell can that man Sickles be doing!"[9]

Even as Sickles' corps advanced to the peach orchard, fate continued to delay Longstreet's attack. The mess caused by Berdan's sharpshooters was soon eclipsed by a second traffic jam, as Major General Lafayette McLaws realized his men were easily visible to the Federal Signal Corps lookout post atop the smaller rocky hill. When he halted his division to find a way to continue moving under cover, Hood's still-advancing division marched directly into the rear of McLaws' men, and the divisions became mixed up together on the road. Eventually, the men managed to navigate the chaos and arrived at their positions to attack, only to find that the situation had changed drastically since that morning. Sickles' men had occupied the peach orchard and were in the process of digging in. McLaws bitterly complained in a letter to his wife: "The report being that the enemy had but two regiments of infantry and one battery at the Peach orchard, on arriving at the vicinity of the Orchard, the enemy was discovered in greater force than was supposed." Historian Harry Pfanz notes that McLaws was known for swearing a blue streak, but even he "must have strained his vocabulary after studying the Federal position along the Emmitsburg Road." His men were under orders to move across the Sherfy peach orchard to hit Cemetery Ridge, and now Sickles and the entire III Corps were squarely in their way.[10]

On McLaws' right, John Bell Hood was also growing more anxious. Elements of Sickles' III Corps had occupied Devil's Den, which was one of the objectives of Hood's advance. A massive tangle of boulders deposited by ancient glacier melt, Devil's Den lay almost squarely at the base of the shorter, rocky hill. Hood sent an aide galloping to Longstreet requesting permission to go around the larger, tree-covered hill to emerge in Sickles' rear and force the abandonment of the peach orchard salient—as well as Cemetery Ridge—while seizing Federal supply trains in the rear. Longstreet, who had spent the better part of July 2 arguing for just such a move, was forced to deny Hood permission to undertake the flanking assault. The movement had been rejected by the commanding general, and Longstreet had been ordered, "to guide my left by the Emmitsburg road." Hood did not give up, however: "I found that in making attack according to orders ... I should have first to encounter and drive off this advance line of battle [Sickles' III Corps]; secondly, at the base and along the slope of the mountain, to confront immense boulders of stone ... which would break our ranks and cause the men to scatter whilst climbing up the rocky precipice." This effort by Hood to convince Longstreet to allow him to flank the Federal Army was again rebuffed, and Hood dispatched Colonel Harry Sellers, "an officer of great courage, but also of marked ability" to plead his case to Longstreet personally. Sellers returned with Longstreet's adjutant, Lieutenant Colonel John Fairfax, for both to repeat the orders to advance on the smaller hill through the "immense boulders of stone." Hood, in a quiet fury, acquiesced to orders, but not before lodging a formal protest against them: "the first and only one I ever made during my entire military career."[11]

As McLaws' first brigade in line, that of Brigadier General Joseph B. Kershaw, debouched from the woods to prepare for the assault, Sickles' artillery opened fire. Kershaw scrambled among his men, ordering them into cover, as McLaws ordered up his division artillery and began a rather lazy artillery duel to try to silence Sickles' cannons at the peach orchard. By now, it was around 3:30pm. From this point forward, notes E. P. Alexander, the head of Longstreet's corps artillery train, "the management of the battle on the Confederate side ... was conspicuously bad."[12]

George Meade had planned to hold a council of war at 3pm with his corps commanders. He had, until that moment, been ignorant of Sickles' advance to the peach orchard and was incensed when he learned of it. Just at that moment, Sickles arrived at headquarters. Meade, as historian Stephen Sears notes, "was not one to tolerate fools gladly, and already his patience was paper-thin after Sickles' repeated puzzlements and complaints about the position assigned him." He ordered Sickles to return to his men and icily informed the New York political general that he would be along shortly to confer with him personally. He then ordered Major General George Sykes to move his V Corps to the left of the army to serve as Sickles' reserve.[13]

As part of the V Corps, the men of Strong Vincent's brigade were roused from where they had been sleeping in the yard of the Deardorff farm to move to the yard of George Weikert's farm in the rear of Sickles' peach orchard salient. They marched swiftly to their new position, only to wind up once more standing and awaiting orders. One soldier of the 83rd Pennsylvania would later claim to the Erie County historian Samuel P. Bates that he heard Vincent mutter to himself as he paced the farmyard: "To-day will either bring me my stars or finish my career as a soldier."[14]

On the edge of Pitzer Woods, Alexander's cannons were attempting to silence their counterparts in Sickles' corps artillery in the peach orchard, with little success. Sickles' position benefitted from its elevation. Captain Nelson Ames of Battery G, 1st New York Light Artillery, noted that, "Their shots directed against us generally struck in front and rebounding passed over our heads." Major General Hunt, Meade's chief of artillery, was personally supervising Sickles' batteries at the peach orchard as Meade arrived for his promised conference with Sickles. The furious Meade was informed that Sickles had simply moved to seize the higher ground to his front. Growing angry, the army commander loudly pointed out that this was "neutral ground, our guns command it as well as the enemy's. The very reason you cannot hold it applies to them." Sickles offered to withdraw to his original position, but it was, Meade declared, too late: "You cannot hold this position, but the enemy will not let you get away without a fight, & it may as well begin now as at any time." Preparing to leave Sickles' position as the shells burst around them, Meade ordered Major General Gouverneur Warren, the chief engineer of the Army of the Potomac, to "examine the condition of affairs" on the left of the line and "if anything serious is going on, attend to it." Warren rode off, accompanied by his staff of three aides, and ascended the smaller, rocky hill, finding it empty of troops except for a detachment of the U.S. Army Signal Corps using the height to observe the Confederate lines.[15]

The rocky face of the smaller hill had been swept clear of trees by local loggers. Its relatively flat top, Warren swiftly realized, would make it a natural strongpoint. The presence of a Confederate battery of artillery upon these heights would force the abandonment of the entire Federal line, from Cemetery Ridge to Culp's Hill. He sent an aide galloping to Captain James Smith's 4th New York Independent Battery, placed just north of Devil's Den, to fire a shot over the woods on Seminary Ridge. Standing atop one of the massive boulders on the crest of the hill, Warren watched through his field glasses as the sun shone off the rifle barrels of Confederate soldiers concealed in the woods as they turned to watch the shot scream overhead. It was approximately 4pm. Across the shallow valley, John Bell Hood stood in his stirrups, brandishing his sword as he bellowed, "Fix bayonets, my brave Texans; forward and take those heights!"[16]

Hood's division roared out of the trees, advancing on Sickles' line. At the far right of Hood's line was Brigadier General Evander M. Law's Alabama Brigade of 1,929 men in five regiments. Law's orders were to find and turn the left flank of the Federal Army, which—as far as Hood could tell—was near the base of the shorter, rocky hill. On the crest of that hill, Gouverneur Warren dispatched Captain Chauncey Reese, one of his orderlies, to Meade's headquarters to request a division to hold the hill. Another orderly, First Lieutenant Ranald Mackenzie, galloped for Sickles' headquarters to request a brigade be detached to secure the hill while Warren awaited further reinforcement. Mackenzie arrived at the Trostle Farm, the site of Sickles' headquarters, and found Sickles chomping a cigar and riding his line of battle as his men fired at "the enemy's line of battle … a mile and a half long." Sickles claimed he could not spare a brigade; his own men were overextended and engaged across the entire line. In a series of events which have never been fully established due to conflicting accounts, while leaving Sickles' headquarters, Lieutenant Mackenzie encountered Major General George Sykes. Hearing Warren's entreaties, Sykes agreed to dispatch a brigade to the hill and sent his own orderly riding to find Brigadier General James Barnes with the command.[17]

As Sykes's aide galloped towards the rear, he found Colonel Strong Vincent astride his horse at the head of his men, who stood in column-of-fours and ready to march to reinforce Sickles. Vincent saw the aide and spurred his horse forward to meet him. Oliver Norton followed his commander:

> Vincent was sitting on his horse at the head of the column, waiting for orders. Seeing Sykes's aide approaching, he rode forward to meet him. I followed with the flag, and distinctly heard the following conversation: "Captain, what are your orders?" The captain replied, "Where is General Barnes?" Vincent said, "What are your orders? Give me your orders." The captain answered, "General Sykes told me to direct General Barnes to send one of his brigades to occupy that hill yonder," pointing to Little Round Top. Vincent said, "I will take the responsibility of taking my brigade there." Returning to the brigade, he directed Colonel Rice, the senior colonel, to bring the brigade to the hill as rapidly as possible, then rode away towards the northwest face of the hill. I followed him.[18]

At the moment of crisis, Vincent seized the initiative and made the decision to leave the rest of the division. This was a gamble. Had Vincent moved his brigade without orders and the Confederates failed to materialize, he would have risked charges of dereliction of duty, or worse.

Major Charles Ross, aide-de-camp to Brigadier General Barnes, according to a friend, vividly recalled that "happening to look back as Barnes led his division down past Devil's Den, [he] saw the rear brigade turning out of column and breasting the slope of Little Round Top, 'General,' he cried, 'Vincent is going away.'"[19]

The four regiments of Vincent's brigade numbered approximately 1,335 men, only a third larger than the paper-strength of a single regiment. Its largest regiment on July 2, 1863, was the 44th New York, with 391 men. Second came the 20th Maine and its 386 men, and third was the 83rd Pennsylvania at 295 men. Smallest of all, the 16th Michigan fielded just 263 men as the regiments double-quicked across the broken, craggy ground in pursuit of their colonel towards the shorter of the two rocky hills. As Vincent's brigade climbed the hill, the III Corps' line was collapsing in on itself. Régis de Trobriand, a French brigadier general who commanded troops under Sickles, claimed that the Confederates "appeared to have the devil in them" during the ferocious fighting along the line of the peach orchard that has since become a proper noun—The Peach Orchard. Sickles went down, severely wounded, when a cannonball all but tore off his leg. Around the same time, John Bell Hood fell with an injury that would paralyze his arm. Command of the Federal III Corps devolved to Major General David B. Birney, and Hood's division to Brigadier General Evander M. Law. Birney began withdrawing the III Corps slowly and methodically through places whose names have since become synonymous with the carnage of the III Corps withdrawal and the efforts of the II and V Corps to hold back the Confederates: the Wheatfield, the Slaughter Pen, the Triangular Field, and Devil's Den.[20]

The Confederate tide kept advancing. Law's brigade passed to the command of its senior colonel, James Sheffield, and was moving further south than the rest of Hood's division. The brigade's stretched line angled towards Devil's Den, where Smith's 4th New York Independent Battery and the 124th New York Infantry were waiting. A private in the 5th Texas, to the left of Law's Alabamans, said: "We were now moving into battle virtually without a leader and wholly ignorant of where the enemy was." John Anderson, a private in the 48th Alabama of Law's brigade, wrote to his wife that, "the shot and shell fell like hail while the miney [sic] balls were whistling around on every side." Hood's Texans and Georgians smashed into Devil's Den in intense hand-to-hand fighting among the towering boulders.[21]

At this moment, Strong Vincent and Oliver Norton were seemingly alone on the rocky hill. The logging path they had used led them to a rocky spur closer to the hill's base than to its crest, on its southern and western slopes. Mounted on their horses, they would have had remarkable views of the fighting along Sickles's collapsing line, as Devil's Den and the Peach Orchard were heavily invested by this time. Norton continued to bear the headquarters' flag aloft while they rode and watched. Suddenly, Confederate shells were screaming through the trees, exploding around them. Vincent turned to Norton and snapped, "They are firing at the flag. Down with that flag, Norton! Damn, it, go behind the rocks with it!" Both men dismounted their horses, and Norton dutifully went behind some of the boulders with his flag, still visible to men coming up the hill from the direction they had come, but not to the Confederates.[22]

Colonel James Rice arrived with the brigade not long after Norton and Vincent had parted company, and Vincent began to place his men along the rocky outcropping. The 44th New York was the first up the hill, followed by the 16th Michigan, 83rd Pennsylvania, and 20th Maine. On a ledge of rocks at the western end of the spur, Vincent and his commanders met to determine their positions. The 44th New York, Vincent said, would hold the right of the line, and the 20th Maine on the left. Colonel Rice objected to his position: "In every battle in which we have been engaged, the Eighty-third and Forty-fourth have fought side by side. I wish it might be so to-day." Butterfield's Twins would not be separated: Vincent ordered Lieutenant Colonel Norval Welch of the 16th Michigan to pass the 44th New York and take its position on the brigade's right. Vincent then ordered his commanders that they must hold their ground "at every hazard," for they were the left of the entire Federal Army.[23]

The men of Vincent's brigade prepared for battle across the rocky spur of the hill soon to be known as Little Round Top. Lieutenant Colonel Norval Welch was "deploying two of [his] largest companies as skirmishers" under the command of Captain Kennison Dygert of the "Brady Sharpshooters," an independent attachment to the regiment, in advance of their main line, covering the wooded hollow between the smaller, rocky hill, and its taller, heavily wooded counterpart. Under the command of Captain Lucius S. Larabee, "Company B was immediately thrown out as skirmishers," wrote Lieutenant Colonel Freeman Conner of the 44th New York. Company D was sent forward from the 83rd Pennsylvania under Captain Chauncey Rogers, and the 20th Maine sent Company B under Captain Walter G. Morrill to the left of their position to guard against an enveloping flank attack. Vincent ordered Lieutenant Nash of his headquarters staff across the valley to the larger hill, to watch the Confederate advance as the rest of the brigade was coming on-line. At the summit of the larger hill, Nash saw at least two Confederate regiments starting to advance up the larger hill, "advancing unopposed and unheralded over Big Round Top."[24]

These were the 15th and 47th Alabama, two regiments of Law's brigade that had drifted south, away from the rest of their unit. The 15th's colonel, William C. Oates, had been told by Brigadier General Law that he would operationally command both regiments if they were to be separated from the rest of the brigade. Swinging towards Devil's Den from the south, Colonel Oates's independent command had come under fire from the 2nd United States Sharpshooters. Turning to engage the green-clad sharpshooters, Oates and his two regiments had pursued half of the marksmen up the large, wooded hill. As the Federal marksmen withdrew, firing as they went, Oates's Alabamans crawled up gargantuan rocks and stumbled between trees in pursuit. They were near exhaustion as they collapsed at the crest of the massive hill, having now added free-hand mountain climbing to the list of their achievements, following the 28-mile march to Gettysburg the night before. Colonel Oates sent a party of 22 men to a spring he had spotted near the base of the hill to fill the two regiments' canteens while he tried to rest the remainder of his men.[25]

Beyond Vincent's brigade, at the crest of the smaller hill, Gouverneur Warren had no clue that any Federal forces had yet arrived on the rocky hill; his anxiety and nerves only increased as the gray tide reached Devil's Den. By his own admission, the first troops he saw arrive were the men of Captain Charles Hazlett's Battery D, 5th United States Light Artillery. Hazlett's guns had been ordered to the summit by Captain Augustus Pearl Martin, commander of the V Corps artillery with the warning of "don't let Sickles get you," and now Hazlett's men—joined by Warren and his staff—hauled the guns to the crest of the hill with handspikes, spurs, and pushing from below. In the valley below, the ragged III Corps line was collapsing rather than withdrawing. The men of the II and V Corps were taking the brunt of the Confederate advance, and the sound of Hazlett's first gun firing from the summit caused a cheer to erupt from blue-clad soldiers fighting near Devil's Den.[26]

At the same time, the skirmishers of the 16th Michigan, 44th New York, and 83rd Pennsylvania were being pushed into the valley between the two hills by advancing Confederates. They had been thrown out by their regiments less than five minutes before, according to Amos Judson. The "Brady Sharpshooters" of the 16th Michigan fired the first Federal shots of the fight to defend this rocky hill at members of the 4th and 5th Texas, who were advancing on the wooded saddle between the hills. In the brief, heated skirmish in the saddle between the hills, Captain Larabee of the 44th New York was killed, and Captain Dygert of the 16th Michigan was captured.[27]

The Texans pursuing the skirmishers had no idea what awaited them within the wooded saddle of land between the two hills. Climbing uphill, over rocks and between trees, they suddenly walked into a wall of lead. The 4th and 5th Texas had wandered into the center-left of the 44th New York and the center-right of the 83rd Pennsylvania. The 44th New York fired the first volley into the 5th Texas, and a soldier of that regiment stated that it was "the most destructive to our line. Every line officer of my regiment is shot down except one man—the major." Another Texan stated that "the enemy was only a short distance up and so near over us that with good aim we could have been shot in the top of the head, either standing or kneeling."[28]

Slightly higher up the rocky hill than his men, Strong Vincent paced behind the 83rd Pennsylvania and 44th New York, watching the Texans stumble back for a moment from the shock of the initial clash before surging forward again, this time joined by the 4th Alabama. Vincent dispatched Lieutenant Clark, another of his aides, to, "go and tell General Barnes to send me reinforcements at once: the enemy are coming against us with an overwhelming force." Vincent was correct; including the two regiments atop the larger hill—being drawn down its slopes by the sounds of combat—the Confederates outnumbered his brigade by over a thousand men.*[29]

As the III Corps gave way at Devil's Den, Confederate marksmen targeted the blue-clad figures on the summit of the rocky hill. A bullet grazed Gouverneur Warren's throat as he and his aides helped to leverage Hazlett's last cannon into position. Anxious to acquire infantry support for Hazlett's gunners and still unaware of the presence of Vincent's brigade, Warren departed the hilltop with his last remaining aide, Lieutenant Washington Roebling,** riding down the northern slope towards Wheatfield Road. There, they met Brigadier General Stephen H. Weed's brigade marching along the road. In a twist of fate, Weed's brigade had been Warren's command before he was promoted to be chief engineer of the Army of the Potomac. Weed had ridden ahead of his brigade to determine its deployment, and Warren reined in his horse alongside the brigade's senior colonel, Patrick O'Rorke, commander of the 140th New York.[30]

O'Rorke, an immigrant from Ireland who had graduated first in his class from West Point in 1861, already had a storied record as a skilled engineer, having overseen the investment and capture of Fort Pulaski, Georgia, in 1862. Now leading the predominantly Irish 140th New York, raised around his adopted home of Rochester, O'Rorke was immediately beseeched by Warren, "Paddy, give me a regiment." O'Rorke shook his head, "General Weed is ahead and expects me to follow him." But Warren would not accept his refusal: "Never mind that, bring your regiment up here and I will take the responsibility." O'Rorke obligingly ordered his regiment to halt and began to re-align it to ascend the northern face of the steep, rocky hill as Warren galloped off in hopes of finding Weed to secure more reinforcements.[31]

---

* Troop numbers for the Confederates taken from eliminating the 48th Alabama (363 men) from the numerical total of Law's brigade (1,929 men) due to its crossing Plum Run and not returning until later to join in the fighting against Vincent's Brigade; and adding the 4th Texas (415 men) and 5th Texas (409 men), all numbers from Petruzzi and Stanley, *The Gettysburg Campaign*, 124.

** Later to gain fame for building the Brooklyn Bridge.

On the southern slopes of Little Round Top, Vincent's brigade had successfully beaten back the first Confederate assault. Confederate Major John Bane of the 4th Texas wrote that it was "impossible to carry the heights by assault with my thinned ranks," and so "ordered my command to fall back in the skirt of timber, the position then occupied being enfiladed by the batteries on the left and exposed to heavy fire of musketry in my immediate front." Lieutenant Colonel King Bryan of the 5th Texas described "the deadly missiles of the enemy, which were being showered like hail upon us" as his regiment fell back from that first assault. But as those Confederates retreated, the 47th and 15th Alabama were finishing their descent from the larger hill, aimed squarely at Vincent's center left. The Federals saw the Confederates approaching before they were ever noticed, and Colonel Joshua Lawrence Chamberlain of the 20th Maine told his men to stand ready.[32]

Colonel William Oates had no idea that he and his men were marching squarely towards Chamberlain's 20th Maine. He ordered Captain Francis Shaaff to take Company A of the 15th Alabama and head east from the saddle between the Round Tops in order to seize Federal wagon trains visible in a farmer's field. By his own later admission, he had both of the regiments under his command "advancing rapidly, without any skirmishers in front" as he attempted to assist the Texans and Alabamans already thrown back by their first failed assault upon Vincent's line by flanking the Federals. "I saw no enemy until within forty or fifty steps of an irregular ledge of rocks," Oates swore, before suddenly "the most destructive fire I ever saw" poured into the two Alabama regiments from the 20th Maine and the 83rd Pennsylvania. Oates's sudden appearance coincided with the reappearance of the 4th and 5th Texas, which had worked to their left and were now coming at the front of the 16th Michigan as the 4th Alabama once more hit the 44th New York and 83rd Pennsylvania. "We advanced up the mountain under a galling fire," wrote Lieutenant Colonel Lawrence H. Scruggs of the 4th Alabama.[33]

The men of Vincent's brigade "stood as firm as the granite boulders which were thickly strewn around," wrote Private William Brown of the 44th New York. Slammed by two Texas regiments, the 16th Michigan shuddered but withstood the blow as it received "a heavy fire" on its exposed position atop bare boulders. The right-most companies of the 44th New York turned their fire on the Texans, helping to cover the front of the men from Michigan. Oliver Norton left his guidon behind the rocks, picked up a fallen musket, and joined the right of the 44th New York's line at the height of the fighting. Colonel Robert Powell of the 5th Texas, lying wounded, recalled that, "The conflict raged with wild ferocity. We were caught in a cul de sac or depressed basin, surrounded on three sides by projecting or shelving rocks surmounted by a stone fence." One of Powell's private soldiers wrote that "the balls are whizzing so thick around us that it looks like a man could hold out a hat and catch it full."[34]

"On came the enemy, running and yelling like fiends, the artillery on Little Round Top making huge gaps in their ranks at every step," reported Amos Judson. "Hundreds of them approached even within fifteen yards of our line, but they approached only to be shot down or hurled back covered with gaping wounds. It was a death grapple in which assailant and assailed seemed resolved to win or fall in the struggle." Philander Platt, a private of Company D, 83rd Pennsylvania, was determined behind his rock: "Now we are fighting on our own native soil, and as for me, I will never [leave] this position alive while there is an enemy in front." Immediately to Platt and Judson's front, Captain William C. Ward of the 4th Alabama lay wounded on the ground from the first assault. He described the second charge of his regiment: "Over their fallen comrades the men rushed up the mountain side, and soon struck the main enemy line, for there was a clash of musketry at close range. Minie [sic] balls were falling through the leaves like hail in a thunderstorm." The Confederates found rocks as well; and from behind cover, Federal and Confederate forces blasted away at each other. But as Captain Albert N. Husted of the 44th New York noted, the Confederates' boulders "afforded considerable protection for the advancing foe, but from which it was very dangerous to retire when the main line retreated." Judson put it more simply: "Taking position behind the rocks, they poured in a deadly fire upon our troops." The fighting was, thought Judson, perhaps the fiercest in the history of warfare.[35]

On the left end of Vincent's line, Chamberlain's 20th Maine was being blasted. Ellis Spear, the 20th's acting major, wrote that, "The fire on both sides was soon hot and men were falling … The color company and colorguard had suffered severely, and the men on the left of the colors had readjusted themselves among the rocks about the salient of the line." Chamberlain himself thought that the Confederates' ferocity "showed their sanguine expectations." Colonel Oates's 15th Alabama "halted but did not break" under the 20th Maine's withering fire, and Lieutenant Colonel Michael J. Bulger of the 47th Alabama fell seriously wounded. The Confederate regiments again pulled back.[36]

A brief lull settled over the valley between the two hills. Chamberlain, anticipating that the Confederates would aim to move around his left, ordered his right wing to "move by the left flank, taking intervals of a pace or two, according to the shelter afforded by rocks or trees, extending so as to cover the whole front then engaged; … the left wing to the left and rear, making a large angle at the color, which was now brought to the point where our left had first rested." Chamberlain also sent his adjutant to Captain Woodward of the 83rd Pennsylvania to request a company in order that he might extend his line further left. Woodward replied that he had no men to spare, but both regimental commanders thinned their ranks to single-file in order to extend the line. As his regiments crept leftwards, Vincent sent his last aide, Captain Amos Judson, running to Major General Sykes's headquarters, pleading for reinforcements.[37]

The Confederates lacked any centralized commander. Elements of two different brigades were assaulting the position held by Vincent's brigade, and the most senior officer on the field and not wounded or killed at that time was Colonel Oates of the 15th Alabama. There was no coordination of strategy among the Confederate forces, just individual regiments flailing forward without cohesion. The 4th and 5th Texas, awkwardly and half-heartedly collaborating on impulse alone, pulled back towards Devil's Den to creep further left, meeting the 48th Alabama. The three regiments aimed themselves squarely at the weakest point of Vincent's line—the approximately 150 men of the 16th Michigan on the bare, bald rocks at Vincent's extreme right at the west-southwest face of the hill. Oates, still nominally in command of both the 15th and 47th Alabama, ordered his lines to extend to his right, preparing to probe for an effort to turn Vincent's left flank. The 4th Alabama withdrew altogether, pulling back up the larger hill and commencing to dig in, because, "owing to the exhausted condition of the men and the roughness of the mountain side, we found it impossible to carry this position," reported Lieutenant Colonel L. H. Scruggs. The 47th Alabama similarly withdrew back up the larger hill upon realizing that the retreat of the 4th Alabama had left its left flank in the air.[38]

As the 4th and 5th Texas, now supported by the 48th Alabama, slammed into the 16th Michigan, the smallest of Vincent's regiments shattered. In his report, Lieutenant Colonel Welch claims that "some one (supposed to be General Weed or Major-General Sykes) called from the extreme crest of the hill to fall back nearer the top, where a much less exposed line could be taken up ... From some misconstruction of orders, and entirely unwarrantable assumption of authority, Lieutenant Kydd ordered the colors back." Neither Stephen Weed nor George Sykes were on the hill at this time, though Welch would insist that he and his regiment did not retreat, but had been ordered back. Others in the brigade were not so charitable. Oliver Norton would, for the rest of his life, accuse Welch and his men of cowardice. Regardless of what prompted the flight, the men of the 16th Michigan were sprinting for the rear as the 44th New York's right-most companies frantically turned their rifles in an effort to check the Confederates surging for the gap in the line. Sergeant Charles Sprague* of the 44th New York, badly wounded in his left shoulder, watched as the 16th Michigan "retired in some confusion." He charged into their midst, and "exhort[ed] them to stand, referring to what the 44th was doing on their left. I was bleeding profusely and very likely a little delirious; my waist belt had broken and I was trying to hold up both my trousers and my wounded arm (which seemed to weigh a ton) with my right arm." Sprague abruptly felt a hand on his uninjured shoulder.[39]

Turning, the wounded sergeant found Vincent standing there. "That will do, Sergeant Sprague," Vincent informed him, "I'll take hold of this." The young brigade commander vaulted down the hill, brandishing the riding crop that had been given to him as a token of his wife, Elizabeth. "Vincent descended from the rock, and with the most superhuman

---

* Charles Ezra Sprague is considered to be one of the fathers of modern accounting, and is a member of The Ohio State University's Accounting Hall of Fame.

exertions of himself and his officers, drove the men to the front, and again the onward surge of the rebel host was checked." Cursing, swearing, and demanding his men return to the line, Vincent whipped some retreating soldiers with the riding crop, before "climbing upon a huge boulder he stands [sic] out alone ten feet above his men." Vincent raised his voice, and bellowed to his men, "Don't give an inch, boys! Don't yield an inch!" Almost as soon as he'd said those words, a minié ball smashed through his left groin, shattering his hip and thigh. Vincent collapsed onto the rock on which he had been standing. As his soldiers sped to his side, he reportedly uttered, "This is the fourth or fifth time they have shot at me, and now they have hit me at last." What progress Vincent had made in stemming the rout of the 16th Michigan was instantly undone; the men began to retreat once more, and it seemed as if the Texans and Alabamans might break Vincent's line at its right.[40]

At this crucial juncture, Colonel Patrick O'Rorke and his 140th New York reached the crest of the rocky hill. Leaping from his horse as he took stock of the situation, O'Rorke drew his sword, brandishing it towards the collapsing 16th Michigan. Captain Porter Farley, the regimental adjutant, stared at the scene before him:

> A great basin lay before us full of smoke and fire, and literally swarming with riderless horses and fighting, fleeing and pursuing men. The air was saturated with the sulphurous fumes of battle and was ringing with the shouts and groans of the combatants. The wild cries of charging lines, the rattle of musketry, the booming of artillery and the shrieks of the wounded were the orchestral accompaniments of a scene very like hell itself.[41]

O'Rorke did not even order his men out of column-of-fours before he thrust the blade of his sword forward, roaring, "Down this way, boys!" and led the charge of the 140th New York to plug the gap left by the 16th Michigan's retreat. As O'Rorke's men drew abreast of the shattered remnants of Welch's 16th Michigan and the 44th New York, the forward ranks fired while their comrades straggled into line of battle. O'Rorke collapsed, instantly dead of a bullet through the neck. His men had saved Vincent's right; the 500 soldiers tipped the balance of the fight back to the Federals, and the Texans and Alabamans withdrew for good after a few minutes more of hot fighting.[42]

Vincent was carried to rest on a boulder behind the position of the 83rd Pennsylvania, adamant that he would not be removed from the field until the battle was decided. With Vincent wounded, command of the brigade devolved upon Colonel James C. Rice of the 44th New York. As the right flank quieted, Rice made his way along the line from his own men to the 83rd Pennsylvania and the 20th Maine, carrying word of Vincent's wounding and his assumption of command. "Colonel Chamberlain and other officers immediately informed me that their commands were out of ammunition. I had at this time neither an aide nor an orderly even to bear a message." Short of men, Rice climbed the hill, seizing "every officer and man in the rear not engaged in the action," and ordering them to run to fetch ammunition for the brigade. He sent more of these *ad hoc* aides running for reinforcements, and unlike Vincent, received some. Brigadier General Samuel W. Crawford sent a reply that five regiments were on the way, led by Colonel Joseph W. Fisher.[43]

The Confederates' next charge would be their last. Only Oates's 15th Alabama remained on the field. The arrival of O'Rorke's reinforcements had pushed back the 4th and 5th Texas and 48th Alabama. Exhaustion and low morale had compelled the 4th and 47th Alabama to withdraw back up the larger hill. Union cannons continued to boom from the summit of the smaller hill, and their shells now harassed the withdrawn Texans and Alabamans on Houck's Ridge. Oates's 15th Alabama had suffered fearful losses, and even the commander's own brother had fallen. But still he was determined to fight. If he could just turn the Federal flank, he was certain he could win. In a desperate throw of the dice, Oates ordered Captain D. B. Waddell to take Company G out even farther to the right of the 15th Alabama and circle around the Federal flank to hit it with enfilade fire as the regiment made its main charge for the flank. Oates's gamble would not pay off.[44]

Across the small valley, Chamberlain was nervous. His men were out of ammunition, and the crescendo of battle in his rear convinced the former college professor that his men were cut off. He no doubt feared that the Confederates had surrounded the hill, and that his men would have to fight their way out. In fact, what Chamberlain had heard were O'Rorke's troops and the arrival of the remainder of Weed's brigade a few minutes later. He saw men in butternut and gray advancing up the hill once more, firing as they came. Oates's detached company suddenly opened on his left with enfilade fire. "Our gallant line writhed & shrunk before the fire it could not repel. It was too evident that we could maintain the defensive no longer," Chamberlain wrote in his official report. Howard Prince, the 20th Maine's regimental historian, recalled that the order to fix bayonets flew along the line "like a bugle note, and down that worn and weary line the word and the action go, like a flash of lighting through the powder-smoke. To the anxious, frenzied heart of every man in that battle-torn array, it came as the chance of life to the drowning … The lines were in motion even before the word of command was completed, and Col. Chamberlain does not know whether he ever finished that order." The right wing of the 20th Maine sprang forward, to the surprise of its left. Ellis Spear recalled that he "saw the line begin to move, I had rec[eive]d no orders to charge, & there was no time to deliberate on the result. The whole line, as far as I could see it, was moving & shouting, or appeared to be, and if any were going forward, all must & I shouted 'forward' & down the slope we plunged." The men of the 20th Maine surged down the hill and slammed into the 15th Alabama in a sudden, sharp melee. Colonel Oates remembered "a Maine man" attempting to seize the Alabamans' colors, only to have Sergeant Pat O'Conner "stove [sic] his bayonet through the head of the Yankee, who fell dead."[45]

Abruptly, fire exploded on Oates's right flank. From behind a stone wall, Captain Morrill and Company B of the 20th Maine emerged, joined by at least a dozen of Colonel Homer Stoughton's 2nd U.S. Sharpshooters and numerous pickets of the other regiments of Vincent's brigade. Oates thought it was an entirely new regiment of Federal troops and that "dismounted cavalry were closing the only avenue of escape on my left rear." Captains Blanton Hill and Frank Park pleaded with Oates to retreat back up the larger hill. Oates recalled, "my dead and wounded were then nearly as great in number as those still on duty. They literally covered the ground. The blood stood in puddles in some places on the rocks; the ground was soaked with the blood of as brave men as ever fell on the red field of battle." Fearing complete encirclement, Oates ordered his regiment to fall back, they did not retreat in confusion before the 20th Maine: a distinction that Oates would argue for the rest of his life. Halfway up the large tree-covered hill in retreat, Oates collapsed of heatstroke and exhaustion, and would have been captured if not dragged to safety by two of his men.[46]

By the time that the 20th Maine executed its famous bayonet charge, the Federal left was in no danger of collapse. The rest of Weed's brigade had hastened to the hill to join with O'Rorke's 140th New York in reinforcing Vincent's brigade, and five more regiments of reinforcements from Crawford's division were just minutes away. These forces pushed the Confederates out of the "Valley of Death" and back to the south and west of the Round Tops by nightfall. Meade had ordered Major General John Sedgwick and the VI Corps to advance and plug the gap between the III and V Corps. William Oates admitted later in life that: "Had I succeeded in capturing Little Round Top isolated as I was I could not have held it ten minutes."[47]

With the hill secured, Vincent at last consented to be moved from the battlefield. He was carried down the slope of the hill he had fought so determinately to defend, to the Jacob Weikert Farm on the Taneytown Road. Weikert, a carpenter by trade, was the cousin of George Weikert, whose farm near the base of Little Round Top the men of Vincent's brigade had rested upon during the early afternoon of July 2. The eight-room stone house and large bank barn had been commandeered by the army as a field hospital. There, Vincent was placed in a room on the ground floor of the farmhouse. Fifteen-year-old Matilda Pierce, a girl from Gettysburg whose had been sent to Weikert's Farm for safety by her parents when they heard the armies were converging on the town, wrote of the scene at the farmhouse: "On this evening the number of wounded brought to the place was indeed appalling. They were laid in different parts of the house. The orchard and space around the buildings were covered with the shattered and dying, and the barn became more and more crowded. The scene had become terrible beyond description." Norton found his commander, pale and unable to speak, lying inside the home, not far from where Brigadier General Stephen H. Weed lay, also badly wounded, also dying.* The two officers Butterfield had sought to promote after Fredericksburg lay expiring within feet of one another, both mortally wounded defending the same hill. Vincent reached out to grasp Norton's hand, and the young private informed his commander that, "the boys are still there, Colonel." Vincent's face "lighted up with pleasure and he pressed my hand. I tried to say a few words expressing my grief, but was too much overcome by the pathetic scene."[48]

* Weed had been mortally wounded when, upon arriving at Little Round Top, he paused to speak to his old friend, Charles Hazlett, at his artillery battery. Weed was shot in the chest—most likely by a Confederate marksman in Devil's Den—and collapsed. As his friend Hazlett bent over to hear Weed's last words, Hazlett was shot through the top of the head, dying instantly. Weed died during the night of July 2.

CHAPTER 10

The Road to Immortality: July 3 to July 7, 1863

> "In the beauty of the lilies Christ was born across the sea,
> With a glory in His bosom that transfigures you and me;
> As he died to make men holy, let us die to make men free,
> While God is marching on.
> Glory, glory, hallelujah! Glory, glory, hallelujah!
> Glory, glory, hallelujah! While God is marching on."
>
> *The Battle Hymn of the Republic*, Julia Ward Howe, 1861[1]

In the inky-black morning of July 3, 1863, Major General George Meade sent a telegram from his headquarters at the Leicester farmhouse to the War Department in Washington. "I would respectfully request that Col. Strong Vincent, Eighty-third Pennsylvania Regiment, be made a brigadier-general of volunteers for gallant conduct on the field yesterday. He is mortally wounded, and it would gratify his friends, as well as myself. It was my intention to have recommended him with others, should he live." Vincent's prophecy in the yard of George Weikert's farmhouse before heading into battle had come true on both counts: He had both received his stars and finished his career as a soldier.[2]

That morning, Major General Daniel Butterfield paid a visit to Vincent, and informed him that Meade had requested his promotion to brigadier general. Vincent asked Butterfield for permission to leave for home at once to recuperate. He had not yet been informed that his wound was mortal. Butterfield consulted with the brigade surgeon, who immediately quashed the idea: "He was told that his removal was entirely impracticable, and was advised to dismiss the idea at once from his mind." Vincent, still pale, still barely able to speak, then requested of his one-time brigade commander, "I want you to send for my wife as soon as possible." Lieutenant John Clark, one of Vincent's adjutants, mounted a horse and galloped to Westminster, Maryland, to telegraph the message to Erie. Another officer rode to Hanover, Pennsylvania, and sent the same message, but "in the confusion and press of business which prevailed," as news of Gettysburg was swamping telegraph lines across the nation, "neither of these messages reached home in time."[3]

At around 1pm on July 3, 1863, Confederate artillery along Seminary Ridge opened fire on the Federal lines in a prelude to the infamous assault now known as Pickett's Charge. As shot and shell rained behind the lines, high profile and priority medical cases, including Vincent, were evacuated to field hospitals further to the rear. Vincent was moved to the farm of Louis A. Bushman, two miles behind Federal lines and about four miles southeast of Gettysburg.[4]

"Vincent talked calmly of death, of his wife, his unborn child, his parents and brother and sister, of the war, and of his country," wrote Vincent's friend, Colonel William Swan. The men of the 83rd Pennsylvania paid their dying colonel a visit on July 4, for "a last glimpse of their beloved leader." Swan reported that, "the clothes which, dyed in his blood, had been cut from his wounded form, were eagerly seized by these devoted men. They cut the cloth into little strips, each man taking a piece to be forever a memorial and a saddest relic of the great Rebellion." The same day, Oliver Norton wrote his father a brief letter that summed up what weighed most heavily upon his thoughts. "I am safe and well. We have met the enemy and given them hell. Colonel Vincent is mortally wounded. Alf Ayres is safe; so is Conway. No time for more."[5]

Confirmation of Vincent's promotion arrived from the War Department at 10:05am on July 4, 1863. That afternoon, the mortally wounded young general was given his stars. He was conscious and aware when they were presented to him.[6]

Amos Judson and John Clark, the two adjutants from the 83rd Pennsylvania, stayed with Vincent, tending to their wounded commander. "He became conscious of his situation, but never uttered a groan nor complaint, and said repeatedly that he suffered no pain. The only times he suffered was when he was moved from one side to the other, and his broken limb was jarred by the operation, though he handled it with all the care and delicacy that it was possible to exercise." Visitors to his death bed included Generals Meade, Sykes, Barnes, "and other prominent officers who had already learned to respect his character as a man and his gallantry on the field of battle." The parade of visitors, however, would stop on July 5: The Army of the Potomac was preparing to pull out of Gettysburg and begin to pursue Robert E. Lee and the Army of Northern Virginia back towards the Potomac and Virginia.[7]

When the news arrived in Erie with news of Strong's grievous wounding, Elizabeth Vincent was seven months pregnant and unable to travel. Bethuel Vincent, however, departed immediately, racing towards Gettysburg to be with his son. Colonel Swan wrote of his friend that, "Vincent had still hope that his father and wife would reach him, and thus was saved from that living death that he otherwise would have suffered while consciousness remained." To those who came to visit him, Vincent joked gently that, "I presume I have done my last fighting."[8]

To his old friend Swan, Vincent seemed more serious, if accepting:

> It was hard for him to die, to be cut off so early, just as he was winning honors that would give so much pleasure to others; it was hard to give up wife and kindred and friends; and it was terrible to linger there alone in that wretched hovel with no dear faces about him. And yet he said he feared not death for himself. He had long been a professed follower of Christ, and felt prepared for future life. But on account of others, death came most unwelcome.[9]

On the evening of July 4, Vincent "fell into a drowsy state, from which he awoke only at long intervals. While asleep, his face wore a troubled expression, as if he suffered, but when awake he uttered no complaint." Amos Judson and John Clark kept up their deathbed vigil, hoping that either Bethuel or Elizabeth would arrive, for Vincent's sake. "Col. Vincent kept slowly but gradually sinking away," Judson wrote. "He seemed inclined to talk but little after the first two days of his illness. So deadening, indeed, had been the blow he received, that he had not the strength to engage in conversation for any length of time."[10]

On July 6, Vincent grew "so weak as to be scarcely able to utter a word above a whisper." Early in the morning on July 7, a courier from the War Department delivered his commission as a brigadier general, signed by President Lincoln and Secretary of War Stanton. He was not conscious to receive it. Shortly before noon on July 7, 1863, and "while the feeble effort to repeat the Lord's Prayer was still lingering upon his lips," Vincent died.[11]

He was 26 years old.

CHAPTER II

The Path to Being Forgotten: The Legacy of Strong Vincent

"Day is done,
Gone the sun,
From the lakes,
From the hill,
From the sky.
All is well,
Safely rest,
God is nigh."

TAPS, LYRICS BY RUKARD HURD, MUSIC BY DANIEL BUTTERFIELD AND OLIVER W. NORTON[1]

Strong Vincent's body departed Gettysburg in the company of Lieutenant Clark on July 8. Oliver Norton wrote to friends at home that, "Colonel Vincent died on the 7th, as brave and gallant a soldier as ever fell ... His loss is felt deeply by the brigade ... No one here can march a brigade as he could. He had less straggling, less of everything evil and more of everything good than any other brigade in the division. Oh, how we loved him." Within hours of the departure of Vincent's remains for Erie, Bethuel Vincent arrived in Gettysburg. A correspondent of *The Erie Weekly Gazette* was present to witness Bethuel's reaction to the news of his son's death: "The intelligence of course fell upon his heart with a crushing power, but burying for the moment his grief at the loss of a beloved son, he turned his attention to other members of the noble 83rd who had met a like fate in the conflict." Through the debris of battle, Bethuel Vincent was guided by locals of Gettysburg to the hill his son had died to defend. At his own expense, Bethuel Vincent ordered the exhumation of the only other officer of the 83rd Pennsylvania to fall at Gettysburg, Captain John Sell,* and paid for his embalming, a coffin, and transport of his remains home. "Our readers will all join us in awarding Mr. V. praise for his conduct in this matter," wrote *The Erie Weekly Gazette*. "It reflected credit upon him as a Citizen, a Patriot and a Christian."[2]

Vincent died before news of his wounding had reached the headlines of the two weekly Erie newspapers. *The Erie Weekly Gazette* ran a column headed "Our Wounded" in its July 9 issue, referencing "Colonel Strong Vincent, who commanded a Brigade ... after distinguishing himself by his bravery and skill, received a severe wound in the thigh from a shell ... His father, B. B. Vincent, Esq., has gone on to take charge of him. We trust his wound may not prove as serious as the despatches [sic] received seem to indicate, though we fear the worst." The next day, July 10, Vincent's body arrived in Erie and was conveyed by Lieutenant Clark to the Vincent family home at Peach and Ninth Streets.[3]

On Monday, July 13, 1863, to the toll of the bells of St. Paul's Episcopal Cathedral just three blocks down Peach Street, Vincent's coffin was removed from his father's home and placed upon a caisson. A United States flag enshrouded the lower part of the coffin; a small silver plaque was attached to the coffin's lid over Vincent's chest. "Col. Strong Vincent. Died July 7th 1863, of wounds received in the battle of Gettysburg. Aged 26 years." Above the plaque, on the bare wood at the head of the coffin, lay Vincent's blue kepi. Across the plaque and the flag lay, at an angle, Vincent's sword in its scabbard. Wreathes of flowers and sprigs of evergreen lay atop the coffin's lower half, on top of the flag. To the muffled roll of the drums, the procession began to move. A detachment of U.S. Regulars led the way, rifles shouldered. They had been dispatched from the provost marshal's headquarters in Waterford, where Vincent had been born and spent the first years of his life. Behind them marched Mehl's Band, the city's first brass band, led by Michael Mehl, originally from Strasbourg in Alsace. Mehl's Band had been the regimental band

* Captain Sell had lost a leg as a result of the fighting on Little Round Top, and had died on July 3.

of the 83rd Pennsylvania until it was discharged by an order from Army of the Potomac headquarters in August 1862. They marched now in final tribute to their fallen commander, playing dirges. Behind Mehl and his band rolled a battery of artillery, six gleaming brass cannons pulled along by their horses in pairs. And behind the cannons came the caisson, draped in mourning crêpe.[4]

The pallbearers marched behind the caisson carrying the remains. Among them was Captain Thomas Austin, Vincent's first commanding officer in Company A of the Erie Regiment. The others included Colonels Benjamin Grant and Matthias Schlaudecker, both veterans of the "Erie Regiment"—Grant had been its lieutenant colonel, and Schlaudecker its major. Lieutenant Colonel David McCreary of the 145th Pennsylvania had similarly served in McLane's 90-day regiment and had himself just fought at Gettysburg in Rose Woods, with his regiment. Captain John W. Reynolds of the 14th United States Infantry and Lieutenant Edward Reed of the 167th Pennsylvania completed the roster of pallbearers. Behind them, led along by "his faithful John," as Elizabeth had once called the Irish-born orderly John Hickey, was Vincent's horse. Decked in the livery of an officer's mount on full parade, with a pair of boots reversed in the stirrups, the riderless horse is an age-old symbol of military funerals.[5]

Behind Vincent's horse came "members of the Bar, Furnace Moulders and Citizens." W. S. Lane, Vincent's law partner and president of the City Common Council, marched behind the coffin of his young associate, as did William Himrod and the Vincents' neighbor, William W. Reed. With these gentlemen of the city, the ironworkers of Vincent, Himrod and Company—in their Sunday best—marched to pay their respects to the young man who had labored on the foundry floor as a teenager doing "almost a man's work." With them were common citizens, come to honor "this gallant young officer." Last of all came carriages, led by one carrying Vincent's widow and parents and another containing his living siblings.[6]

At St. Paul's Episcopal Cathedral on Sixth Street, Vincent's coffin was removed from the caisson by the pallbearers and conveyed into the sanctuary, where Reverend John F. Spalding preached, as *The Erie Weekly*

Gazette, called it, "an address … calculated from its pervading spirit to console afflicted relatives and friends, bearing testimony as it did to the pure and noble character of the deceased, and the patriotism and gallantry which signalized his short but brilliant career." The text of this sermon, sadly, does not seem to have survived. As the bell tolled once more, Vincent's remains were removed from the cathedral and returned to the caisson. The funeral cortege turned left onto Sassafras Street and followed it to Eighteenth Street. Turning right, they processed to Chestnut Street and the gatehouse of Erie Cemetery. Carried by the pallbearers to the gravesite, Vincent's casket was stripped of flowers, flag, hat, and sword before it was lowered into the ground. The regulars fired a gun salute over the grave, and Strong Vincent was left to repose in the soil of his hometown.[7]

The Erie Observer, the local Democratic organ, spared some column inches in its July 18, 1863, edition to note that, "The correspondents of the New York papers all unite in attributing to Gen. Vincent the most determined gallantry and the ablest military qualities during the recent battles at Gettysburg." Quoting the *New York Times*, the piece continues: "Great grief is expressed in the army at his loss, he was everywhere admired and respected as an accomplished gentleman and gallant soldier."[8]

The center column of the July 23, 1863, edition of *The Erie Weekly Gazette* was given over to an elegiac poem—"Don't Yield an Inch, Boys!"—written in tribute to Vincent. Its last stanza trumpeted Vincent's fame to posterity:

> No chance can dim his garlands fair:
> No time can touch his clustering hair;
> But ever in immortal youth,
> In Love, Fidelity and Truth,
> Upon that monumental Rock,
> VINCENT the Brave through time shall stand!
> And on that rock inscribed shall be
> In letter bright,
> With living light,
> "*Vivere Sat Vincere*!"*[9]

---

* "To conquer is to live enough!"

On September 29, 1863, Elizabeth Carter Vincent gave birth to a baby girl at her in-laws' home in Erie. The girl, named Blanche Strong Vincent by her mother, came into Elizabeth's life at a time when she was distraught with grief. "Lizzie rather dreads to sleep as she often dreams of her husband's death," wrote Elizabeth's friend Sarah Porter. Elizabeth's sister, Sarah Doremus, had come to stay with her and the Vincents for a time; and it was Sarah Doremus who informed Sarah Porter of Blanche's birth: "I hasten to send you the good tidings that Lizzie Vincent has a little girl," wrote Porter to a mutual friend. "Mrs. Doremus writes that she was very ill, but is doing well … she does not seem disappointed that she has not a son and speaks of Strong's delight as if he were only absent on duty." But tragedy was not yet finished with Elizabeth Vincent. On September 20, 1864—nine days short of her first birthday—Blanche Strong Vincent died unexpectedly of an unknown cause, tragically nothing unusual in an era of higher childhood mortality, and was subsequently buried with the father she had never met.[10]

By the fall of 1864, the battlefield at Gettysburg was already becoming a destination for the curious. John G. Frey, a local farmer, was doing land office business serving as a guide for the tourists who arrived in the town. He made certain to always lead his clients to the rocky hill south of town, and up its steep face. There, near the summit, he led them to a large, flat-topped boulder with an inscription carved into it by the point of a bayonet, and subsequently highlighted with paint in its recesses: "Col. Strong Vincent Fell Here, Com'd 3d Brig. 1st div. 5th corps, July 2d 1863." Telling his clients of Vincent's brigade and its determined fight for the hill, Frey led his clients back down the slopes and over to Devil's Den, where he showed them the grave of a Confederate soldier, explaining that, "this particular Rebel had been killed by two of Berdan's sharpshooters on July 2 because he had been the one who had shot Colonel Strong Vincent." While sharpshooters were certainly active in Devil's Den at the time Vincent was shot, it is impossible to know whence the shot that wounded him came, whether a marksman or an errant shot from the 4th or 5th Texas or 48th Alabama.[11]

On July 25, 1878, a group of veterans from Vincent's brigade departed from the main reunion on the battlefield and ascended the rocky heights

The marble marker on Little Round Top marking the spot where Strong Vincent stood to watch the fighting, and then was placed after he fell wounded. This is a reproduction of the original marker at Gettysburg. The original, damaged by weather, now resides in the Heritage Room of the Raymond M. Blasco, MD Memorial Library in Erie, Pennsylvania. (*Author's collection*)

they had fought to defend 15 years before. The hill had a name now: Little Round Top. Gathering on a rocky ridge surrounded by trees, closer to the base of the hill than its top, they unveiled a marble slab engraved with a V Corps Maltese Cross and carrying the inscription, "Third Brigade, First Division, Fifth Corps. General Strong Vincent, wounded July 2; died July 7, 1863." It was the first monument placed on the battlefield outside of the Gettysburg National Military Cemetery.[12]

The veterans of the 83rd Pennsylvania dedicated their monument on the battlefield on September 12, 1889. A 23-foot combination of Quincy granite and bronze, the life-sized statue of Strong Vincent drawing his sword appears to stare defiantly towards Big Round Top and the positions of the Confederate regiments that assaulted his line. Due to Pennsylvania's regulations upon its regiments' monuments, however, Vincent is not identified by name in any way upon the monument. By the time the monument was dedicated, the rocky spur of Little Round Top where Vincent's men had held the line had come to be cartographically known as "Vincent's Spur." At the dedication ceremony on September 12, the guests of honor were Elizabeth Carter Vincent and the Reverend Boyd Vincent, who was now Episcopal Bishop of Cincinnati. Twenty-six years after her husband's death, Elizabeth Vincent still resided with his family, living with his brother as his housekeeper and friend in Cincinnati. Elizabeth Vincent died on April 14, 1914, nearly 51 years after her husband had died. She had never remarried. Her reputation as an intelligent and resourceful woman was well-earned. She published several books in her lifetime, ranging from *Mary, the Mother of Jesus* to translations of Franz Delitzsch's theological treatises, travel memoirs, art history tomes, and more. Her body was returned to Erie, and buried beside her husband and young child.[13]

By the time of Elizabeth Vincent's death, her husband's legacy was being subsumed by that of his one-time subordinate, Joshua Lawrence Chamberlain. Oliver Norton, Vincent's faithful bugler and color-bearer, became so incensed by the amount of popular credit for the victory flowing to Chamberlain that he attempted to set the record straight. He began publishing his accounts of the fighting in 1900, and his books fiercely countered the notion that it had been Chamberlain who saved the Union. Norton's *Strong Vincent and His Brigade at Gettysburg* and *The Attack and Defense of Little Round Top, Gettysburg, July 2, 1863* were both intended to counteract the narrative that Chamberlain promoted. Ellis Spear, who had grown disenchanted with Chamberlain, soon became one of Norton's staunchest allies in his fight for justice for Strong Vincent. In the first letter of what would become a prodigious correspondence, Spear fumed to Norton about Chamberlain's recently published "Through Blood and Fire at Gettysburg" in *Hearst's Magazine*. "The credit of that fight has been unjustly taken by another officer. That other officer was the Colonel of my regiment, who is still living, a man of facile pen and tongue. It has also seemed to me a robbery of Vincent when the avenue of that point in the field was called 'Chamberlain Avenue' when it should have been called 'Vincent Avenue.'"[14]

Spear and Norton's indignation would only increase as Chamberlain's reputation grew. Following the posthumous publication of Chamberlain's *The Passing of the Armies*, Spear vented his spleen to Norton, "I have not read it through; like yourself, I was disgusted though not unprepared … I knew Chamberlain in college in '54 to '58. He had the same infirmity then, notoriously of inability to tell the truth always."[15]

Norton carried his criticism of Chamberlain to the public. In the introduction of *The Attack and Defense of Little Round Top*, he noted that, "It should be possible for those who remain … to recognize the sincerity and valor of their foes, to put aside all hatred and prejudice … In what the author has to say he hopes to do this. This attitude will not oblige him, in cases where writers have in his opinion deliberately misrepresented the facts to cover their own misconduct, to refrain from pointing this out." The criticism of Chamberlain is veiled; it reads more openly as a swipe at Lieutenant Colonel Norval Welch's cowardice. Context is required to reveal Norton's criticism of Chamberlain. From around 1890, Chamberlain had been involved with a very nasty—and very public—feud with his old adversary, William C. Oates of the 15th Alabama, regarding the placement of the Confederate regiment's monument on Little Round Top. Chamberlain kept blocking its placement, furiously arguing that the Confederates had never reached that point of the hill; Oates doubled down, repeatedly claiming that they had. Oates fumed in one letter to William M. Robbins, the sole Southerner on the Gettysburg Battlefield Commission, "He is like many others on both sides at this late date who are disposed to make themselves the whole push." As a result of this feud, there remains no monument to the 15th Alabama to this day at Gettysburg.[16]

Informing Norton of a conversation he had once witnessed, Spear reported that Chamberlain had corrected a group of students that he had "held" Little Round Top rather than just fought there as the students had claimed. "Knowing so well the facts, it seemed to me like robbing the dead. Of course he should have said, 'No, that honor belongs to Strong Vincent.' But as a matter of fact, he was himself the author of all these stories." In another letter, Spear claims that Chamberlain's "literary ability was of a high order, and he always had a gracious manner, but was absolutely unable to tell the truth and was of inordinate vanity. As far as he could, he robbed Vincent."[17]

Ellis Spear died in 1917. Oliver Norton followed him in 1920. With their passing, Vincent's two most strident defenders were gone, and Chamberlain's reputation grew largely without challenge in subsequent decades.

In 1930, the 85-year-old Reverend Boyd Vincent, Episcopal Bishop of the Diocese of Southern Ohio, traveled to Erie, Pennsylvania, one final time. The city of his birth had changed dramatically in the decades since he had moved to Pittsburgh to become a priest in 1876 following the death of his father. One of its most visible changes was the reason for his presence. In 1928, the City of Erie School District had begun construction on a new high school to serve students on the west side of the city. It was now ready to be opened. The massive Grecian-columned façade of the building resembled a temple more than a high school, and Bishop Vincent had been asked to provide the dedicatory address for the new Strong Vincent High School in a ceremony on October 24, 1930. In the program for the dedication ceremony, a photograph of Strong Vincent stared out at the reader above a quote from a letter of his: "Surely the right will prevail. To break this land in twain is monstrous and impossible." The school remains in operation today, as Strong Vincent Middle School. Fittingly, the school mascot is The Colonels.[18]

On Erie's bayfront, a stone's throw from Commodore Oliver Hazard Perry's 1813 flagship *Niagara*, stands a life-sized bronze statue of Vincent. The bronze hero holds his riding crop raised as if he were exhorting the men of the 16th Michigan back to their place in line on Little Round Top. The statue was dedicated in 1998 as part of the City of Erie's bicentennial celebration. Nearby, a massive steel girder of the World Trade Center casts long shadows over the bronze Vincent as the sun sinks to the west, the native son overshadowed by national tragedy.

The house in which Vincent was born was destroyed by fire in the late 20th century, and his family's home in Waterford has been gone for decades. On July 2, 2021, a small monument was unveiled at Vincent's birthplace: a tablet bearing his photograph and an inscription referring to his birth and childhood in Waterford. None of the family's homes remain in Erie. The site of their mansion at Ninth and Peach Streets is now the bookstore for Gannon University. The Erie Grand Army of the Republic Post, which had been named "Strong Vincent Post" in his honor, ceased operation with the deaths of Erie's last veterans of the Grand Army.

In Erie Cemetery, Strong Vincent's grave lies on a shady knoll in a circular plot centered around a stone Celtic cross. Buried beside and around him are his siblings, his parents, his grandparents, his wife, and his daughter. A small American flag flutters in the breeze on either side of his headstone, which reads simply, "Brig. Gen'l. Strong Vincent. Killed at Gettysburgh Holding Little Round Top. 1837–1863."

Yet Vincent has been largely forgotten, both by historians and by the general public. He has been eclipsed by Chamberlain, who himself would write to Oliver Norton, saying that, "[Vincent] was a noble man, and I have not known an abler commander in his grade. Nothing could exceed his skill and energy in taking the position on Little Round Top

Brigadier General Strong Vincent's grave in Erie Cemetery, Erie, Pennsylvania. Note the Lincoln pennies left face-up on the headstone as a mark of respect for his military service. (*Author's collection*)

and the confidence he inspired in his subordinates. To this the result of the fight on the left at Round Top is very largely due." Chamberlain was not alone in writing to Norton in praise of Vincent in the early years of the 20th century. "No man who lived and fought in the battle of Gettysburg did more for his country than Vincent," declared Daniel Butterfield. Daniel Sickles stated, "Colonel Vincent's part in the operations of that day, on the left of the Union lines, was distinguished by excellent judgement, prompt movements, and signal gallantry." Henry Tremain, who had commanded the 73rd New York during the battle, said, "too much recognition cannot be given by this country to the skill and heroism of General Vincent's supreme effort and sacrifice." Perhaps the highest compliment, however, was that paid by the enemy. Confederate Lieutenant General James Longstreet wrote to Norton: "It gives me pleasure to state in reference to the worth of Little Round Top to the Union Army at Gettysburg, it was everything to the success of the Union battle. General Vincent's prompt action in moving to save that point, held it, and was the means of getting the battle to his side."[19]

Strong Vincent's name is familiar to too few of the millions of men and women who visit Gettysburg or who have a passing interest in the American Civil War. While Chamberlain was awarded the Congressional Medal of Honor and became a major general, Strong Vincent's commission to brigadier general was never even ratified by the United States Senate. Chamberlain has come to dominate the story and, in doing so, has suppressed the history of the greatest battle of the American Civil War. And it is not just the story of Strong Vincent that is quashed by the heroic narrative centered on the commander of the 20th Maine, it is that of Patrick O'Rorke and Stephen Weed, Captain John Sell, and innumerable privates and non-commissioned officers who fell that day, whose story is forgotten behind the heroism of the boys from Maine.

Without Vincent, however, none of them would have given their lives to defend Little Round Top. The counterfactual must be, if Vincent had not seized the initiative—had not moved his brigade without orders to do so and had waited for those orders to come—how many would have died trying to fight their way up a Little Round Top held by the Confederates? Vincent's men had been on-line on the hill for less than five minutes before the Confederates were driving in their pickets. Had Vincent delayed for orders, the roles would have been reversed and perhaps the entire battle of Gettysburg lost, as the Confederates fortified Little Round Top and placed artillery upon its summit.

The rock sporting the inscription spotted by those first battlefield tourists in 1864 still marks the spot where Vincent fell on Little Round Top. It is located beside the massive, castle-like monument to the 12th and 44th New York on the southern crest of the hill. Millions pass it by without a glance, be they local schoolchildren racing for the stairs to the observation deck of the New York monument or foreign tourists marveling over the spectacular views of the rolling foothills of the Appalachian Mountains from Little Round Top's summit.

To walk Vincent's line, one must head down the steep, sheer rocks to the monument of the 16th Michigan on a promontory jutting from Little Round Top towards Devil's Den, and make one's way along an unkempt path full of downed trees and rabbit warrens. Beneath you

The inscription on the boulder where Strong Vincent fell wounded at Little Round Top. First recorded by battlefield tourists in 1864, the engraving is believed to have been made by a soldier's bayonet and is contemporaneous to the battle. (*Author's collection*)

drops Vincent's Spur, the wall of rocks that the Confederate tide crashed against. The white marble marker placed in 1878 stands where Vincent stood to watch the battle unfold beneath him when he sent his aides running for reinforcements, and where he laid after he had been wounded and refused to be removed from the field. Crossing Sykes Avenue, one ascends to the lines of the 20th Maine, and, if feeling adventurous, can walk an even more poorly maintained trail than the first where the paved path to the main 20th Maine Monument intersects Wright Avenue, to a moss-covered and somewhat overgrown marker for the position of Chamberlain's wayward Company B under Captain Walter Morrill.

The only place one will encounter other human beings on this walk, from Vincent's right to the left, will be the main monument of the 20th Maine. Without dispute, the men from Maine performed an heroic feat on July 2, 1863. Their unorthodox bayonet charge broke the last Confederate regiment attacking the brigade. But it is erroneous to claim, as has been done for decades by everyone from Ken Burns to Sir John Keegan, that their bayonet charge saved the Federal left flank.

Strong Vincent saved the Union that day. He—and he alone—deserves the lion's share of the credit for the defense of Little Round Top on July 2, 1863. Without his decision to seize the initiative, to move his brigade without orders, there would have been no 20th Maine in place to make a bayonet charge. There would have been no gap in the line for Colonel O'Rorke and the 140th New York to plug. There would have been no infantry support for the Federal battery or for the signal post, or for Gouverneur Warren to famously stand on his boulder to peer over Devil's Den with his field glasses. His courage throughout the war, his devotion to the entwined causes of Union and liberty, his dedication to staying in the field—denying himself an unquestionable boon in a post-war career to do so—render Strong Vincent a far more sterling example of personal heroism, moral rectitude, and of privilege set aside in the struggle for the Union than does the example of the self-promoting Joshua Lawrence Chamberlain.

Historians are servants of the truth. Their job is to consult the primary sources and interpret their meaning, to decode and scry the motivations and the thoughts behind them. It is irrefutable that Joshua Lawrence

Chamberlain engaged in five decades of reputation-building after the battle of Gettysburg to make himself, in the words of his adversary Colonel Oates, "the whole push" of the action on the left flank of the Federal Army. His own second-in-command, Ellis Spear, condemned him, saying that, "as far as he could, he robbed Vincent." Dr. Frank Varney, in his book *General Grant and the Rewriting of History*, while examining falsehoods in Grant's memoirs that have colored histories of the Civil War for decades, notes that, "the argument might be made that historians have not blindly followed Grant, but that they have instead formed their own conclusions based on the evidence. But a close look at the primary sources indicates a sharp discrepancy between what too many historians have said and what the sources tell us." The same might apply to Chamberlain. His memoirs, memorials, and essays on Gettysburg have colored examinations of the battle of Gettysburg for nearly 16 decades. An examination of the primary sources, rather than simple reliance on Chamberlain's accounts, shows the clear legitimacy of Strong Vincent to the title of "Savior of the Federal Left" that has so often been attributed to Chamberlain.[20]

It is long, long past time that this forgotten man be returned to his central place in the historical narrative.

The monument to the 83rd Pennsylvania at Gettysburg National Military Park. Officially, the statue atop the monument is a generic officer, but newspaper coverage of the monument's construction confirms that it is a bronze statue of Strong Vincent. (*Author's collection*)

APPENDIX

The Origins of the "Chamberlain Myth"

> "History is written for the most part from the outside. Truth often suffers distortion by reason of the point of view of the narrator, some pre-occupation of his judgement or fancy not only as to relative merits but even as to facts in their real relations. An interior view may not be without some personal coloring. But it must be of interest, especially in important transactions, to know how things appeared to those actually engaged in them."
>
> BREVET MAJOR GENERAL JOSHUA LAWRENCE CHAMBERLAIN,
> *THE PASSING OF THE ARMIES*, 1915[1]

Over the preceding pages, I have examined the life and service of Brigadier General Strong Vincent, the man whose life and sacrifice have been sublimated to the story of his subordinate, then-Colonel Joshua Lawrence Chamberlain. As stated in both the introduction and the conclusion of this work, the restoration of Strong Vincent to his rightful role as the hero and savior of Little Round Top is not an effort to slur or diminish the immense heroism and bravery of Chamberlain and his 20th Maine. The laurels of Little Round Top are more than substantial enough to be passed around among the various claimants. The ingenuity of the 20th Maine's legendary bayonet charge at the zenith of the fighting remains a hallmark story of courage and audacity under fire in the annals of the military history of the United States of America.

The discipline of history is, however, built upon the bedrock of truth. Even if historical objectivity is the metaphorical windmill at which generations of Don Quixotes will endlessly tilt, the duty of historians is to do their level best to present an unvarnished portrait of the truth.

As such, while Joshua Lawrence Chamberlain has been presented as the romantic *beau idéal* of an American hero for more than a century and a half, that story is built, in large part, upon fabrication. In the conclusion of this work, I quote a passage from Dr. Frank Varney's *General Grant and the Rewriting of History*: "The argument might be made that historians have not blindly followed Grant, but that they have instead formed their own conclusions based on the evidence. But a close look at the primary sources indicates a sharp discrepancy between what too many historians have said and what the sources tell us." If one accepts the premise that history—and historians—have discounted Strong Vincent for nearly 160 years, the logical next question one must ask oneself is, "How?" Dr. Varney presents a detailed and cogent template for how to examine the submersion of truth within myth in his study of Lieutenant General Ulysses S. Grant's use of his Personal Memoirs to tear down men whom Grant harbored grudges against, principally William S. Rosecrans and Gouverneur K. Warren. While I do not believe that Chamberlain harbored a grudge against Vincent, the template established by Dr. Varney is a useful one to employ to examine the development of what, hereafter, I shall refer to as the Chamberlain myth.[2]

The foundations of the Chamberlain myth were laid by Joshua Chamberlain himself in the years following the conclusion of the American Civil War. In the immediate post-war years, Chamberlain undertook a speaking tour throughout New England and other northern states, delivering a series of lectures on the fighting on Little Round Top and his roles in the Petersburg and Appomattox campaigns. Chamberlain published a pair of articles on Fredericksburg and Gettysburg for the 50th anniversaries of the battles in 1912 and 1913 in *Cosmopolitan* and *Hearst* magazines, and published his memoirs of Appomattox, *The Passing of the Armies*, posthumously in 1915.[3]

Speaking tours, magazine articles, and memoirs were not altogether unusual when it came to the Civil War generation; North or South, one could barely throw a quarter without striking some memoir of the conflict in the decades following 1865. What was unusual, however, was Joshua Chamberlain himself. The professor from Bowdoin College in Maine possessed a deep and a burning ambition and, it can be argued, more than a little vanity. During the fall of 1863, Chamberlain began a very public and very vocal campaign to get himself promoted to the rank of brigadier general. Organizing contacts throughout the military and civilian spheres, he let loose a "firestorm of endorsements" at the War Department while keeping his involvement in the campaign under cover. He bitterly complained during his tenure as brigade commander following the death of Brigadier General James Clay Rice in 1864 that commanding a brigade without the pay raise and allowances of a general's star was "an 'injustice' that 'quite cancelled the complement' of having been given responsibility for the brigade." During his post-war lecture tour, Chamberlain would be welcomed to auditoriums by Georg Friedrich Handel's "See the Conqu'ring Hero Comes" from his oratorio *Judas Maccabaeus*, drawing comparison with both the warrior of antiquity for whom the oratorio was named and to Prince William Augustus, Duke of Cumberland, for whose victory at Culloden Handel had written the oratorio. When other veterans of the fighting for Little Round Top began to publish their memoirs and stories—whether in books or in newspapers across the country—historian Glenn LaFantasie notes that Chamberlain's public remarks on the fighting throughout the 1880s were "uncharacteristically defensive, and more than a little peevish."[4]

Perhaps the most damning indictment of Chamberlain's post-war conduct, however, comes in a letter from Ellis Spear, the acting major of the 20th Maine at Gettysburg and one-time close friend to Chamberlain. Writing to Oliver Norton, the life-long defender of the legacy of Strong Vincent, following Chamberlain's death, Spear dismissed *The Passing of the Armies*, stating bluntly that, "I knew Chamberlain in college in '54 to '58. He had the same infirmity then, notoriously of inability to tell the truth always."[5]

The perception among his peers and fellow veterans of the fighting on July 2, 1863, that Joshua Lawrence Chamberlain was somehow not telling the truth should give historians pause. Regardless of whether one wholly accepts the accuracy and reliability of Ellis Spear's narrative—several historians have discounted Spear as a source due to thinly sourced accusations of senility—the accusation of Chamberlain's dishonesty should carry weight. In the introduction to his unpublished memoirs, Spear writes somewhat acidly that, "the actors in these affairs owe to posterity a just and truthful account of what they saw without unjust disparag[e]ment to others and without boasting or misrepresentations of one's own services."[6]

It thus becomes the duty of the historian to examine the documentary record of the fighting on July 2, 1863, and to ascertain whether Spear's accusations are with or without merit. Even Thomas Desjardin, the modern historian of the 20th Maine whose 1995 *Stand Firm Ye Boys from Maine* has become a modern classic on the fighting on Little Round Top, concedes that the classic story of Chamberlain as the savior of the Federal left at Gettysburg is "full of easily disproved details. A story that is as much construction as it is fact." How does one separate fact from fiction, however, when nearly 16 decades of romanticism and pop culture have saturated it to the point where the morass of myth can barely be dislodged?[7]

The Chamberlain myth came into the world not with a whimper, but with a roar. Its genesis—the first stone laid upon the foundation built by Joshua Chamberlain himself with his speaking tour—came in the most unlikely of places. In the 1870s, in the pages of the Southern Historical Society Papers, James Longstreet and William C. Oates were in the midst of a battle royale. In its fifth volume, the publication included a reprint of Lieutenant General Longstreet's "Account of the Campaign and Battle" of Gettysburg, which had run the previous November in the *Philadelphia Times*. In his account of the fighting, Longstreet pointedly remarked on the combat along the slopes of Little Round Top, specifically singling out how "the force thrown upon this point was so strong as to seize our right, as it were, in a vise." Longstreet's article is concerned with the protection of his reputation. By the latter half of the 1870s, the myth of the "Lost Cause" of the Confederacy was ascendant, and a good chunk of Longstreet's article is spent refuting accusations that he was the cause of the Confederate defeat at Gettysburg: specifically singling out Jubal Early and William N. Pendleton for criticism.[8]

This article, however, struck a nerve with William C. Oates, the commander of the 15th Alabama, who responded with a sharply worded article of his own in the subsequent publication. Oates's

"Gettysburg—The Battle on the Right" would be the cornerstone for the modern association of the fight for Little Round Top with the singular heroism of Joshua Lawrence Chamberlain. In the introduction to his article, Oates lays the fault of the defeat squarely at the foot of some unnamed commander—Longstreet, of course—stating firmly that, "the army under Lee was never much stronger numerically, nor its condition better than at Gettysburg. The rank and file were never more confident of success. I therefore conclude that some one 'blundered.'" Oates continues to voice his support for Jubal Early's accusations against Longstreet, now outright naming his former commander, to state that "[Longstreet] is responsible for the loss of the battle, and that ground cannot be fairly designated by any other term than that of the want of generalship." From there on, Oates's article is a standard history of the role of his regiment in the fighting of July 2, 1863, similar to that found in his later memoir *The War Between the Union and the Confederacy and its Lost Opportunities*—with one surprising difference. In his account of the zenith of the fighting, Oates inserts a startling statistic: "Of 644 men and 42 officers, I had lost 343 men and 19 officers." Historians J. David Petruzzi and Steven A. Stanley, in their numerical study of the Gettysburg campaign which has been referred to throughout this work, calculate the number of men taken into combat by the 15th Alabama not to have exceeded 499 men, and that their casualties were 18 killed, 77 wounded, 83 missing.[9]

Oates would, himself, later attempt to correct this mistake. In his 1905 memoir, he wrote that he had neglected to exclude from his tally the men from Company A, whom he had detached to attempt to seize Federal wagons beyond the Round Tops; the men he had sent to fill the regiment's canteens; and the number who collapsed of exhaustion and heatstroke after more than 12 hours of marching and mountain-climbing. Stating that his regiment actually numbered "less than four hundred officers and men" when they assaulted Chamberlain and the 20th Maine, Oates then owned up to the discrepancy: "In the hasty manner of writing my report I took as a basis of the strength of my regiment its last muster before we began the march to Pennsylvania. I also wrote the article after the war on the same basis, which was a mistake."[10]

It was this incorrect math which allowed the next layer of stone to be laid upon the myth of the 20th Maine. Oates's figure of 686 officers and men for the 15th Alabama was swiftly seized upon by two writers. Howard Prince, the 20th Maine's regimental historian, would use the number as evidence of the overwhelming odds that the men of Maine stalwartly stood against. Petruzzi and Stanley's same numerical study of the campaign which gives us our figures for the 15th Alabama lists the 20th Maine as taking into battle no more than 386 men on July 2. Recalling Oates's comment that his command went into battle with "less than four hundred officers and men," it must be that the 20th Maine and 15th Alabama were more or less equally matched in terms of manpower on the afternoon of July 2.[11]

The second writer to capitalize on Oates's 686-man misestimate, however, would do far more damage to historical understanding than Captain Prince. The Reverend Theodore Gerrish had served as a private soldier in Company H, 20th Maine, during the war, and his memoirs were published in 1882 as *Army Life: A Private's Reminiscences of the Civil War.* The 20th Maine's bestselling 20th-century historian, John J. Pullen, stated that "many books are built upon other books; and in writings on the Civil War, few books have been built upon more often than those of Theodore Gerrish." Gerrish's style is simple and direct: a frequent use of the personal "I" throughout the text as he recounts what he saw, felt, heard, and experienced in the Army of the Potomac from 1862 to 1865. Indeed, this author makes use of Gerrish's memoirs when discussing the battle of Fredericksburg. But, abruptly, Gerrish's personal "I" vanishes as he begins to talk about Gettysburg, and the group "we" replaces it. What could explain the sudden, drastic shift in tone for the memoir that has been referenced by everyone from Pullen to Ken Burns to Michael Shaara?[12]

Thomas Desjardin has the simple, honest, almost scandalous answer: Gerrish was not with the 20th Maine at Gettysburg. He was in an army hospital in Philadelphia. At best, then, Gerrish's account of Gettysburg is second-hand; at worst, it might be entirely a creation of Gerrish. It is not an eyewitness account, even as Gerrish speaks of events he plainly could not have witnessed, such as his tentmate staggering from a mortal wound; the dying words of Captain Land; two wounded sergeants falling together. All of this is suddenly presented once more with the personal "I." It is in the depths of Gerrish's highly suspect account, as well, that several persistent stories of the fighting on Little Round Top are first documented to appear: the claim that there were 10 Alabamans for every man from Maine; that rifle barrels were close enough to touch at the height of the fighting; that it was Holman Melcher, not Joshua Chamberlain, who led the bayonet charge; and that the 20th Maine hesitated before its famous charge.[13]

In 1882, Gerrish's account met with immediate pushback from members of the 20th Maine. James Nichols, the former commander of Company K, 20th Maine, published an open letter to Gerrish in the Lincoln County News blasting the account of Gettysburg as "a work of fiction." Even Colonel Chamberlain, it appears, had some issue with Gerrish's account of the battle. Preserved in the Maine State Archives in Augusta is fragment of a letter from Chamberlain to Gerrish containing Chamberlain's personal recollections of the moment the order to charge was given, seemingly pugnaciously challenging Gerrish's assertion of both hesitation in the ranks and Melcher's leading the charge.[14]

At the close of the 1880s, the War Department's ongoing publication *The War of the Rebellion* finally reached the Gettysburg campaign. In its 27th volume, part one of three relating to Gettysburg, Chamberlain's official report of the battle of Gettysburg, dated July 6, 1863, was published for the first time. In this report, Chamberlain uses the name "Little Round Top" to refer to the hill where the battle had taken place. To us in the 21st century, this is perfectly ordinary; we use that very name to refer to the hill. For a document supposedly written in 1863, this should instantly raise suspicion, particularly when viewed in conjunction with Chamberlain's personal correspondence from the period. Two letters dated July 6, 1863, and one dated July 18, 1863, feature references to the hill as either "Wolf Hill" or "Sugar Loaf Hill." The name "Round Top" is only used in reference to the larger hill across the small valley from the hill that Vincent's brigade fought to defend. Why the discrepancy? Little Round Top did not have a name until 1867, notes Desjardin.[15]

Furthermore, Desjardin—in his volume on the memory and cultural impact of the battle of Gettysburg—discusses how Chamberlain's official report states that, "Captain Billings, Lieutenant Kendall, and Lieutenant Linscott are officers whose loss we deeply mourn." This would, as Desjardin notes, have been deeply surprising to Captain Charles Billings and Lieutenant Arad Linscott, neither of whom had died as of July 6. Billings died on July 15, and Linscott on July 27.[16]

Desjardin discusses how, when the War Department was preparing *The War of the Rebellion* for publication, it discovered the report of the 20th Maine missing from departmental files and wrote to Chamberlain in March of 1884 requesting:

> the report along with a formal certificate 'that it is an exact copy of the report made by you in the first instance.' ... This copy of his report was in Chamberlain's handwriting and had very few corrections—strange when considering that he wrote it in haste just a few days after the battle while the army was on the march. Despite these conditions, he wrote it in eloquent style comprising just over 2,500 words.[17]

This is, without a doubt, remarkable—to the point of incredulity. While Joshua Lawrence Chamberlain is best remembered as a citizen-soldier, a professor of rhetoric turned general, to presume that words simply flow from the brain to the page with little need for emendation for even the most gifted and acclaimed writers is simply, categorically, wrong. The truth of the matter, as both common sense and Desjardin would tell us, is simple—the report submitted by Chamberlain for publication in the official records of the American Civil War is not the report he authored in 1863. That official report, nearly a thousand words shorter than the one published more than 25 years later, still exists in one place that we know of, the Maine State Archives in Augusta. Attached to a letter addressed to the adjutant general of Maine, Brigadier General John Hodson, the original report makes no reference to the name "Little Round Top" or to officers who were not yet dead as of the time of writing as being dead. Similarly, it lacks much of the rhetorical flourish of the sort present in Chamberlain's "original" report dispatched to the War Department in 1884.[18]

What does this mean for our understanding of the fighting on Little Round Top on July 2, 1863? For generations, historians have viewed *The War of the Rebellion* as the baseline for Civil War history. While the OR, to use a common shorthand for "Official Records," is not without its flaws, it is generally a foundation for everyone from acclaimed and tenured academics to students writing a term paper for an undergraduate class. The assumption is there that these documents were taken from the archives of the War Department, curated by army officers appointed to the task, and then published, as with the long-running *Foreign Relations of the United States* series from the State Department.

Yet within *The War of the Rebellion*'s first volume on the Gettysburg campaign, there are four pages whose veracity is now thoroughly debased. More than likely, they are the four pages most looked at by generations of historians given the voluminous amount of literature which focuses upon the battle for Little Round Top. The report of Joshua Lawrence Chamberlain, submitted in 1884, is a fraud and a forgery insofar as it was postdated to July 6, 1863, and written with two decades of hindsight.

It bears remembering the comments earlier referred to by the historian Glenn LaFantasie about Chamberlain in the 1880s as more accounts of the fighting on Little Round Top began to be disseminated: He was "uncharacteristically defensive, and more than a little peevish." Is this doctored report another example of Chamberlain's defensiveness and peevishness relating to broader interest in accounts relating to the fighting on the Federal left?[19]

This question will, more than likely, never be answered. There is likely no "smoking gun" letter from Chamberlain explaining why he certified a fraudulent report as accurate to the War Department. It must, however, be noted that Chamberlain consciously made the choice to—at the very least—rewrite his original 1863 report with the benefits of hindsight. This speaks to a man determined to protect his own legacy and his own image as the heroic warrior of Round Top, an image that had earned him four terms as governor of Maine, had secured him the presidency of his alma mater, Bowdoin College, and had led to his being able to embark upon speaking tours across several states.

As the monuments ascended at Gettysburg—beginning with the small marble tablet marking the location where Strong Vincent lay wounded during the latter phases of the combat—Chamberlain was lionized as the man who saved the left at Gettysburg. His oration at the dedication of the 20th Maine's monument is quoted as the opening lines of an audio tour of the battlefield sold at the National Park Service visitor center to this day. By the beginning of the 20th century, Chamberlain was once more, in a sense, fighting the battle of July 2, 1863. He engaged in a very bitter, very protracted feud with his old adversary, Colonel William C. Oates of the 15th Alabama, regarding the placement of the regiment's monument on Little Round Top. Oates sought to site the memorial at the furthest point of his advance, where Captain Waddell and Company G had circled around the 20th Maine to launch enfilading fire during Oates's last, desperate attack. Chamberlain vehemently protested the selection of the monument site, alleging vocally and stridently that the Alabamans had never reached that point. The site selected for the monument to the 15th Alabama would have been uphill from that of the 20th Maine—a symbolic victory, at least, for Oates, who had insisted for decades that his men had been close to breaking through Chamberlain's line. Oates's commentary on Chamberlain's behavior in this conflict is quoted in the final chapter of this work, but is reprinted here for argumentative cohesion: "He is like many others on both sides at this late date who are disposed to make themselves the whole push."[20]

In 1912, following his brouhaha with Oates, Chamberlain published the article "My Story of Fredericksburg" in *Cosmopolitan Magazine* to commemorate the 50th anniversary of that battle. This was followed the next year by the appearance of "Through Blood and Fire at Gettysburg" in *Hearst Magazine*. Both of these articles must be treated with immense caution by historians seeking to use them, for both articles ran in magazines edited by William Randolph Hearst, the infamous father of "Yellow Journalism" who may or may not (depending upon which historian one consults) have helped kickstart the Spanish-American War simply as a means of selling papers. The Hearst editors' sensationalist tendencies are clearly on display in both articles, from the vignette of Chamberlain sleeping in a pile of corpses for warmth on the slopes of Marye's Heights, to the bizarre appearance of the ghost of George Washington while on the march to Gettysburg. While these articles in particular are what drove the wedge between Chamberlain and his old friend, Ellis Spear, it is worth noting that it is obvious that even a man as arguably vainglorious and self-indulgent as Chamberlain would hardly conjure up a ghost story in an account of the battle of Gettysburg. It is instead the self-congratulatory tone of both articles that resulted in the split between the men; the articles present war as heroic and gallant, and Spear, writing his own memoirs, recalled war as an assemblage of horrors, grief, and tragedy.

As the original manuscripts of both articles have been lost, it is impossible to tell how much of the preening and self-congratulatory rhetoric is Chamberlain's and how much was inserted by the Hearst editors. It is possible that Chamberlain was as disgusted by the articles as Spear and Norton were in their fulminatory correspondence following Chamberlain's death. Indeed, for the Gettysburg article at least, we possess evidence of Chamberlain's dissatisfaction with it as it appeared in its published form: "The Hearst editors so mutilated and 'corrected' my 'Gettysburg,' so I have not tried to get copies," Chamberlain stated flatly to someone requesting a copy of the article from him. To Elliot Dill, former adjutant general of Maine, Chamberlain was even more blunt: "[the article] is much curtailed and changed by the insertion of 'connective tissue' by the editor." Regardless, the Gettysburg article has come to be one of the definitive accounts of the fighting on Little Round Top, reprinted and repackaged in stand-alone paperbacks and anthologies for decades.[21]

With Chamberlain's death in 1914 at the age of 85, the Chamberlain myth settled into a relative period of malaise. The first flicker of revival—and its broader escape into the popular imagination—came in 1938, when the novelist Kenneth Roberts released *Trending into Maine*, a travelogue regarding his love for his native state. Within the volume, a chapter entitled "Maine Stories I'd Like to Write" contained the story of the 20th Maine on Little Round Top. John J. Pullen, Chamberlain's biographer and a 20th-century regimental historian of the 20th Maine, somewhat wryly notes that "a few pages about that regiment were almost entirely about Joshua Chamberlain." A decade later, rebutting Arnold J. Toynbee's assertions that Maine was an antiquated backwater, Roberts, in a *Saturday Evening Post* article, highlighted Mainers and their historic, civilized accomplishments, including Joshua Chamberlain's defense of Little Round Top.[22]

From Roberts, it is only a short jump to 1957 and the publication of Pullen's *The Twentieth Maine: A Volunteer Regiment in the Civil War.* While Pullen, in his own examination of Chamberlain's legacy, modestly refers to the work as "far from being a best-seller," the book remains a frequent guest in bibliographies on the battle of Gettysburg, including this one. The following year, Pullen's regimental history of the 20th Maine was abridged by Reader's Digest Condensed Books, and interest in Chamberlain and his regiment exploded. Within two years, the first biography of Chamberlain—*Soul of a Lion* by Willard M. Wallace—had appeared.[23]

In 1974, novelist and professor Michael Shaara published *The Killer Angels.* This novel, which won the Pulitzer Prize for Fiction in 1975, has never been out of print and has been assigned as required course reading everywhere from high schools to the U.S. Army War College. Though Shaara's vivid and gripping prose, a phantasm of the battle of Gettysburg is brought to life in the imaginations of readers across the United States, men, women, and children, young and old—all transfixed by the hallowed, haunted ground in southcentral Pennsylvania. Central to the novel is Joshua Lawrence Chamberlain, his portrayal taken from Pullen's regimental history, which itself draws heavily upon Chamberlain's own papers, report, and the memoirs of Theodore Gerrish.

Chamberlain's ascent could not now be stopped. In 1990, documentarian Ken Burns's nine-episode documentary, *The Civil War,* was broadcast on PBS stations across the United States, partially as a result of the producer's interest in the Civil War being sparked by Shaara's novel. As a consequence, Chamberlain and the 20th Maine became the only Federal soldiers present on Little Round Top in the minds of the millions of Americans who tuned in to watch Burns's series. The documentary sparked a renaissance of the American Civil War, and in the vanguard of that renaissance rode Joshua Lawrence Chamberlain.

When *The Killer Angels* film adaptation, *Gettysburg*, was released in 1993, with Hollywood star Jeff Daniels portraying Chamberlain, Chamberlain's narrative of Little Round Top was once more given supremacy. The role of Colonel Strong Vincent—barely more than a glorified cameo for English actor Maxwell Caulfield—was so ancillary as to be almost impossible to distinguish in the war epic if one was not watching specifically for it, despite Caulfield's superb performance with the approximately 10 lines he was given.

My undergraduate advisor once stated flatly to a student railing against the concept of bigotry that, "No matter how hard you try, you can't kill an idea." That is, at this point, what Joshua Lawrence Chamberlain has become—an idea. He has transcended the pages of history and fiction with almost disconcerting ease. As he exists now—in paintings by artists in their Gettysburg galleries, on coffee mugs, staring out from book jackets, T-shirts, beer bottles, postcards—Chamberlain has become more idea than man. He represents the romanticized idea of a hero, a man who set aside his own life and his own career to step forward at his country's call, exhibited immense bravery, and then returned to civilian life after being awarded repeatedly for his gallantry. It is a neat, wholesome, all-American image, what we all want to imagine good people deserve when they take up so dirty and bloody a business as war. For millions, Chamberlain has only the faintest basis in reality—a novel based partially upon a regimental history based partially upon doctored reports and likely fraudulent memoirs; a film based upon a novel based upon .... To return to my earlier metaphor, then, it is for historians to tilt at the windmill of Chamberlain, not because we seek to undercut a story that has become synonymous with Gettysburg, not because of Chamberlain's ambition or vanity, but because of the necessity of presenting, as best as we can, truth. This is not to say that I believe the 20th Maine or Chamberlain should be consigned to the dust heap of history—quite the opposite. Their role at Gettysburg was integral to the successful defense of Little Round Top, beyond a shadow of a doubt. Where the difficulties arise is contextualizing their efforts on the left of Vincent's line as only a part of Vincent's line, and realizing that Vincent—not Chamberlain—was the hero of the hour.

Bibliography

Primary Sources

"A Brave Man in Moulded Clay." *The Boston Globe* (Boston, MA), July 31, 1888.

Adams, S. J. *We Are Coming Father Abraham 300,000 More.* Boston: Henry Tolman & Co., 1862. M1640.A. Civil War Sheet Music Collection, Library of Congress. https://www.loc.gov/item/ihas.200000811.

Alexander, Edward Porter. *Military Memoirs of a Confederate: A Critical Narrative.* New York: Charles Scribner's Sons, 1907.

Alleman, Tillie Pierce. *At Gettysburg, or What a Girl Saw and Heard of the Battle: A True Narrative.* New York: W. Lake Borland, 1889. http://digital.library.upenn.edu/women/alleman/gettysburg/gettysburg.html.

Ames, Nelson. *History of Battery G, First Regiment, New York Light Artillery.* Marshalltown, IA: Marshall Printing Company, 1900.

Anderson, John. John Anderson to E. P. Anderson, July 17, 1863. Quoted in Laine and Penny, *Law's Alabama Brigade in the War Between the Union and the Confederacy.* Shippensburg, PA: White Mane, 1996.

"A Visit to Camp Wilkins." *The Erie Weekly Gazette* (Erie, PA), May 23, 1861.

Bane, John P. "Report of Major John P. Bane, Fourth Texas Infantry." In *Operations in North Carolina, Virginia, West Virginia, Maryland, Pennsylvania, and Department of the East. June 3–August 3, 1863.* Edited by Lieut. Col. Robert N. Scott, 410–11. Vol. 27, Part 2 of *The War of the Rebellion: A Compilation of the Official Records of the Union and Confederate Armies.* Washington: Government Printing Office, 1889.

Berdan, Hiram. "Report of Col. Hiram Berdan, First U.S. Sharpshooters, commanding First and Second U.S. Sharpshooters." In *Reports-Operations in North Carolina, Virginia, West Virginia, Maryland, Pennsylvania, and Department of the East. June 3–August 3, 1863: The Gettysburg Campaign, etc.* Edited by Lieut. Col. Robert N. Scott, 514–16. Vol. 27, Part 1 of *The War of the Rebellion: A Compilation of the Official Records of the Union and Confederate Armies.* Washington: Government Printing Office, 1889.

Bradbury, William B. and M. A. Kidder. *Marching Along: The Popular Army Song and Chorus.* New York: Firth, Pond & Co., 1862. M1640.B. Civil War Sheet Music Collection, Library of Congress. https://www.loc.gov/item/ihas.200001220.

Branch, Lawrence O. "Report of Brig. Gen. L. O'B. Branch, C.S. Army, of engagement May 27, with congratulations from General R. E. Lee" In *Reports-The Peninsular Campaign, Virginia. March 17–September 2, 1862.* Edited by Lieut. Col. Robert N. Scott, 740–3. Vol. 11, Part 1 of *The War of the Rebellion: A Compilation of the Official Records of the Union and Confederate Armies.* Washington: Government Printing Office, 1884.

Brooks, Noah. *Mr. Lincoln's Washington: Selections from the Writings of Noah Brooks, Civil War Correspondent.* Edited by P. J. Staudenraus. New York: Thomas Yoseloff, 1967.

Brown, William H. "On Gettysburg Field: A View from Little Round Top During the Progress of the Battle." *The Philadelphia Weekly Times*, March 17, 1882.

Bryan, King. "Report of Lieut. Col. K. Bryan, Fifth Texas Infantry." In *Operations in North Carolina, Virginia, West Virginia, Maryland, Pennsylvania, and Department of the East. June 3–August 3, 1863.* Edited by Lieut. Col. Robert N. Scott, 411–12. Vol. 27, Part 2 of *The War of the Rebellion: A Compilation of the Official Records of the Union and Confederate Armies.* Washington: Government Printing Office, 1889.

Buford, John. John Buford to Colonel Alexander, A.A.G. Cavalry Corps, June 6, 1863. In *Reports–Operations in North Carolina, Virginia, West Virginia, Maryland, Pennsylvania, and Department of the East. June 3–August 3, 1863: The Gettysburg Campaign, etc.* Edited by Lieut. Col. Robert N. Scott, 14. Vol. 27, Part 3 of *The War of the Rebellion: A Compilation of the Official Records of the Union and Confederate Armies.* Washington: Government Printing Office, 1889.

——. John Buford to John Reynolds, June 30, 1863—10:30 p.m. In *Reports-Operations in North Carolina, Virginia, West Virginia, Maryland, Pennsylvania and Department of the East. June 3–August 3, 1863: The Gettysburg Campaign, etc.* Edited by Lieut. Col. Robert N. Scott, 923. Vol. 27, Part 1 of *The War of the Rebellion: A Compilation of the Official Records of the Union and Confederate Armies.* Washington: Government Printing Office, 1889.

——. John Buford to Alfred Pleasonton, June 30, 1863—10:40 p.m. In *Reports-Operations in North Carolina, Virginia, West Virginia, Maryland, Pennsylvania and Department of the East. June 3–August 3, 1863: The Gettysburg Campaign, etc.* Edited by Lieut. Col. Robert N. Scott, 924. Vol. 27, Part 1 of *The War of the Rebellion: A Compilation of the Official Records of the Union and Confederate Armies.* Washington: Government Printing Office, 1889.

Burnside, Ambrose E. Ambrose E. Burnside to General G. W. Cullum, November 7, 1862. In *Correspondence–Operations in Northern Virginia, West Virginia, Maryland, and Pennsylvania. September 3–November 14, 1862.* Edited by Lieut. Col. Robert N. Scott, 552–4. Vol. 19, Part 2 of *The War of the Rebellion: A Compilation of the Official Records of the Union and Confederate Armies.* Washington: Government Printing Office, 1887.

——. "Report of the Operations of the Army of the Potomac, Nov. 7 1862 – Jan. 25, 1863." In *Operations in Northern Virginia, West Virginia, Maryland, and Pennsylvania. November 15, 1862–January 25, 1863.* Edited by Lieut. Col. Henry M. Lazelle,

82–97. Vol. 21 of *The War of the Rebellion: A Compilation of the Official Records of the Union and Confederate Armies.* Washington: Government Printing Office, 1884.

Butterfield, Daniel. Daniel Butterfield to Oliver Norton, February 19, 1901. In *Strong Vincent and His Brigade at Gettysburg, July 2, 1863.* Chicago: O. L. Deming, 1909.

——. "Report of Brig. Gen. Daniel Butterfield, U.S. Army, as General of the Trenches, April 27" In *Reports-The Peninsular Campaign, Virginia. March 17–September 2, 1862.* Edited by Lieut. Col. Robert N. Scott, 384–8. Vol. 11, Part 1 of *The War of the Rebellion: A Compilation of the Official Records of the Union and Confederate Armies.* Washington: Government Printing Office, 1884.

——. Daniel Butterfield to Hon. E. M. Stanton, December 17, 1862. In *Reports, Union Correspondence, Etc.* Edited by Maj. George W. Davis, Mr. Leslie J. Perry, and Mr. Joseph W. Kirkley, 959. Vol. 51, Part 1 of *The War of the Rebellion: A Compilation of the Official Records of the Union and Confederate Armies.* Washington: Government Printing Office, 1897.

——. Daniel Butterfield to Major-General Hancock, July 1, 1863–1:10 p.m. In *Reports -Operations in North Carolina, Virginia, West Virginia, Maryland, Pennsylvania, and Department of the East. June 3–August 3, 1863: The Gettysburg Campaign, etc.* Edited by Lieut. Col. Robert N. Scott, 461. Vol. 27, Part 3 of *The War of the Rebellion: A Compilation of the Official Records of the Union and Confederate Armies.* Washington: Government Printing Office, 1889.

Campbell, Hugh S. "Reports of Lieut. Col. Hugh S. Campbell, Eighty-third Pennsylvania Infantry, of the battle of Gaines' Mill, engagement at Turkey Bridge, and battle of Malvern Hill." In *Reports-The Peninsular Campaign, Virginia. March 17–September 2, 1862.* Edited by Lieut. Col. Robert N. Scott, 343–7. Vol. 11, Part 2 of *The War of the Rebellion: A Compilation of the Official Records of the Union and Confederate Armies.* Washington: Government Printing Office, 1884.

Caspar Trepp Papers Collection, MS670.25. New-York Historical Society Library, New York, New York, United States of America.

Chamberlain, Joshua Lawrence. *Joshua L. Chamberlain: A Life in Letters.* Edited by Thomas Desjardin. Oxford: Osprey Press, 2012.

——. *Through Blood & Fire: Selected Civil War Papers of Major General Joshua Chamberlain.* Edited by Mark Nesbitt. Mechanicsburg, PA: Stackpole Books, 1996.

——. Joshua Chamberlain to George Herendeen, July 6, 1863. Joshua L. Chamberlain Correspondence, Maine State Archives. https://digitalmaine.com/chamberlain_corr/4.

——. Joshua Chamberlain to Theodore Gerrish, circa 1882. Joshua L. Chamberlain Correspondence, Maine State Archives. https://digitalmaine.com/chamberlain_corr/56.

——. Joshua Chamberlain to "Mrs. Eckstrom," May 28, 1913. Folger Library Special Collections, Chamberlain Family Papers, University of Maine.

——. Joshua Chamberlain to Elliott Dill, June 12, 1913. Records of the Adjutant General of Maine, Maine State Archives.

——. Joshua Chamberlain to O. W. Norton, January 15, 1910. In *Army Letters 1861–1865, Being Extracts from Private Letters to Friends from a Soldier in the Field During the Late Civil War, With an Appendix Containing Copies of Some Official Documents, Papers, and Addresses of Later Date*. Chicago: O. L. Deming, 1903. Reprint: Dayton, OH: Morningside, 1995.

——. "My Story of Fredericksburg." In *"Bayonet! Forward:" My Civil War Reminiscences*, edited by Stan Clark. Gettysburg, PA: Stan Clark Military Books, 1994.

——. *The Passing of the Armies: An Account of the Final Campaign of the Army of the Potomac, Based upon Personal Reminiscences of the Fifth Army Corps*. New York: G. P. Putnam's Sons, 1915.

——. "Report of Col. Joshua L. Chamberlain, Twentieth Maine Infantry." In *Reports—Operations in North Carolina, Virginia, West Virginia, Maryland, Pennsylvania, and the Department of the East. June 3–August 3, 1863: The Gettysburg Campaign, etc.* Edited by Lieut. Col. Robert N. Scott, 622–6. Vol 27, Part 1 of *The War of the Rebellion: A Compilation of the Official Records of the Union and Confederate Armies.* Washington: Government Printing Office, 1889.

Conner, Freeman. "Report of Lieut. Col. Freeman Conner, Forty-fourth New York Infantry." In *Reports–Operations in North Carolina, Virginia, West Virginia, Maryland, Pennsylvania, and Department of the East. June 3–August 3, 1863: The Gettysburg Campaign, etc.* Edited by Lieut. Col. Robert N. Scott, 630–1. Vol. 27, Part 1 of *The War of the Rebellion: A Compilation of the Official Records of the Union and Confederate Armies.* Washington: Government Printing Office, 1889.

"Correspondence." *Crawford Journal* (Meadville, PA), November 26, 1861.

Dawes, Rufus R. "With the Sixth Wisconsin at Gettysburg." The Gettysburg Discussion Group. Accessed November 13, 2020. http://www.gdg.org/Research/MOLLUS/mollus18.html.

Dearing, Gilbert H. *Chronological History of the 17th Regiment of New York Infantry Volunteers*. Sing Sing, NY: Sunnyside Printing Co., 1894.

Donohoe, Michael T. "Report of Col. Michael T. Donohoe, Tenth New Hampshire Infantry." In *Operations in Northern Virginia, West Virginia, Maryland, and Pennsylvania. November 15, 1862–January 25, 1863.* Edited by Lieut. Col. Henry M. Lazelle, 337–8. Vol. 21 of *The War of the Rebellion: A Compilation of the Official Records of the Union and Confederate Armies*. Washington: Government Printing Office, 1884.

Farley, Porter. "Bloody Round Top: The Key to the Position at the Battle of Gettysburg." *The National Tribune* (Washington, D.C.), May 3, 1883.

Fletcher, William A. *Rebel Private, Front and Rear: Experiences and Observations from the Early Fifties and Through the Civil War*. Beaumont, TX: The Greer Print, 1908.

Foote, Daniel. "Letter from Washington – Arrival of the Erie Regiment." *The Erie Weekly Gazette* (Erie, PA), September 26, 1861.

Foster, Stephen Collins. Manuscript "Willie Has Gone to War," 1862. CAM. FHC.2011.01. Foster Hall Collection, Center for American Music, University of Pittsburgh Library.

——. *Was My Brother in the Battle?* New York: Horace Waters, 1862. M3.3.F7 W22 1862. The Library of Congress Celebrates the Songs of America, Library of Congress, Washington, D.C. https://www.loc.gov/item/2011567048.

Franklin, William B. "Reports of Brig. Gen. William B. Franklin, U.S. Army, commanding division." In *Reports–The Peninsular Campaign, Virginia. March 17–September 2, 1862.* Edited by Lieut. Col. Robert N. Scott, 614–17. Vol. 11, Part 1 of *The War of the Rebellion: A Compilation of the Official Records of the Union and Confederate Armies.* Washington: Government Printing Office, 1884.

"General Strong Vincent." *The Erie Weekly Gazette* (Erie, PA), July 16, 1863.

"General Orders No. 194." In *Reports–Operations in North Carolina, Virginia, West Virginia, Maryland, Pennsylvania and Department of the East. June 3–August 3, 1863: The Gettysburg Campaign, etc.* Edited by Lieut. Col. Robert N. Scott, 396. Vol. 27, Part 3 of *The War of the Rebellion: A Compilation of the Official Records of the Union and Confederate Armies.* Washington: Government Printing Office, 1889.

Gerrish, Theodore. *Army Life: A Private's Reminiscences of the Civil War.* Portland, ME: Hoyt, Fogg & Donham, 1882.

Gregg, David McMurtrie. "Reports of Brig. Gen. David McM. Gregg, U.S. Army, commanding Second Division." In *Reports–Operations in North Carolina, Virginia, West Virginia, Maryland, Pennsylvania, and Department of the East. June 3–August 3, 1863: The Gettysburg Campaign, etc.* Edited by Lieut. Col. Robert N. Scott, 949–61. Vol. 27, Part 1 of *The War of the Rebellion: A Compilation of the Official Records of the Union and Confederate Armies.* Washington: Government Printing Office, 1889.

Griffin, Charles. "Report of Brig. Gen. Charles Griffin, U.S. Army, commanding First Division." In *Operations in Northern Virginia, West Virginia, Maryland, and Pennsylvania. November 15, 1862–January 25, 1863.* Edited by Lieut. Col. Henry M. Lazelle, 404–5. Vol. 21 of *The War of the Rebellion: A Compilation of the Official Records of the Union and Confederate Armies.* Washington: Government Printing Office, 1884.

Halleck, Henry W. Henry Halleck to Joseph Hooker, June 27, 1863—8 p.m. In *Reports–Operations in North Carolina, Virginia, West Virginia, Maryland, Pennsylvania, and Department of the East. June 3–August 3, 1863: The Gettysburg Campaign, etc.* Edited by Lieut. Col. Robert N. Scott, 60. Vol. 27, Part 1 of *The War of the Rebellion: A Compilation of the Official Records of the Union and Confederate Armies.* Washington: Government Printing Office, 1889.

——. Henry W. Halleck to George G. Meade, June 27, 1863. In *Reports–Operations in North Carolina, Virginia, West Virginia, Maryland, Pennsylvania, and Department of the East. June 3–August 3, 1863: The Gettysburg Campaign, etc.* Edited by Lieut. Col. Robert N. Scott, 60. Vol. 27, Part 1 of *The War of the Rebellion: A Compilation of the Official Records of the Union and Confederate Armies.* Washington: Government Printing Office, 1889.

Hendrick, Mr. L. A. "Mr. L. A. Hendrick's Letters." *New York Daily Herald* (New York, NY), June 26, 1863.

Hill, Edward. "The Last Charge at Fredericksburg." In *A Biographical Memorial of General Daniel Butterfield, Including Many Addresses and Military Writings.* Edited by Julia Lorrilard Butterfield, 301–11. New York: The Grafton Press, 1904.

Hood, John Bell. *Advance and Retreat: Personal Experiences in the United States and Confederate Armies.* New Orleans: The Hood Orphan Memorial Fund, G. T. Beauregard 1880. Reprint: Bloomington, IN: Indiana University Press, 1959.

Hooker, Joseph. Joseph Hooker to Abraham Lincoln, June 5, 1863. In *Reports-Operations in North Carolina, Virginia, West Virginia, Maryland, Pennsylvania, and Department of the East. June 3–August 3, 1863: The Gettysburg Campaign, etc.* Edited by Lieut. Col. Robert N. Scott, 30. Vol. 27, Part 1 of *The War of the Rebellion: A Compilation of the Official Records of the Union and Confederate Armies.* Washington: Government Printing Office, 1889.

——. Joseph Hooker to Major-General Halleck, June 27, 1863. In *Reports–Operations in North Carolina, Virginia, West Virginia, Maryland, Pennsylvania, and Department of the East. June 3–August 3, 1863: The Gettysburg Campaign, etc.* Edited by Lieut. Col. Robert N. Scott, 60. Vol. 27, Part 1 of *The War of the Rebellion: A Compilation of the Official Records of the Union and Confederate Armies.* Washington: Government Printing Office, 1889.

——. Joseph Hooker to Major-General Halleck, June 27, 1863—1 p.m. In *Reports – Operations in North Carolina, Virginia, West Virginia, Maryland, Pennsylvania, and Department of the East. June 3–August 3, 1863: The Gettysburg Campaign, etc.* Edited by Lieut. Col. Robert N. Scott, 60. Vol. 27, Part 1 of *The War of the Rebellion: A Compilation of the Official Records of the Union and Confederate Armies.* Washington: Government Printing Office, 1889.

Howard, Oliver Otis. *Autobiography of Oliver Otis Howard, Major General United States Army.* 2 vols. New York: Baker & Taylor, 1907.

Howe, Julia Ward. *The Battle Hymn of the Republic.* Philadelphia: The Supervisory Committee for Recruiting Colored Regiments, 1863. 98101743. Rare Book and Special Collections Division, Library of Congress, Washington, D.C. https://www.loc.gov/item/98101743.

Hunt, Henry J. "The Second Day at Gettysburg." In *Retreat from Gettysburg*, edited by Robert U. Johnson and Clarence C. Buel, 290–312. Vol. 3 of *Battles and Leaders of the Civil War: Being for the Most Part Contributions by Union and Confederate Officers.* New York: Castle Books, 1956.

Husted, Captain A. N. "Gettysburg in Perspective." In *A History of the Forty-Fourth Regiment, New York Volunteer Infantry, in the Civil War, 1861–1865*, edited by Eugene A. Nash, 297–303. Chicago: R. R. Donnelly & Sons, 1911.

Hutchinson, Jesse Jr. *"Get Off the Track!" A Song for Emancipation.* Boston: Published by the Author, 1844. 012.156. The Lester S. Levy Sheet Music Collection, Sheridan Libraries and University Museums, Johns Hopkins University. https://levysheetmusic.mse.jhu.edu/collection/012/156.

Jähr, G. H. G. *Manual of Homœpathic Medicine in Two Parts. Part II: Therapeutical and Symptomatological Repertory.* Trans. P. F. Curie, M. D. London: Hippolyte Baillière, 1847.

Judson, Amos M. *History of the Eighty-Third Regiment Pennsylvania Volunteers*. Erie, PA: B. F. H. Lynn, 1865.

Keeler, Francis D. *War Letters Written During the Rebellion*. Saginaw, MI: Julian A. Keeler, 1895.

King, Charles. Charles King to Oliver Norton, January 21, 1910. In *Army Letters 1861–1865, Being Extracts from Private Letters to Friends from a Soldier in the Field During the Late Civil War, With an Appendix Containing Copies of Some Official Documents, Papers, and Addresses of Later Date*. Chicago: O. L. Deming, 1903. Reprint: Dayton, OH: Morningside, 1995.

L. C. B. "Don't Yield an Inch, Boys!" *The Erie Weekly Gazette* (Erie, PA), July 23, 1863.

Lincoln, Abraham. *The Collected Works of Abraham Lincoln*. Edited by Roy P. Basler, Marion Dolores Pratt and Lloyd A. Dunlap. 9 vols. New Brunswick, NJ: Rutgers University Press, 1953–5.

"Local Notices." *The Erie Weekly Gazette* (Erie, PA), May 1, 1861.

"Local Paragraphs." *The Erie Weekly Gazette* (Erie, PA), August 7, 1862.

"Local Paragraphs." *The Erie Weekly Gazette* (Erie, PA), July 16, 1863.

Longstreet, James. *From Manassas to Appomattox: Memoirs of the Civil War in America*. Philadelphia: J. B. Lippincott, 1896.

——. James Longstreet to Oliver Norton, December 6, 1901. In *Strong Vincent and His Brigade at Gettysburg, July 2, 1863*. Chicago: O. L. Deming, 1909.

——. "Lee's Right Wing at Gettysburg." In *Retreat from Gettysburg*, edited by Robert U. Johnson and Clarence C. Buel, 339–53. Vol. 3 of *Battles and Leaders of the Civil War: Being for the Most Part Contributions by Union and Confederate Officers*. New York: Castle Books, 1956.

——. "General James Longstreet's Account of the Campaign and Battle." *Southern Historical Society Papers* 5, no 1 (1878): 54–86.

Magruder, John B. "J. Bankhead Magruder to General Lee." In *Reports–The Peninsular Campaign, Virginia. March 17–September 2, 1862*. Edited by Lieut. Col. Robert N. Scott, 422. Vol. 11, Part 3 of *The War of the Rebellion: A Compilation of the Official Records of the Union and Confederate Armies*. Washington: Government Printing Office, 1884.

Martin, Augustus P. "Little Round-Top: By A. P. Martin, Commanding Artillery Brigade, 5th Corps." *The Fulton Democrat* (McConnellsburg, PA), September 20, 1900.

Martindale, John H. "Report of Brig. Gen. John H. Martindale, U.S. Army, commanding First Brigade." In *Reports–The Peninsular Campaign, Virginia. March 17–September 2, 1862*. Edited by Lieut. Col. Robert N. Scott, 701–7. Vol. 11, Part 1 of *The War of the Rebellion: A Compilation of the Official Records of the Union and Confederate Armies*. Washington: Government Printing Office, 1884.

McClellan, George B. *Report of Maj.-Gen. George B. McClellan, August 4, 1863, with an Account of the Campaign in Western Virginia*. New York: Sheldon and Company, 1864.

——. *The Civil War Papers of George B. McClellan: Selected Correspondence, 1860–1865*. Edited by Stephen W. Sears. New York: Ticknor and Fields, 1989.

McLaws, Lafayette. Lafayette McLaws to Emily McLaws, July 7, 1863. In *The Civil War: The Third Year as Told by Those Who Lived It*, edited by Brooks D. Simpson. New York: Library of America, 2013.

Meade, George G. George G. Meade to James Barnes, May 28, 1863. In *Correspondence–Operations in Northern Virginia, West Virginia, Maryland, and Pennsylvania, January 26–June 3, 1863.* Edited by Lieut. Col. Robert N. Scott, 535–6. Vol. 22, Part 2 of *The War of the Rebellion: A Compilation of the Official Records of the Union and Confederate Armies.* Washington: Government Printing Office, 1889.

——. George G. Meade to Brig. Gen. S. Williams, May 31, 1863. In *Correspondence–Operations in Northern Virginia, West Virginia, Maryland, and Pennsylvania, January 26–June 3, 1863.* Edited by Lieut. Col. Robert N. Scott, 572–3. Vol. 22, Part 2 of *The War of the Rebellion: A Compilation of the Official Records of the Union and Confederate Armies.* Washington: Government Printing Office, 1889.

———. George G. Meade to James Barnes, June 19, 1863. Manuscript. The New-York Historical Society. *General James Barnes Collection: Correspondence, Military Records, Sketches & Personal Papers, 1861–1869.*

——. George G. Meade to Henry W. Halleck, June 28, 1863. In *Reports–Operations in North Carolina, Virginia, West Virginia, Maryland, Pennsylvania, and Department of the East. June 3–August 3, 1863: The Gettysburg Campaign, etc.* Edited by Lieut. Col. Robert N. Scott, 61. Vol. 27, Part 1 of *The War of the Rebellion: A Compilation of the Official Records of the Union and Confederate Armies.* Washington: Government Printing Office, 1889.

——. George G. Meade to Henry W. Halleck, July 3, 1863. In *Reports–Operations in North Carolina, Virginia, West Virginia, Maryland, Pennsylvania, and Department of the East. June 3–August 3, 1863: The Gettysburg Campaign, etc.* Edited by Lieut. Col. Robert N. Scott, 1041. Vol. 27, Part 1 of *The War of the Rebellion: A Compilation of the Official Records of the Union and Confederate Armies.* Washington: Government Printing Office, 1889.

——. *The Life and Letters of George Gordon Meade, Major-General United States Army.* Edited by Col. George Meade. 2 vols. New York: Charles Scribner's Sons, 1913.

Morell, George W. "Report of Brig. Gen. George W. Morell, U.S. Army, commanding division." In *Reports–The Peninsular Campaign, Virginia. March 17–September 2, 1862.* Edited by Lieut. Col. Robert N. Scott, 698–701. Vol. 11, Part 1 of *The War of the Rebellion: A Compilation of the Official Records of the Union and Confederate Armies.* Washington: Government Printing Office, 1884.

"Mrs. Strong Vincent and Boyd Vincent …" *Pittsburgh Dispatch* (Pittsburgh, PA), September 13, 1889.

Nash, Eugene Arus. *A History of the Forty-Fourth Regiment, New York Volunteer Infantry, in the Civil War, 1861–1865.* Chicago: R. R. Donnelly & Sons, 1911.

Nichols, James. *Lincoln County News* (Lincoln County, ME), April 1882.

Norton, Frank H. *Porter's Division Song (The Army of the Free).* Washington, D.C.: Philp & Solomons Metropolitan Bookstore, c. 1862. The John M. Sell Civil War Collection. Special Collections and Archives. California State University Northridge Library.

Norton, Oliver Willcox. *Army Letters 1861–1865, Being Extracts from Private Letters to Friends from a Soldier in the Field During the Late Civil War, With an Appendix Containing Copies of Some Official Documents, Papers, and Addresses of Later Date.* Chicago: O. L. Deming, 1903. Reprint: Dayton, OH: Morningside, 1995.

——. *Strong Vincent and His Brigade at Gettysburg, July 2, 1863.* Chicago: O. L. Deming, 1909.

——. *The Attack and Defense of Little Round Top, Gettysburg, July 2, 1863.* New York: Neale, 1913. Reprint, Gettysburg, PA: Stan Clark Military Books, 1992.

Oates, William C. *The War Between the Union and the Confederacy and its Lost Opportunities; With a History of the 15th Alabama Regiment and the Forty-Eight Battles in which it was Engaged.* New York: Neale, 1905.

——. "Gettysburg—The Battle on the Right." *Southern Historical Society Papers* 6, No. 1 (1878): 172–82.

——. William C. Oates to William M. Robbins, April 1, 1902. Quoted in LaFantasie, "Joshua Chamberlain and the American Dream." In *The Gettysburg Nobody Knows*, edited by Gabor S. Boritt, 31–55. Oxford: Oxford University Press, 1997.

Office of the Auditor General of the Commonwealth of Pennsylvania. *Annual Report of the Auditor General of the State of Pennsylvania and of the Tabulations and Deductions from the Reports of the Rail Road and Canal Companies for the Year 1867.* by John F. Hartranft, Auditor General and Lane S. Hart, Rail-Road Clerk. Harrisburg, PA: Singerly & Myers State Printers, 1868.

"On Little Round Top." *The Evening Republican* (Meadville, PA), August 27, 1889.

"On the Field at Gettysburg." *Harrisburg Telegraph* (Harrisburg, PA), May 31, 1878.

"Our Wounded." *The Erie Weekly Gazette* (Erie, PA), July 9, 1863.

Platt, Philander. "On Little Round Top: The Bitter, Obstinate, Victorious Struggle Made by Vincent's Brigade to Save Our Left." *The National Tribune* (Washington, D.C.), April 11, 1907.

Porter, Fitz John. "Report of Maj. Gen. Fitz John Porter, U.S. Army, as Director of the Siege of Yorktown from April 7–May 5" In *Reports–The Peninsular Campaign, Virginia. March 17–September 2, 1862.* Edited by Lieut. Col. Robert N. Scott, 311–16. Vol. 11, Part 1 of *The War of the Rebellion: A Compilation of the Official Records of the Union and Confederate Armies.* Washington: Government Printing Office, 1884.

Powell, R. M. "With Hood at Gettysburg." *The Philadelphia Weekly Times*, December 13, 1884.

Prince, Howard L. "Captain Howard L. Prince's Address." 1889. In *With a Flash of His Sword: The Writings of Major Holman S. Melcher, 20th Maine Infantry*, edited by William B. Styple. Kearny, NJ: Belle Grove, 1994.

——. "Twentieth Maine Regiment" In *Maine at Gettysburg: Report of Maine Commissioners, Prepared by The Executive Committee.* Edited by Charles Hamlin, Greenlief T. Stevens and George W. Verrill. Portland, ME: Lakeside Press, 1898.

"Proclamation of the President of the United States." *The Erie Weekly Gazette* (Erie, PA), April 18, 1861.

Program of Dedication: Strong Vincent High School, Erie, Pennsylvania, October 24, 1930. Event Program. The Dana Massing Collection.

"RECRUITS WANTED!" *Crawford Journal* (Meadville, PA), July 30, 1861.

"Return of the Erie Regiment." *The Erie Weekly Gazette* (Erie, PA), July 25, 1861.

Rittenhouse, Benjamin F. *The Battle of Gettysburg as Seen From Little Round Top: A Paper Read Before the District of Columbia Commandery of the Military Order of the Loyal Legion of the United States, May 4, 1887.* Washington: Judd & Detweiler Printers, 1887.

Rice, James C. "Reports of Col. James C. Rice, Forty-fourth New York Infantry, commanding regiment and Third Brigade." In *Reports–Operations in North Carolina, Virginia, West Virginia, Maryland, Pennsylvania, and Department of the East. June 3–August 3, 1863: The Gettysburg Campaign, etc.* Edited by Lieut. Col. Robert N. Scott, 616–20. Vol. 27, Part 1 of *The War of the Rebellion: A Compilation of the Official Records of the Union and Confederate Armies.* Washington: Government Printing Office, 1889.

Rice, John F. to "Len & Lib," March 3/5, 1862. The Erie County Historical Society. The John F. Rice Letters.

Roberts, Charles W. "Report of Col. Charles W. Roberts, Second Maine Infantry, of engagement May 27." In *Reports–The Peninsular Campaign, Virginia. March 17–September 2, 1862.* Edited by Lieut. Col. Robert N. Scott, 707–10. Vol. 11, Part 1 of *The War of the Rebellion: A Compilation of the Official Records of the Union and Confederate Armies.* Washington: Government Printing Office, 1884.

Robertson, John. *Michigan in the War.* Lansing, MI: W. S. George & Co., State Printers and Binders, 1882.

Roebling, Washington. *Wash Roebling's War: Being a Selection from the Unpublished Civil War Letters of Washington Augustus Roebling*, edited by Earl Schenck Miers. Newark, DE: The Spiral Press, 1961.

Root, George F. *The Battle Cry of Freedom.* Chicago: Root & Cady, 1862. 0012_003259_000275. University of Tennessee Sheet Music Collection, University of Tennessee, Knoxville, Special Collections, University of Tennessee. https://digital.lib.utk.edu/collections/islandora/object/utsmc%3A18221.

Sawyer, Charles Carroll and Henry Tucker. *Weeping, Sad and Lonely, or When This Cruel War is Over.* Brooklyn: Sawyer & Thompson, 1863. M1640.T. Civil War Sheet Music Collection, Library of Congress. https://www.loc.gov/item/ihas.200002105.

Scruggs, Lawrence Houston. "Report of Lieut. Col. L. H. Scruggs, Fourth Alabama Infantry." In *Operations in North Carolina, Virginia, West Virginia, Maryland, Pennsylvania, and Department of the East. June 3–August 3, 1863.* Edited by Lieut. Col. Robert N. Scott, 391–2. Vol. 27, Part 2 of *The War of the Rebellion: A Compilation of the Official Records of the Union and Confederate Armies.* Washington: Government Printing Office, 1889.

Sell, John M. John M. Sell to "Dear Father & Mother," October 29, 1861. The John M. Sell Civil War Collection. Special Collections and Archives. California State University Northridge Library.

———. John M. Sell to "Dear Father & Mother," March 29, 1863. The John M. Sell Civil War Collection. Special Collections and Archives. California State University Northridge Library.

———. John M. Sell to William J. Sell, March 26, 1863. The John M. Sell Civil War Collection. Special Collections and Archives. California State University Northridge Library.

———. John M. Sell to William J. Sell, June 3, 1863. The John M. Sell Civil War Collection. Special Collections and Archives. California State University Northridge Library.

Sheffield, James L. "Report of Col. James L. Sheffield, Forty-eighth Alabama Infantry." In *Operations in North Carolina, Virginia, West Virginia, Maryland, Pennsylvania, and Department of the East. June 3–August 3, 1863*. Edited by Lieut. Col. Robert N. Scott, 395–6. Vol. 27, Part 2 of *The War of the Rebellion: A Compilation of the Official Records of the Union and Confederate Armies.* Washington: Government Printing Office, 1889.

Sickles, Daniel E. Daniel E. Sickles to Oliver Norton, November 21, 1901. In *Strong Vincent and His Brigade at Gettysburg, July 2, 1863*. Chicago: O. L. Deming, 1909.

Spear, Ellis. Ellis Spear to Oliver Norton, July 5, 1913. In *Army Letters 1861–1865, Being Extracts from Private Letters to Friends from a Soldier in the Field During the Late Civil War, With an Appendix Containing Copies of Some Official Documents, Papers, and Addresses of Later Date.* Chicago: O. L. Deming, 1903. Reprint: Dayton, OH: Morningside, 1995.

———. Ellis Spear to Oliver Norton, January 18, 1916. In *With a Flash of His Sword: The Writings of Major Holman S. Melcher, 20th Maine Infantry*, edited by William B. Styple. Kearny, NJ: Belle Grove, 1994.

———. Ellis Spear to Oliver Norton, February 1, 1916. In *With a Flash of His Sword: The Writings of Major Holman S. Melcher, 20th Maine Infantry*, edited by William B. Styple. Kearny, NJ: Belle Grove, 1994.

———. *The Civil War Recollections of General Ellis Spear*, edited by Michael H. Alpert, Andrea C. Hawkes, Marie H. McCosh, Abbott Spear, and Craig L. Symonds. Orono, ME: University of Maine Press, 1997.

———. "The Left at Gettysburg." *The National Tribune* (Washington, D.C.), June 12, 1913.

Sprague, Charles E. Charles Sprague to Oliver Norton, January 16, 1910. In *Army Letters 1861–1865, Being Extracts from Private Letters to Friends from a Soldier in the Field During the Late Civil War, With an Appendix Containing Copies of Some Official Documents, Papers, and Addresses of Later Date*. Chicago: O. L. Deming, 1903. Reprint: Dayton, OH: Morningside, 1995.

Stevens, Charles Augustus. *Berdan's United States Sharpshooters in the Army of the Potomac, 1861–1865*. St. Paul, MN: Price-McGill, 1892.

Stevens, John W. *Reminiscences of the Civil War: A Soldier in Hood's Texas Brigade, Army of Northern Virginia*. Hillsboro, TX: Hillsboro Mirror Print, 1902.

Stoughton, Homer R. "Report of Maj. Homer R. Stoughton, Second U.S. Sharpshooters." In *Reports–Operations in North Carolina, Virginia, West Virginia, Maryland, Pennsylvania, and Department of the East. June 3–August 3, 1863: The Gettysburg Campaign, etc.* Edited by Lieut. Col. Robert N. Scott, 518–19. Vol. 27, Part 1 of *The War of the Rebellion: A Compilation of the Official Records of the Union and Confederate Armies.* Washington: Government Printing Office, 1889.

Swan, William W. "Strong Vincent." In *Harvard Memorial Biographies*, 66–81. Boston: Welch, Bigelow and Company, 1866.

"The Camp on the Battle Field." *Harrisburg Daily Independent* (Harrisburg, PA), July 26, 1878.

"The Late General Vincent." *The Erie Observer* (Erie, PA), July 18, 1863.

Thompson, John Reuben. *Richmond is a Hard Road to Travel.* New Orleans: Blackmar & Co., 1863. conf0339. Historic American Sheet Music, David M. Rubenstein Rare Book & Manuscript Collection, Duke University. https://library.duke.edu/digitalcollections/hasm_conf0339.

Tremain, Henry E. Henry E. Tremain to Oliver Norton, November 23, 1901. In *Strong Vincent and His Brigade at Gettysburg, July 2, 1863.* Chicago: O. L. Deming, 1909.

Townsend, E. D. "General Orders No. 182." In *Correspondence–Operations in Northern Virginia, West Virginia, Maryland, and Pennsylvania. September 3–November 14, 1862.* Edited by Lieut. Col. Robert N. Scott, 545. Vol. 19, Part 2 of *The War of the Rebellion: A Compilation of the Official Records of the Union and Confederate Armies.* Washington: Government Printing Office, 1887.

Trobriand, Régis de. *Four Years with the Army of the Potomac*, translated by George K. Dauchy. Boston: Ticknor and Company, 1889.

United States Congress. *Report of the Joint Committee on the Conduct of the War at the Second Session Thirty-Eighth Congress.* Benjamin F. Wade, Zachariah Chandler, Benjamin F. Harding, Daniel W. Gooch, George W. Julian, Moses F. Odell, and Benjamin F. Loan. 3 vols. Washington: Government Printing Office, 1865.

United States War Department. *Revised United States Army Regulations of 1861, With an Appendix Containing the Changes and Laws Affecting Army Regulations and Articles of War to June 25, 1863.* Washington D.C.: Government Printing Office, 1863.

Vincent, Boyd. *Our Family of Vincents: A History, Genealogy, and Biographical Notices.* Cincinnatti, OH: Privately Printed by Stewart Kidd, & Co., 1924.

Vincent, John F. John F. Vincent to D. McConaughy, Esq., November 30, 1863. Quoted in Nevins and Styple *What Death More Glorious: A Biography of General Strong Vincent.* Kearny, NJ: Belle Grove, 1997.

Vincent, Strong. "Report of Col. Strong Vincent, Eighty-third Pennsylvania Infantry." In *Operations in Northern Virginia, West Virginia, Maryland, and Pennsylvania. November 15, 1862–January 25, 1863.* Edited by Lieut. Col. Henry M. Lazelle, 412–14. Vol. 21 of *The War of the Rebellion: A Compilation of the Official Records of the Union and Confederate Armies.* Washington: Government Printing Office, 1884.

——. "Report of Col Strong Vincent, Eighty-third Pennsylvania Infantry." In *Reports -Operations in Northern Virginia, West Virginia, Maryland, and Pennsylvania, January 26–June 3, 1863*. Edited by Lieut. Col. Robert N. Scott, 521–2. Vol. 25, Part 1 of *The War of the Rebellion: A Compilation of the Official Records of the Union and Confederate Armies.* Washington: Government Printing Office, 1889.

——. Strong Vincent to Capt. Davis, A.A.G., May 30, 1863. Letter. The New-York Historical Society. *General James Barnes Collection: Correspondence, Military Records, Sketches & Personal Papers, 1861–1869.*

——. Strong Vincent to James Barnes, June 1, 1863. Letter. The New-York Historical Society. *General James Barnes Collection: Correspondence, Military Records, Sketches & Personal Papers, 1861–1869.*

——. "Report of Col. Strong Vincent, Eighty-third Pennsylvania Infantry, commanding Third Brigade." In *Reports–Operations in North Carolina, Virginia, West Virginia, Maryland, Pennsylvania, and Department of the East. June 3–August 3, 1863: The Gettysburg Campaign, etc.* Edited by Lieut. Col. Robert N. Scott, 613–15. Vol. 27, Part 1 of *The War of the Rebellion: A Compilation of the Official Records of the Union and Confederate Armies.* Washington: Government Printing Office, 1889.

War Department. Bureau of Military Justice. Court Martial Case Files, 12/1800–10/1894. "Trepp, Casper–Lieutenant Colonel, U.S. Sharp Shooters, 1st." 1815145 – LL-188. Records of the Office of the Judge Advocate General (Army), 1792–2010. National Archives Building, Washington, D.C..

Ward, W. C. "Incidents and Personal Experiences on the Battlefield at Gettysburg." *Confederate Veteran* 8, No. 8 (August, 1900): 345–9.

Warren, Gouverneur K. Gouverneur Warren to Captain Porter Farley, July 13, 1872. In *The Attack and Defense of Little Round Top, Gettysburg, July 2, 1863*, edited by Oliver Willcox Norton. New York: Neale, 1913. Reprint, Gettysburg, PA: Stan Clark Military Books, 1992.

——. Gouverneur Warren to Captain Porter Farley, July 24, 1872. In *The Attack and Defense of Little Round Top, Gettysburg, July 2, 1863*, edited by Oliver Willcox Norton. New York: Neale, 1913. Reprint, Gettysburg, PA: Stan Clark Military Books, 1992.

Welch, Norval E. "Report of Lieut. Col. Norval E. Welch, Sixteenth Michigan Infantry." In *Reports–Operations in North Carolina, Virginia, West Virginia, Maryland, Pennsylvania, and Department of the East. June 3–August 3, 1863: The Gettysburg Campaign, etc.* Edited by Lieut. Col. Robert N. Scott, 627–8. Vol. 27, Part 1 of *The War of the Rebellion: A Compilation of the Official Records of the Union and Confederate Armies.* Washington: Government Printing Office, 1889.

Woodward, Orpheus S. "Report of Capt. Orpheus S. Woodward, Eighty-third Pennsylvania Infantry." In *Reports-Operations in North Carolina, Virginia, West Virginia, Maryland, Pennsylvania, and Department of the East. June 3–August 3, 1863: The Gettysburg Campaign, etc.* Edited by Lieut. Col. Robert N. Scott, 632. Vol. 27, Part 1 of *The War of the Rebellion: A Compilation of the Official Records of the Union and Confederate Armies.* Washington: Government Printing Office, 1889.

Secondary Sources

Anderson, Fred S. *A History of the School District of the City of Erie, Pa., 1795–1970.* Erie, PA: The School District of the City of Erie, 1975.

Bates, Samuel P. *History of Erie County, Pennsylvania. Containing a History of the County; Its Townships, Towns, Villages, Schools, Churches, Industries, Etc.; Portraits of Early Settlers and Prominent Men; Biographies; History of Pennsylvania, Statistical and Miscellaneous Matters.* Chicago: Warner, Beers, & Co., 1884.

Bell, Andrew McIllwaine. *Mosquito Soldiers: Malaria, Yellow Fever, and the Course of the American Civil War.* Baton Rouge, LA: Louisiana State University Press, 2010.

Brooks, Victor. *The Fredericksburg Campaign: October 1862–January 1863.* Conshohocken, PA: Combined Publishing, 2000.

Brown, Richard H. "'Not Well and Not Sick' of the Chickahominy Fever: Hollis Wrisley's Civil War." *The Massachusetts Review* 46, No. 4 (Winter, 2005/2006): 558–86.

Carlyon, David. *Dan Rice: The Most Famous Man You've Never Heard Of.* New York: Public Affairs, 2001.

"Chronology of Major Events Leading to Secession Crisis." Sixteen Months to Sumter: Newspaper Editorials on the Path to Secession. American Historical Association, 2007. Accessed October 2, 2020. https://www.historians.org/teaching-and-learning/teaching-resources-for-historians/sixteen-months-to-sumter/chronology.

Coco, Gregory A. *A Strange and Blighted Land: Gettysburg: The Aftermath of a Battle.* El Dorado Hills, CA: Savas Beatie, 2017.

——. *A Vast Sea of Misery: A History and Guide to the Union and Confederate Field Hospitals at Gettysburg; July 1–November 20, 1863.* El Dorado Hills, CA: Savas Beatie, 2017.

Coddington, Edwin B. *The Gettysburg Campaign: A Study in Command.* New York: Touchstone, 1997.

Crawford, Kim. *The 16th Michigan Infantry.* Dayton, OH: Morningside, 2002.

Desjardin, Thomas A. *Stand Firm Ye Boys from Maine: The 20th Maine and the Gettysburg Campaign.* 15th Anniversary Edition. New York: Oxford University Press, 2009.

——. *These Honored Dead: How the Story of Gettysburg Shaped American Memory.* Cambridge, MA: Da Capo, 2003.

DiCiccio, Carmen. *Coal and Coke in Pennsylvania.* Harrisburg, PA: Pennsylvania Historical and Museum Commission, 1996.

Fishel, Edwin C. "Pinkerton and McClellan: Who Deceived Whom?" *Civil War History* 34, No. 2 (June 1988): 115–42.

Glatthaar, Joseph T. *General Lee's Army: From Victory to Collapse.* New York: Free Press, 2008.

Gottfried, Bradley M. *Brigades of Gettysburg: The Union and Confederate Brigades at the Battle of Gettysburg.* New York: Skyhorse, 2012.

Guelzo, Allen C. *Gettysburg: The Last Invasion*. New York: Alfred A. Knopf, 2013.

Hearn, Chester G. *Lincoln and McClellan at War*. Baton Rouge, LA: Louisiana State University Press, 2012.

Hess, Earl J. *Field Armies and Fortifications in the Civil War: The Eastern Campaigns, 1861–1864*. Chapel Hill, NC: University of North Carolina Press, 2005.

Huntington, Tom. *Searching for George Gordon Meade: The Forgotten Victor of Gettysburg*. Mechanicsburg, PA: Stackpole, 2012.

Kahan, Paul. *Amiable Scoundrel: Simon Cameron, Lincoln's Scandalous Secretary of War*. Lincoln, NE: Potomac Books, 2016.

Keller, Kate Van Winkle. "What are the Real Words to 'Yankee Doodle?'" Colonial Music Institute, Washington Library, Center for Digital History, George Washington's Mount Vernon. December 2001. https://www.mountvernon.org/library/digitalhistory/colonial-music-institute/essays/real-words-to-yankee-doodle.

LaFantasie, Glenn. "Joshua Chamberlain and the American Dream." In *The Gettysburg Nobody Knows*, edited by Gabor S. Boritt, 31–55. New York: Oxford University Press, 1997.

——. *Twilight at Little Round Top: July 2, 1863–The Tide Turns at Gettysburg*. New York: Vintage Civil War Library, 2005.

Laine, J. Gary and Morris Penny. *Law's Alabama Brigade in the War Between the Union and the Confederacy*. Shippensburg, PA: White Mane, 1996.

"Legacy." Miss Porter's School. Miss Porter's School. Accessed Sept. 30, 2020. https://www.porters.org/legacy.

Longacre, Edward G. *Lee's Cavalrymen: A History of the Mounted Forces of the Army of Northern Virginia, 1861–1865*. Norman, OK: University of Oklahoma Press, 2012.

——. *Lincoln's Cavalrymen: A History of the Mounted Forces of the Army of the Potomac, 1861–1865*. Norman, OK: University of Oklahoma Press, 2012.

——. *The Man Behind the Guns: A Military Biography of General Henry J. Hunt, Chief of Artillery, Army of the Potomac*. Cambridge, MA: Da Capo Press, 2003.

——. *Joshua Chamberlain: The Soldier and the Man*. Cambridge, MA: Da Capo Press, 1999.

Mackowski, Chris, Kristopher D. White and Daniel T. Davis. *Don't Give an Inch: The Second Day at Gettysburg, July 2, 1863–From Little Round Top to Cemetery Ridge*. Emerging Civil War Series. El Dorado Hills, CA: Savas Beatie, 2016.

Matteson, John. *A Worse Place than Hell: How the Civil War Battle of Fredericksburg Changed a Nation*. New York: W. W. Norton, 2021.

Nevins, James H. and William B. Styple. *What Death More Glorious: A Biography of General Strong Vincent*. Kearny, NJ: Belle Grove, 1997.

O'Reilly, Francis Augustín. *The Fredericksburg Campaign: Winter War on the Rappahannock*. Baton Rouge, LA: Louisiana State University Press, 2006.

Petruzzi, J. David and Steven A. Stanley. *The Gettysburg Campaign in Numbers and Losses: Synopses, Orders of Battle, Strengths, Casualties, and Maps, June 9–July 14, 1863*. El Dorado Hills, CA: Savas Beatie, 2012.

Pfanz, Harry W. *Gettysburg–The Second Day*. Chapel Hill, NC: The University of North Carolina Press, 1987.

Pullen, John J. *The Twentieth Maine: A Classic Story of Joshua Chamberlain and His Volunteer Regiment*. Mechanicsburg, PA: Stackpole, 2008.

——. *Joshua Chamberlain: A Hero's Life and Legacy*. Mechanicsburg, PA: Stackpole Books, 1999.

Rable, George C. *Fredericksburg! Fredericksburg!* Chapel Hill, NC: The University of North Carolina Press, 2002.

Ramold, Steven J. *Baring the Iron Hand: Discipline in the Union Army*. DeKalb, IL: Northern Illinois University Press, 2010.

Robertson, William Glenn. "The Peach Orchard Revisited: Daniel Sickles and the Third Corps on July 2, 1863." In *The Second Day at Gettysburg: Essays on Confederate and Union Leadership*, edited by Gary W. Gallagher. Kent, OH: Kent State University Press, 1993.

Schellhammer, Michael. *The 83rd Pennsylvania Volunteers in the Civil War*. Jefferson, NC: McFarland, 2003.

Schultz, Duane. "Jove's Thunder: The Federals' Fredericksburg Scorecard: Shameful Orgy of Destruction, Wretched Loss." *America's Civil War* 30, No. 5 (July, 2017): 44–51.

Sears, Stephen W. *Chancellorsville*. Boston: Houghton-Mifflin, 1996.

——. *Gettysburg*. New York: Mariner, 2003.

——. *To the Gates of Richmond: The Peninsula Campaign*. New York: Ticknor & Fields, 1992.

Smith, Karlton. "How Not to Conduct a Reconnaissance: Capt. Samuel R. Johnston, July 2, 1863–Part 1." *From the Fields of Gettysburg: The Blog of Gettysburg National Military Park*. March 12, 2015. Accessed October 16, 2018. https://npsgnmp.wordpress.com/2015/03/12/how-not-to-conduct-a-reconnaissance-capt-samuel-r-johnston-july-2-1863-part-i.

——. "'To Consider Every Contingency:' Lt. Gen. James Longstreet, Capt. Samuel R. Johnston, and the factors that affected the reconnaissance and countermarch, July 2, 1863," Lecture, Gettysburg, PA, April 8, 2006. National Park Service History eLibrary, The Gettysburg Seminars. http://npshistory.com/series/symposia/gettysburg_seminars/11/essay4.pdf.

Stonesifer, Roy P. *Brigadier General Strong Vincent: A Hero of Gettysburg*. Erie, PA: Strong Vincent Commemoratives Committee of the Greater Erie Bicentennial Commission, 1995.

Tagg, Larry. *The Generals of Gettysburg: The Leaders of America's Greatest Battle*. Cambridge, MA: Da Capo, 2003.

Trulock, Alice Rains. *In the Hands of Providence: Joshua L. Chamberlain and the American Civil War*. Chapel Hill, NC: The University of North Carolina Press, 1992.

Varney, Frank P. *General Grant and the Rewriting of History: How the Destruction of General William S. Rosecrans Influenced Our Understanding of the Civil War.* El Dorado Hills, CA: Savas Beatie, 2013.

Villanueva, Jari. "Lyrics or Words to Taps." The Taps Bugler: Jari Villanueva, Taps Historian and Professional Bugler, January 11, 2020. Accessed November 14, 2020. https://www.tapsbugler.com/lyrics-or-words-to-taps.

Warner, Ezra. *Generals in Blue: Lives of the Union Commanders*. Baton Rouge: Louisiana State University Press, 1964.

——. *Generals in Grey: Lives of the Union Commanders*. Baton Rouge: Louisiana State University Press, 1959.

Wert, Jeffry D. *The Sword of Lincoln: The Army of the Potomac*. New York: Simon & Schuster, 2005.

Whitman, Benjamin. *Nelson's Biographical Dictionary and Historical Reference Book of Erie County, Pennsylvania. Containing a Condensed History of Pennsylvania, of Erie County, and of the Several Cities, Boroughs and Townships in the County; also Portraits and Biographies of the Governors since 1790 and of Numerous Representative Citizens.* Erie, PA: S. B. Nelson, 1896.

Notes

1 Frank H. Norton, *Porter's Division Song (The Army of the Free)* (Washington, D.C.: Philp & Solomons Metropolitan Bookstore, c. 1862), Box 1, Folder 15, The John M. Sell Civil War Collection, Special Collections and Archives, California State University Northridge Library.

Introduction

1 Oliver Willcox Norton, *The Attack and Defense of Little Round Top* (New York: Neale, 1913; Reprint Gettysburg, PA: Stan Clark Military Books, 1992), 267. Citations refer to the SCMB edition.

2 "Mrs. Strong Vincent and Boyd Vincent …" *Pittsburgh Dispatch* (Pittsburgh, PA), Sept. 13, 1889; "On Little Round Top," *Evening Republican* (Meadville, PA), Aug. 27, 1889; "The Camp on the Battle Field," *Harrisburg Daily Independent* (Harrisburg, PA), July 26, 1878; "A Brave Man In Moulded Clay," *Boston Globe* (Boston, MA), July 31, 1888; "On the Field at Gettysburg," *Harrisburg Telegraph* (Harrisburg, PA), May 31, 1878.

3 Thomas A. Desjardin, *These Honored Dead: How the Story of Gettysburg Shaped American Memory* (Cambridge, MA: Da Capo Press, 2003), 129.

4 James H. Nevins and William B. Styple, *What Death More Glorious: A Biography of General Strong Vincent* (Kearny, NJ: Belle Grove, 1997); Roy P. Stonesifer, *Brigadier General Strong Vincent: A Hero of Gettysburg* (Erie, PA: Strong Vincent Commemorative Committee of the Greater Erie Bicentennial Commission, 1995).

5 Glenn LaFantasie, "Joshua Chamberlain and the American Dream," in *The Gettysburg Nobody Knows*, ed. Gabor S. Boritt (Oxford: Oxford University Press, 1997), 40.

1. The Strongs and the Vincents: Early Life, Education, and Courtship

1 Jesse Hutchinson, Jr., *"Get Off the Track!" A Song for Emancipation* (Boston: Published by the Author, 1844), 012.156, The Lester S. Levy Sheet Music Collection, Sheridan Libraries and University Museums, Johns Hopkins University.

2 Boyd Vincent, *Our Family of Vincents: A History, Genealogy, and Biographical Notices* (Cincinnati, OH: Privately Printed by Stewart Kidd Company, 1927), 32; Ibid., 68; Ibid., 56.

3 Samuel P. Bates, *History of Erie County, Pennsylvania. Containing a History of the County; Its Townships, Towns, Villages, Schools, Churches, Industries, Etc.; Portraits of Early Settlers and Prominent Men; Biographies; History of Pennsylvania, Statistical and Miscellaneous Matters* (Chicago: Warner, Beers & Co., 1889), 967; Boyd Vincent, *Our Family of Vincents*, 91; Bates, *History of Erie County*, 959–60; Boyd Vincent, *Our Family of Vincents*, 58; Bates, *History of Erie County*, 679.

4 Nevins and Styple, *What Death More Glorious*, 12; Bates, *History of Erie County*, 499; Benjamin Whitman, *Nelson's Biographical Dictionary and Historical Reference Book of Erie County, Pennsylvania. Containing a Condensed History of Pennsylvania, of Erie County, and of the Several Cities, Boroughs and Townships in the County; also Portraits and Biographies of the Governors since 1790 and of Numerous Representative Citizens* (Erie, PA: S. B. Nelson, 1896), 582–4.

5 Boyd Vincent, *Our Family of Vincents*, 58; Ibid., 86; Carmen DiCiccio, *Coal and Coke in Pennsylvania* (Harrisburg, PA: Historical and Museum Commission, 1996), 47.

6 Boyd Vincent, *Our Family of Vincents*, 87–8.

7 Ibid.; Ibid., 58; Ibid., 87; Bates, *History of Erie County*, 535.

8 William W. Swan, "Strong Vincent" in *Harvard Memorial Biographies*, Vol. 2 (Cambridge, MA: Sever and Francis, 1866), 66; Boyd Vincent, *Our Family of Vincents*, 58; Swan, "Strong Vincent," 66; Boyd Vincent, *Our Family of Vincents*, 58.

9 Swan, "Strong Vincent," 66; Boyd Vincent, *Our Family of Vincents*, 88; Stonesifer, *Strong Vincent*, 3.

10 "Legacy," Miss Porter's School, Miss Porter's School, accessed Sept. 30, 2020.

11 Stonesifer, *Strong Vincent*, 3; Nevins and Styple, *What Death More Glorious*, 16; Ibid., 17.

12 Swan, "Strong Vincent," 66; Boyd Vincent, *Our Family of Vincents*, 88; Swan, "Strong Vincent," 67.

13 Ibid.

14 Ibid.; Nevins and Styple, *What Death More Glorious*, 18; Michael Schellhammer, *The 83rd Pennsylvania Volunteers in the Civil War* (Jefferson, NC: McFarland, 2003), 22.

15 Swan, "Strong Vincent," 67; Bates, *History of Erie County*, 326; Ibid., 535; Ibid., 896; Office of the Auditor General of the Commonwealth of Pennsylvania, *Annual Report of the Auditor General of the State of Pennsylvania and of the Tabulations and Deductions from the Reports of the Rail Road and Canal Companies for the Year 1867*, John F. Hartranft, Auditor General and Lane S. Hart, Rail-Road Clerk (Harrisburg, PA: Singerly & Myers State Printers, 1868), 284.

16 Swan, "Strong Vincent," 67; Bates, *History of Erie County*, 381; Ibid., 326; Boyd Vincent, *Our Family of Vincents*, 58.

17 "Chronology of Major Events Leading to Secession Crisis," Sixteen Months to Sumter: Newspaper Editorials on the Path to Secession, American Historical Association, 2007, accessed October 2, 2020.

2. Lieutenant Vincent of the Erie Regiment: January to August 1861

1 Handwritten Manuscript, "Willie Has Gone to War" by Stephen Collins Foster, 1862, CAM.FHC.2011.01, Foster Hall Collection, Center for American Music, University of Pittsburgh Library.

2 "Chronology of Major Events Leading to Secession Crisis".

3 Schellhammer, *The 83rd Pennsylvania*, 15.

4 "Proclamation of the President of the United States," *The Erie Weekly Gazette* (Erie, PA), April 18, 1861; Schellhammer, *The 83rd Pennsylvania*, 15–16; Ibid., 20; Ibid., 8; Nevins and Styple, *What Death More Glorious*, 22.

5 Amos M. Judson, *History of the Eighty-Third Regiment Pennsylvania Volunteers* (Erie, PA: B. F. H. Lynn, 1865), 21; Schellhammer, *The 83rd Pennsylvania*, 20; Ibid., 16.

6 Nevins and Styple, *What Death More Glorious*, 22; "Local Notices," *Erie Weekly Gazette* (Erie, PA), May 1, 1861.

7 Judson, *History of the Eighty-Third*, 22; Boyd Vincent, *Our Family of Vincents*, 58; Judson, *History of the Eighty-Third*, 22; Oliver Willcox Norton, Oliver Norton to "Sister L.", May 10, 1861, in *Army Letters 1861–1865, Being Extracts from Private Letters to Friends from a Soldier in the Field During the Late Civil War, With an Appendix Containing Copies of Some Official Documents, Papers, and Addresses of Later Date* (Chicago: O. L. Deming, 1903; Reprint Dayton, OH: Morningside, 1995), 10. Citations refer to the Morningside edition.

8 Judson, *History of the Eighty-Third*, 22; Schellhammer, *The 83rd Pennsylvania*, 16; "A Visit to Camp Wilkins," *Erie Weekly Gazette* (Erie, PA), May 23, 1861; Judson, *History of the Eighty-Third*, 22.

9 Ibid.

10 Oliver Norton, *The Attack and Defense of Little Round Top*, 283.

11 Judson, *History of the Eighty-Third*, 22; Ibid.; Oliver Norton, Oliver Norton to "Mother," June 22, 1861, *Army Letters*, 16–18; Judson, *History of the Eighty-Third*, 23.

12 Schellhammer, *The 83rd Pennsylvania*, 17–18.

13 "Return of the Erie Regiment," *The Erie Weekly Gazette* (Erie, PA), July 25, 1861; Judson, *History of the Eighty-Third*, 23; Schellhammer, *History of the 83rd Pennsylvania*, 18.

14 Jeffry D. Wert, *The Sword of Lincoln: The Army of the Potomac* (New York: Simon & Schuster, 2005), 26–8; Schellhammer, *History of the 83rd Pennsylvania*, 19.

3. The 83rd Pennsylvania: August 1861 to March 1862

1 William B. Bradbury and M. A. Kidder, *Marching Along: The Popular Army Song and Chorus* (New York: Firth, Pond & Co., 1862), M1640.B, Civil War Sheet Music Collection, Library of Congress, Washington, D.C.

2 "Recruits Wanted!" *Crawford Journal* (Meadville, PA), July 30, 1861; Bates, *History of Erie County*, 466; Schellhammer, *The 83rd Pennsylvania*, 19; Swan, "Strong Vincent," 68; Bates, *History of Erie County*, 466.

3 Ibid.; David Carlyon, *Dan Rice: The Most Famous Man You've Never Heard Of* (New York: Public Affairs, 2001), 410–11.

4 Schellhammer, *The 83rd Pennsylvania*, 24; Judson, *The Eighty-Third Pennsylvania*, 24; Schellhammer, 20; Ibid., 24.

5 Nevins and Styple, *What Death More Glorious*, 27; George B. McClellan, George McClellan to Edwin M. Stanton, February 3, 1862, in *Report of Maj.-Gen. George B. McClellan, August 4, 1863, with an Account of the Campaign in Western Virginia* (New York: Sheldon and Company, 1864), 103; Chester G. Hearn, *Lincoln and McClellan at War* (Baton Rouge, LA: Louisiana State University Press, 2012), 50–1; Ibid., 36–9; Wert, *The Sword of Lincoln*, 36.

6 George B. McClellan, George B. McClellan to Ellen McClellan, July 27, 1861, in *The Civil War Papers of George B. McClellan: Selected Correspondence, 1860–1865*, ed. Stephen W. Sears (New York: Ticknor and Fields, 1989), 70.

7 Nevins and Styple, *What Death More Glorious*, 27; Wert, *The Sword of Lincoln*, 35.

8 Schellhammer, *The 83rd Pennsylvania*, 28; Judson, *History of the Eighty-Third*, 24; Daniel Foote, "Letter from Washington–Arrival of the Erie Regiment," *The Erie Weekly Gazette*, September 26, 1861.

9 Schellhammer, *The 83rd Pennsylvania*, 28; Judson, *History of the Eighty Third*, 24; Oliver Norton, Oliver Norton to "Sister L.," September 30, 1861, *Army Letters*, 23.

10 Judson, *History of the Eighty Third*, 24; Schellhammer, *The 83rd Pennsylvania*, 28; Oliver Norton, Oliver Norton to "Sister L.," September 30, 1861, *Army Letters*, 24; Schellhammer, *The 83rd Pennsylvania*, 30–4; Oliver Norton, Oliver Norton to "Dear Friends at Home," October 4, 1861, *Army Letters*, 25.

11 Ezra J, Warner, "Fitz John Porter," *Generals in Blue: Lives of the Union Commanders* (Baton Rouge, LA: Louisiana State University Press, 1964), 378–80.

12 Warner, "Daniel Butterfield," *Generals in Blue*, 62–3.

13 Judson, *History of the Eighty-Third*, 24–5; Gilbert H. Dearing, *Chronological History of the 17th Regiment of New York Infantry Volunteers* (Sing Sing, NY: Sunnyside Printing Co., 1894), 19; Kim Crawford, *The Sixteenth Michigan Infantry* (Dayton, OH: Morningside, 2002), 12–40.

14 Oliver Norton, Oliver Norton to "Friend P-s", October 26, 1861, *Army Letters*, 29; Judson, *History of the Eighty*-Third, 25; Eugene Arus Nash, *A History of the Forty-Fourth Regiment, New York Volunteer Infantry, in the Civil War, 1861–1865* (Chicago: R. R. Donnelly & Sons, 1911), 44–5.

15 Ibid., 9.

16 Ibid., 45–6.

17 Schellhammer, *The 83rd Pennsylvania*, 37–8.

18 Nevins and Styple, *What Death More Glorious*, 163; Ezra J. Warner, "James Clay Rice," *Generals in Blue: Lives of the Union Commanders* (Baton Rouge, LA: Louisiana State University Press, 1964), 400–1.

19 John M. Sell to "Dear Father & Mother," October 29, 1861, Box 1, Folder 18, The John M. Sell Civil War Collection, Special Collections and Archives, California State University Northridge Library.

20 Norton, *Attack and Defense*, 284.

21 Schellhammer, *The 83rd Pennsylvania*, 38; Nash, *History of the Forty-Fourth*, 55; "Correspondence," *Crawford Journal* (Meadville, PA), November 26, 1861; Oliver Norton, Oliver Norton to "Friend P-s," November 15, 1861, *Army Letters*, 33.

22 Judson, *History of the Eighty-Third*, 25; Ibid., 25–6; Schellhammer, *The 83rd Pennsylvania*, 38–42.

23 Ibid., 44; Nevins and Styple, *What Death More Glorious*, 28; Swan, "Strong Vincent," 68; Nevins and Styple, *What Death More Glorious*, 30.

24 Judson, *History of the Eighty-Third*, 26.

25 Ibid.

26 Schellhammer, *The 83rd Pennsylvania*, 44–5; Nash, *History of the Forty-Fourth*, 53; Oliver Norton, Oliver Norton to "Sister L.," January 7, 1862, *Army Letters*, 39.

27 Judson, *History of the Eighty-Third*, 26; Letter of Miss Sarah Porter, quoted in Nevins and Styple, *What Death More Glorious*, 30.

28 Judson, *History of the Eighty-Third*, 26; Oliver Norton, Oliver Norton to "Sister L.," January 17, 1862, *Army Letters*, 40–1; Hearn, *Lincoln and McClellan at* War, 66; Wert, *Sword of Lincoln*, 56–7; Stephen W. Sears, *To the Gates of Richmond: The Peninsula Campaign* (New York: Houghton Mifflin Harcourt, 1992), 4–5; Schellhammer, *The 83rd Pennsylvania*, 48.

29 Schellhammer, *The 83rd Pennsylvania*, 46–7.

30 Hearn, *Lincoln and McClellan at War*, 66; Ibid.; George B. McClellan, George B. McClellan to Ellen McClellan, c. October 11, 1861, *Civil War Papers of George B. McClellan*, 106; George B. McClellan, George B. McClellan to Ellen McClellan, November 17, 1861, *Civil War Papers of George B. McClellan*, 135.

31 Paul Kahan, *Amiable Scoundrel: Simon Cameron, Lincoln's Scandalous Secretary of War* (Lincoln, NE: Potomac Books, 2016), 145; Wert, *Sword of Lincoln*, 56–7; Abraham Lincoln, President's General War Order No. 1, January 27, 1862, in *The Collected Works of Abraham Lincoln*, ed. Roy P. Basler, Marion Dolores Pratt and Lloyd A. Dunlap (New Brunswick, NJ: Rutgers University Press, 1953), 5:111–12.

32 Sears, *To the Gates of Richmond*, 4–5; Schellhammer, *The 83rd Pennsylvania*, 48.

33 John Rice, John Rice to "Len & Lib," March 3/5, 1862, Letter, From the Erie County Historical Society.

34 McClellan, *Report of Maj.-Gen. George B. McClellan*, 123; Oliver Norton, Oliver Norton to "Cousin L.," March 17, 1862, *Army Letters*, 59; Judson, *History of the Eighty-Third*, 27.

35 McClellan, *Report of Maj.-Gen. George B. McClellan*, 128; Sears, *To the Gates of Richmond*, 17.; Ibid., 18; Wert, *The Sword of Lincoln*, 63–4.

4. The Swamps of the Chickahominy: Late March to September 1862

1 John Reuben Thompson, *Richmond is a Hard Road to Travel* (New Orleans: Blackmar & Co, 1863), conf0339, Historic American Sheet Music, David M. Rubenstein Rare Book & Manuscript Collection, Duke University.

2 Wert, *Sword of Lincoln*, 66.

3 Nash, *History of the 44th New York*, 61; Judson, *History of the Eighty-Third*, 28; Nash, *History of the 44th New York*, 61–2.
4 Wert, *Sword of Lincoln*, 66; Hearn, *Lincoln and McClellan at War*, 112; Judson, *History of the Eighty-Third*, 28.
5 Hearn, *Lincoln and McClellan at War*, 111.
6 Judson, *History of the Eighty-Third*, 29.
7 Oliver Norton, Oliver Norton to "Sister L.," March 29, 1862, *Army Letters*, 63–4.
8 Schellhammer, *The 83rd Pennsylvania*, 54.
9 McClellan, *Report of Maj.-Gen. George B. McClellan*, 159; Ibid., 162; George B. McClellan, George B. McClellan to Ellen McClellan, April 4, 1862, in *The Civil War Papers of George B. McClellan*, 228.
10 John B. Magruder, "J. Bankhead Magruder to General Lee," April 5, 1862, in *The War of the Rebellion: A Compilation of the Official Records of the Union and Confederate Armies* (Washington: Government Printing Office, 1884), Vol. 11, Part 3, 422; Sears, *To the Gates of Richmond*, 37–8.
11 McClellan, *Report of Maj.-Gen. George B. McClellan*, 166–7.
12 Sears, *To the Gates of Richmond*, 37; Hearn, *Lincoln and McClellan at War*, 112–13.
13 George B. McClellan, George B. McClellan to Abraham Lincoln, April 5, 1862, in *The Civil War Papers of George B. McClellan*, 228.
14 Abraham Lincoln, Abraham Lincoln to George B. McClellan, April 6, 1862, *Collected Works of Abraham Lincoln*, 5:182; George B. McClellan, George B. McClellan to Edwin M. Stanton, April 7, 1862, in *The Civil War Papers of George B. McClellan*, 232; George B. McClellan, George B. McClellan to Ellen McClellan, April 6, 1862, in *The Civil War Papers of George B. McClellan*, 230; George B. McClellan, George B. McClellan to Ellen McClellan, April 8, 1862, in *The Civil War Papers of George B. McClellan*, 234.
15 Schellhammer, *The 83rd Pennsylvania*, 55–6; Swan, "Strong Vincent," 69; Nash, *History of the Forty-Fourth New York*, 67–8; Judson, *History of the Eighty-Third*, 32.
16 Daniel Butterfield, "Report of Brig. Gen. Daniel Butterfield, U.S. Army, as General of the Trenches, April 27," in *The War of the Rebellion: A Compilation of the Official Records of the Union and Confederate Armies* (Washington: Government Printing Office, 1884), Vol. 11, Part 1, 385–8.
17 Fitz John Porter, "Report of Maj. Gen. Fitz John Porter, U.S. Army, as Director of the Siege of Yorktown from April 7–May 5," in *The War of the Rebellion: A Compilation of the Official Records of the Union and Confederate Armies* (Washington: Government Printing Office, 1884), Vol. 11, Part 1, 311–16; Judson, *History of the Eighty-Third*, 32.
18 Porter, "Report of Maj. Gen. Fitz John Porter, U.S. Army, as Director …", 313–14.
19 Ibid., 314–15.
20 George B. McClellan, George B. McClellan to Edwin M. Stanton, May 4, 1862 – 7 pm, in *The Civil War Papers of George B. McClellan*, 254; Sears, *To the Gates of Richmond*, 67–70; Ibid., 72–82; Ibid., 84–6; William B. Franklin, "Reports of Brig. Gen. William B. Franklin, U.S. Army, commanding division," in *The War of*

the Rebellion: A Compilation of the Official Records of the Union and Confederate Armies (Washington: Government Printing Office, 1884), Vol. 11, Part 1, 617; McClellan, *Report of Maj. Gen. George B. McClellan*, 191; Judson, *History of the Eighty-Third*, 33.

21 Ibid., 33–5, parentheses in the original.

22 Ibid.

23 Ibid., 35.

24 Ibid.

25 Strong Vincent, Strong Vincent to Elizabeth Vincent, April 1863, in Swan, "Strong Vincent," 73.

26 Schellhammer, *The 83rd Pennsylvania*, 63; Oliver Norton, Oliver Norton to "Sister L.," May 23, 1862, in *Army Letters*, 79; Sears, *To the Gates of Richmond*, 95.

27 Ibid; Crawford, *The 16th Michigan Infantry*, 130; Francis D. Keeler, Francis Keeler to Mary Bailey, May 16, 1862, in *War Letters Written During the Rebellion* (Saginaw, MI: Julian A. Keeler, 1895), 68; Sears, *To the Gates of Richmond*, 95.

28 Sears, *To the Gates of Richmond*, 103; Judson, *History of the Eighty-Third*, 36.

29 Edwin C. Fishel, "Pinkerton and McClellan: Who Deceived Whom?" *Civil War History* 34, No. 2 (June 1988): 125–7; Sears, *To the Gates of Richmond*, 60; George B. McClellan, George B. McClellan to Abraham Lincoln, May 14,1862, in *The Civil War Papers of George B. McClellan*, 264.

30 Ezra J. Warner, "George Webb Morell," in *Generals in Blue*, 330–1; Judson, *History of the Eighty-Third*, 36; Schellhammer, *The 83rd Pennsylvania*, 67; McClellan, *Report of Maj.-Gen. George B. McClellan*, 211; Nash, *History of the Forty-Fourth New York*, 73; Oliver Norton, Oliver Norton to "Dear Friends at Home," May 26, 1862, in *Army Letters*, 81–2; Thomas Stockton, Stockton Diary, May 22–24, 1862, quoted in Crawford, *The 16th Michigan*, 135.

31 Judson, *History of the Eighty-Third*, 36; George W. Morell, "Report of Brig. Gen. George W. Morell, U.S. Army, commanding division," in *The War of the Rebellion: A Compilation of the Official Records of the Union and Confederate Armies* (Washington: Government Printing Office, 1884), Vol. 11, Part 1, 698–701; Wert, *Sword of Lincoln*, 91; Sears, *To the Gates of Richmond*, 114; Morell, "Report of Brig. Gen George W. Morell," 699.

32 Sears, *To the Gates of Richmond*, 114; Morell, "Report of Brig. Gen. George W. Morell," 699; Ezra J. Warner, "Lawrence O'Bryan Branch," in *Generals in Grey*, 31.

33 Lawrence O. Branch, "Report of Brig. Gen. Lawrence O'B. Branch, C.S. Army, of engagement May 27, with congratulations from General R. E. Lee," in *The War of the Rebellion: A Compilation of the Official Records of the Union and Confederate Armies* (Washington: Government Printing Office, 1884), Vol. 11, Part 1, 740–3; Nash, *History of the Forty-Fourth New York*, 74.

34 Morell, "Report of Brig. Gen. George W. Morell," 699–700, Parentheses original to Gen. Morell's report; John H. Martindale, "Report of Brig. Gen. John H. Martindale, U.S. Army, commanding First Brigade," in *The War of the Rebellion: A Compilation of the Official Records of the Union and Confederate Armies* (Washington: Government Printing Office, 1884), Vol. 11, Part 1, 701–7.

35 Charles W. Roberts, "Report of Col. Charles W. Roberts, Second Maine Infantry, of engagement May 27," in *The War of the Rebellion: A Compilation of the Official Records of the Union and Confederate Armies* (Washington: Government Printing Office, 1884), Vol. 11, Part 1, 707–10; Sears, *To the Gates of Richmond*, 116; Judson, *History of the Eighty-Third*, 37; Morell, "Report of Brig. Gen. George W. Morell," 700; Oliver Norton, Oliver Norton to "Brother and Sister," June 2, 1862, in *Army Letters*, 84.

36 McClellan, "George B. McClellan to Edwin M. Stanton," May 28, 1862, in *The Civil War Papers of George B. McClellan*, 279; McClellan, "George B. McClellan to Ellen McClellan," May 28, 1862, in *The Civil War Papers of George B. McClellan*, 280.

37 Judson, *History of the Eighty-Third*, 38; Sears, *To the Gates of Richmond*, 138–40; Ibid., 145.

38 Richard H. Brown, "'Not Well and Not Sick' of the Chickahominy Fever: Hollis Wrisley's Civil War," *The Massachusetts Review*, 46, No. 4 (Winter 2005/2006): 578–81; Sears, *To the Gates of Richmond*, 163–5; Swan, "Strong Vincent," 69.

39 Shellhammer, *The 83rd Pennsylvania*, 99; Hugh S. Campbell, "Reports of Lieut. Col. Hugh S. Campbell, Eighty-third Pennsylvania Infantry, of the battle of Gaines' Mill, engagement at Turkey Bridge, and Battle of Malvern Hill," in *The War of the Rebellion: A Compilation of the Official Records of the Union and Confederate Armies* (Washington: Government Printing Office, 1884), Vol. 11, Part 2, 343–7; Schellhammer, *The 83rd* Pennsylvania, 95–6; Norton, *Army* Letters, 339; Schellhammer, *The 83rd Pennsylvania*, 20; Judson, *History of the Eighty-Third*, 122.

40 Swan, "Strong Vincent," 69; Schellhammer, *The 83rd Pennsylvania*, 99; Swan, "Strong Vincent," 70; Nevins and Styple, *What Death More Glorious*, 35; Boyd Vincent, *Our Family of Vincents*, 59; Swan, "Strong Vincent," 70; Nevins and Styple, *What Death More Glorious*, 35; Judson, *History of the Eighty Third*, 49.

41 Swan, "Strong Vincent," 70; Nevins and Styple, *What Death More Glorious*, 35.

42 Elizabeth Vincent, Elizbeth Vincent to Sarah Porter, in Nevins and Styple, *What Death More Glorious*, 37–8.

43 "Local Paragraphs," *The Erie Weekly Gazette* (Erie, PA), August 7, 1862.

44 Letter of Dr. Brandes, quoted in Nevins and Styple, *What Death More Glorious*, 36; G. H. G. Jähr, *Manual of Homœpathic Medicine in Two Parts: Part I: Materia Medica. Part II: Therapeutical and Symptomatological Repertory* (London: Hippolyte Baillière, 1847), 435.

45 Judson, *History of the Eighty-Third*, 117; Elizabeth Vincent, Elizabeth Vincent to Sarah Porter, in Nevins and Styple, *What Death More Glorious*, 38.

46 Ibid., 39–40.

47 Ibid., 36–41.

48 Ibid., 41.

49 Wert, *Sword of Lincoln*, 173; Schellhammer, *The 83rd Pennsylvania*, 131; Norton, "Two Bugle Calls," in *Army Letters*, 323–9.

5. October 1862 to January 1863: Colonel Vincent

1 George F. Root, *The Battle Cry of Freedom* (Chicago: Root & Cady, 1862), 0012_003259_000275, University of Tennessee Sheet Music Collection, University of Tennessee, Knoxville, Special Collections, University of Tennessee.
2 Hearn, *Lincoln and McClellan at War*, 197–203; Abraham Lincoln, "Abraham Lincoln to George B. McClellan," in *The Collected Works of Abraham Lincoln*, 5:474.
3 Schellhammer, *The 83rd Pennsylvania*, 134; Swan, "Strong Vincent," 70; Schellhammer, *The 83rd Pennsylvania*, 135.
4 Steven J, Ramold, *The Iron Hand: Military Discipline in the Union Army* (DeKalb, IL: Northern Illinois University Press, 2010), 54–62); Ibid., 346–7.
5 Judson, *History of the Eighty Third*, 55.
6 Wertz, *Sword of Lincoln*, 178; Judson, *History of the Eighty-Third*, 55.
7 E. D. Townsend, "General Orders No. 182," in *The War of the Rebellion: A Compilation of the Official Records of the Union and Confederate Armies* (Washington: Government Printing Office, 1887), Vol. 19, Part 2, 545
8 Warner, "Fitz John Porter," in *Generals in Blue*, 378–80; Schellhammer, *The 83rd Pennsylvania*, 136; Ezra J. Warner, "Joseph Hooker," in *Generals in Blue*, 233–5.
9 Norton, Oliver Norton to "Sister L.," December 6, 1862, in *Army Letters*, 127–8.
10 Judson, *History of the Eighty-Third*, 55; George C. Rable, *Fredericksburg! Fredericksburg!* (Chapel Hill, NC: The University of North Carolina Press, 2002), 19; George G. Meade, "George Meade to Mrs. George G. Meade," November 9, 1862, in *The Life and Letters of George Gordon Meade, Major-General United States Army*, ed. Col. George Meadc (New York: Charles Scribner's Sons, 1913), 1:325; Rable, *Fredericksburg! Fredericksburg!*, 57.
11 Ibid., 57–60; Ambrose E. Burnside, "Ambrose Burnside to General G. W. Cullum," November 7, 1862, in *The War of the Rebellion: A Compilation of the Official Records of the Union and Confederate Armies* (Washington: Government Printing Office, 1887), Vol. 19, Part 2, 552; Crawford, *The 16th Michigan*, 227.
12 Schellhammer, *The 83rd Pennsylvania*, 138–9; Judson, *History of the Eighty-Third*, 57; Francis Augustín O'Reilly, *The Fredericksburg Campaign: Winter War on the Rappahannock* (Baton Rouge: Louisiana State University Press, 2006), 7–8; Oliver Norton, Oliver Norton to "Sister L.," December 6, 1862, in *Army Letters*, 127.
13 O'Reilly, *The Fredericksburg Campaign*, 30; Ibid., 30–2; Rable, *Fredericksburg! Fredericksburg!*, 87–8; O'Reilly, *The Fredericksburg Campaign*, 7–8.
14 Earl J. Hess, *Field Armies & Fortifications in the Civil War: The Eastern Campaigns, 1861–1864*, (Chapel Hill: The University of North Carolina Press, 2005), 157.
15 Strong Vincent, Strong Vincent to Lieut. J. H. Barnet, October 14, 1862, in *What Death More Glorious*, 129; Strong Vincent, Strong Vincent to Lt. Lansing, AAAG, November 1, 1862, in *What Death More Glorious*, 130; Strong Vincent, Strong Vincent to Lt. Lansing, A.A.A.G, November 1, 1862, in *What Death More Glorious*, 131; Strong Vincent, Strong Vincent to Col Pulston, November 21, 1862, in *What Death More Glorious*, 131–2.

16 Strong Vincent, Strong Vincent to Surgeon General King, November 28, 1862, in *What Death More Glorious*, 132; Strong Vincent, Strong Vincent to Gen. S. Thomas, November 28, 1862, in *What Death More Glorious*, 133, Parentheses original to Vincent's letter.

17 Rable, *Fredericksburg! Fredericksburg!*, 88; Crawford, *The 16th Michigan*, 232; Rable, *Fredericksburg! Fredericksburg!*, 136.

18 O'Reilly, *The Fredericksburg Campaign*, 57–67; Edwin G. Longacre, *The Man Behind the Guns: A Military Biography of General Henry J. Hunt, Chief of Artillery, Army of the Potomac* (Cambridge, MA: Da Capo Press, 2003), 129.

19 Duane Schultz, "Jove's Thunder: The Federals' Fredericksburg Scorecard: Shameful Orgy of Destruction, Wretched Loss," *America's Civil War* 30, no. 5 (July 2017): 48; Longacre, *The Man behind the Guns*, 129–31.

20 Rable, *Fredericksburg! Fredericksburg!*, 162; Victor Brooks, *The Fredericksburg Campaign: October 1862–January, 1863*, (Conshohocken, PA: Combined, 2000), 94.

21 James Longstreet, *From Manassas to Appomattox: Memoirs of the Civil War in America* (Philadelphia: J. B. Lippencott, 1896), 302; Edward Porter Alexander, *Military Memoirs of a Confederate: A Critical Narrative* (New York: Charles Scribner's Sons, 1907), 290–1.

22 Oliver Norton, Oliver Norton to "Sister L.," December 20, 1862, in *Army Letters*, 130; Nash, *History of the Forty-Fourth*, 112–13; Joshua L. Chamberlain, "My Story of Fredericksburg," in *"Bayonet! Forward:" My Civil War Reminiscences*, ed. Stan Clark (Gettysburg, PA: Stan Clark Military Books, 1994), 3.

23 O'Reilly, *The Fredericksburg Campaign*, 77–8.

24 Rable, *Fredericksburg! Fredericksburg!*, 168–71.

25 Oliver Norton, Oliver Norton to "Sister L.," December 16, 1862, in *Army Letters*, 130; Ellis Spear, *The Civil War Recollections of General Ellis Spear*, eds. Abbott Spear, Andrea C. Hawkes, Marie H. McCosh, Craig L. Symonds, and Michael Alpert (Orono, ME: The University of Maine Press, 1997), 19.

26 John Matteson, *A Worse Place Than Hell: How the Civil War Battle of Fredericksburg Changed A Nation* (New York: W. W. Norton, 2021), 214.

27 Ambrose Burnside, "Report of the Operations of the Army of the Potomac, Nov. 7, 1862 – Jan. 25, 1863," in *The War of the Rebellion: A Compilation of the Official Records of the Union and Confederate Armies* (Washington: Government Printing Office, 1887), Vol. 21, 90; O'Reilly, *The Fredericksburg Campaign*, 247–8; Ibid., 250–75.

28 Holman Melcher, Holman Melcher to Nathaniel Melcher, December 19, 1862, in *With a Flash of His Sword: The Writings of Major Holman S. Melcher, 20th Maine Infantry*, ed. William B. Styple (Kearny, NJ: Belle Grove, 1994), 11.

29 O'Reilly, *The Fredericksburg Campaign*, 263; Ezra J. Warner, "Charles Griffin," in *Generals in Blue*, 190–1; O'Reilly, *The Fredericksburg Campaign*, 263; Judson, *History of the Eighty-Third*, 58; Spear, *The Civil War Recollections of General Ellis Spear*, 299; Charles Griffin, "Report of Brig. Gen. Charles Griffin, U.S. Army, commanding

First Division," in *The War of the Rebellion: A Compilation of the Official Records of the Union and Confederate Armies* (Washington: Government Printing Office, 1887), Vol. 21, 405.

30 Edward Hill, "The Last Charge at Fredericksburg," in *A Biographical Memorial of General Daniel Butterfield, Including Many Addresses and Military Writings*, ed. Julia Lorrilard Butterfield (New York: The Grafton Press, 1904), 303; Theodore Gerrish, *Army Life: A Private's Reminiscences of the Civil War* (Portland, ME: Hoyt, Fogg & Donham, 1882), 76; Ellis Spear, *Civil War Recollections*, 300; Joshua Lawrence Chamberlain, Joshua Chamberlain to Fannie Chamberlain, December 17, 1862, in *Joshua L. Chamberlain: A Life in Letters*, ed. Thomas Desjardin (Oxford: Osprey, 2012), 179; Judson, *History of the Eighty-Third*, 58.

31 Hill, "The Last Charge at Fredericksburg," 303; Judson, *History of the Eighty-Third*, 58.

32 O'Reilly, *The Fredericksburg Campaign*, 383–4; Strong Vincent, "Report of Col. Strong Vincent, Eighty-third Pennsylvania," in *The War of the Rebellion: A Compilation of the Official Records of the Union and Confederate Armies* (Washington: Government Printing Office, 1887), Vol. 21, 413; Judson, *History of the Eighty-Third*, 58; Michael T. Donohoe, "Report of Col. Michael T. Donohoe, Tenth New Hampshire Infantry," in *The War of the Rebellion: A Compilation of the Official Records of the Union and Confederate Armies* (Washington: Government Printing Office, 1887), Vol. 21, 337.

33 O'Reilly, *The Fredericksburg Campaign*, 385–6; Strong Vincent, "Report of Col. Strong Vincent, Eighty-third Pennsylvania," in *The War of the Rebellion: A Compilation of the Official Records of the Union and Confederate Armies* (Washington: Government Printing Office, 1887), Vol. 21, 413; Gerrish, *Army Life*, 78.

34 Edward G. Longacre, *Joshua Chamberlain: The Soldier and the Man* (Cambridge, MA: Da Capo, 1999), 92–4; Chamberlain, "My Story of Fredericksburg," 7; Holman Melcher, Holman Melcher to Nathaniel Melcher, December 19, 1862, in *With a Flash of His Sword*, 14–15; Judson, *History of the Eighty-Third*, 58–9; Joshua Chamberlain to Fannie Chamberlain, December 17, 1862, in *Joshua L. Chamberlain: A Life in Letters*, 180.

35 Oliver Norton to "Sister L.," December 20, 1862, in *Army Letters*, 129; Judson, *History of the Eighty-Third*, 59–60; Crawford, *The 16th Michigan*, 250–2; Swan, "Strong Vincent," 71–2; Nevins and Styple, *What Death More Glorious*, 49–50.

6. "I Enlisted to Fight": January to April 1863

1 Charles Carroll Sawyer and Henry Tucker, *Weeping, Sad and Lonely, or When This Cruel War is Over* (Brooklyn: Sawyer & Thompson, 1863), M1640.T, Civil War Sheet Music Collection, The Library of Congress, Washington, D.C..

2 Wertz, *Sword of Lincoln*, 204; Oliver Norton to "Sister L.," December 20, 1862, in *Army Letters*, 129; Schellhammer, *The 83rd Pennsylvania*, 150.

3 Daniel Butterfield, Daniel Butterfield to E. M. Stanton, December 17, 1862, in *The War of the Rebellion: A Compilation of the Official Records of the Union and

Confederate Armies (Washington: Government Printing Office, 1897), Vol. 51, Part 1, 959.

4 Nevins and Styple, *What Death More Glorious*, 54; Norton, *Attack and Defense of Little Round Top*, 285; Swan, "Strong Vincent," 72; Wert, *Sword of Lincoln*, 213–15; Nevins and Styple, *What Death More Glorious*, 54–5.

5 Wert, *Sword of Lincoln*, 216–20; Ezra J. Warner, "George Gordon Meade," in *Generals in Blue*, 315–17; Tom Huntington, *Searching for George Gordon Meade: The Forgotten Victor of Gettysburg* (Mechanicsburg, PA: Stackpole, 2013), 186; Ibid., ix.

6 Schellhammer, *The 83rd Pennsylvania*, 154.

7 Strong Vincent, Strong Vincent to Dr. James King, January 7, 1863, in *What Death More Glorious*, 135; Strong Vincent, Strong Vincent to Hon. Saml. B. Thomas, December 26, 1862, in *What Death More Glorious*, 134; Strong Vincent, Strong Vincent to Capt. Estes, A.A.A. Genl., January 10, 1863, in *What Death More Glorious*, 136–7; Strong Vincent, Strong Vincent to "General", January 14, 1863, in *What Death More Glorious*, 137–8.

8 Strong Vincent, Strong Vincent to Capt. J. P. Sherborne, A.A.G., January 26, 1863, in *What Death More Glorious*, 138; Strong Vincent Strong Vincent to Capt. Estes, A.A.A.G., March 11, 1863, in *What Death More Glorious*, 139.

9 Swan, "Strong Vincent," 73; Nevins and Styple, *What Death More Glorious*, 55; Ramold, *Baring the Iron Hand*, 302; Ibid, 312.

10 Charles Augustus Stevens, *Berdan's United States Sharpshooters in the Army of the Potomac, 1861–1865* (St. Paul, MN: Price-McGill, 1892) 1–25; Nevins and Styple, *What Death More Glorious*, 55.

11 Records of the Court Martial of Lieutenant Colonel Caspar Trepp, 1st U.S.S.S., 1863, MS670.25, Box 1, Folder 3, Court martial papers, New-York Historical Society Archives, New York, New York, United States; Court Martial Case File "Trepp, Casper–Lieutenant Colonel, U.S. Sharp Shooters, 1st", 1863, 1815145-LL188, War Department, Bureau of Military justice, Records of the Office of the Judge Advocate General (Army), National Archives, Washington, D.C., United States.

12 Ibid.; "General Orders No. 23" March 2, 1863, in Records of the Court Martial of Lieutenant Colonel Caspar Trepp, 1st U.S.S.S., 1863, MS670.25, Box 1, Folder 3, Court martial papers, New-York Historical Society Archives, New York, New York, United States.

13 Ibid.

14 "General Orders No. 31" March 27, 1863, in Records of the Court Martial of Lieutenant Colonel Caspar Trepp, 1st U.S.S.S., 1863, MS670.25, Box 1, Folder 3, Court martial papers, New-York Historical Society Archives, New York, New York, United States.

15 Ramold, *Baring the Iron Hand,* 310–11; Swan, "Strong Vincent," 73–4.

16 Crawford, *The 16th Michigan*, 290–7.

17 Schellhammer, *The 83rd Pennsylvania*, 154.

18 Strong Vincent, Strong Vincent to Dr. James King, March 24, 1863, in *What Death More Glorious*, 142.

19 Strong Vincent, Strong Vincent to Capt. Estis, A.A.A. Genl., March 24, 1863, in *What Death More Glorious*, 143; Oliver Norton, Oliver Norton to "Sister L.," April 8, 1863, in *Army Letters*, 147–9.

20 John M. Sell to "Dear Father & Mother," March 29, 1863, Box 1, Folder 30, The John M. Sell Civil War Collection, Special Collections and Archives, California State University Northridge Library; John M. Sell to William J. Sell, March 26, 1863, Box 1, Folder 12, The John M. Sell Civil War Collection, Special Collections and Archives, California State University Northridge Library.

21 Wert, *The Sword of Lincoln*, 230.

7. "I Wish He Were a Brigadier-General": May to June 1863

1 S. J. Adams, *We Are Coming Father Abraham 300,00 More* (Boston: Henry Tolman & Co., 1862), M1640.A, Civil War Sheet Music Collection, The Library of Congress, Washington, D.C..

2 Judson, *History of the Eighty-Third*, 62.

3 Strong Vincent, Strong Vincent to Elizabeth Vincent, April 1863, in Swan, "Strong Vincent," 73.

4 Wertz, *Sword of Lincoln*, 231–6; George Meade, George G. Meade to Mrs. George Meade, May 7, 1863, in *The Life and Letters of George Gordon Meade*, 1:371.

5 Oliver Norton, Oliver Norton to "Sister L.," May 8, 1863, in *Army Letters*, 149; Judson, *History of the Eighty-Third*, 62.

6 Stephen W. Sears, *Chancellorsville* (Boston: Houghton-Mifflin, 1996), 233–5; Joseph T. Glatthaar, *General Lee's Army: From Victory to Collapse* (New York: Free Press, 2008), 245–7.

7 Wert, *Sword of Lincoln*, 221.

8 Oliver Otis Howard, *Autobiography of Oliver Otis Howard, Major General United States Army* (New York: Baker & Taylor, 1907), 1:366; Sears, *Chancellorsville,* 281–307.

9 Wert, *Sword of Lincoln,* 244–52; Judson, *History of the Eighty-Third*, 62–3; Strong Vincent, "Report of Col. Strong Vincent, Eighty-third Pennsylvania Infantry," in *The War of the Rebellion: A Compilation of the Official Records of the Union and Confederate Armies* (Washington: Government Printing Office, 1889), Vol. 25, Part 1, 522.

10 Noah Brooks, *Mr. Lincoln's Washington: Selections from the Writings of Noah Brooks, Civil War Correspondent*, ed. P. J. Staudenraus (New York: Thomas Yoseloff, 1967), 179–80; Wert, *Sword of Lincoln*, 254; Oliver Norton, Oliver Norton to "Mother," May 10, 1863, in *Army Letters* 151.

11 Judson, *History of the Eighty-Third,* 63; Crawford, *The 16th Michigan,* 315–17; Nevins and Styple, *What Death More Glorious*, 59; Schellhammer, *The 83rd Pennsylvania*, 162.

12 Strong Vincent, "General Orders No. 1" in *What Death More Glorious,* 150; Strong Vincent, "General Orders No. 2," in *What Death More Glorious*, 150–1; Strong Vincent, "General Orders No. 3," in *What Death More Glorious*, 151–3.

13 Oliver Norton, Oliver Norton to "Sister L.,' May 27, 1863, in *Army Letters*, 155; United States War Department, *Revised United States Army Regulations of 1861, With an Appendix Containing the Changes and Laws Affecting Army Regulations and Articles of War to June 25, 1863* (Washington, D.C.: Government Printing Office, 1863), 73.

14 Ezra J. Warner, "James Barnes," in *Generals in Blue*, 20–1; George G. Meade, George Meade to Brig. Gen. James Barnes, in *The War of the Rebellion: A Compilation of the Official Records of the Union and Confederate Armies* (Washington: Government Printing Office, 1889), Vol. 25, Part 2, 535; Schellhammer, *The 83rd Pennsylvania*, 162–3.

15 "Picketing on the Rappahannock," in *History of the Forty-Fourth New York*, 322; Judson, *History of the Eighty-Third*, 63; Strong Vincent, Strong Vincent to Capt. Davis, A.A.G., May 30, 1863, Letter, From New-York Historical Society, *General James Barnes Collection: Correspondence, Military Records, Sketches & Personal Papers, 1861–1869.*

16 George G. Meade, George Meade to Brig. Gen. S. Williams, May 31, 1863, in *The War of the Rebellion: A Compilation of the Official Records of the Union and Confederate Armies* (Washington: Government Printing Office, 1889), Vol. 25, Part 2, 572.

17 "Picketing on the Rappahannock," in *History of the Forty-Fourth New York*, 322; Judson, *History of the Eighty-Third*, 63; Norton, Oliver Norton to "Cousin L.," June 1, 1863, in *Army Letters,* 156–7; Judson, *History of the Eighty-Third*, 63.

18 Strong Vincent, Strong Vincent to Capt. Davis, A.A.G., June 1, 1863, Letter, From New-York Historical Society, *General James Barnes Collection: Correspondence, Military Records, Sketches & Personal Papers, 1861–1869.*

19 John M. Sell to William J. Sell, June 3, 1863, Box 1, Folder 15, The John M. Sell Civil War Collection, Special Collections and Archives, California State University Northridge Library.

20 Strong Vincent, Strong Vincent to Capt. Davis, A.A.G., June 4, 1863, in *What Death More Glorious*, 153–4.

21 Edwin B. Coddington, *The Gettysburg Campaign: A Study in Command* (New York: Touchstone, 1997), 13–25; Glatthaar, *General Lee's Army*, 268–9.

22 Joseph Hooker, Joseph Hooker to Abraham Lincoln, June 5, 1863, in *The War of the Rebellion: A Compilation of the Official Records of the Union and Confederate Armies* (Washington: Government Printing Office, 1889), Vol. 27, Part 1, 30; Abraham Lincoln, Abraham Lincoln to Joseph Hooker, June 5, 1863, in *The Collected Works of Abraham Lincoln*, 6:249.

23 John Buford, John Buford to Colonel Alexander, A.A.G. Cavalry Corps, June 6, 1863, in *The War of the Rebellion: A Compilation of the Official Records of the Union and Confederate Armies* (Washington: Government Printing Office, 1889), Vol. 27,

Part 3, 14; Wert, *Sword of Lincoln*, 260–2; Edward G. Longacre, *Lee's Cavalrymen: A History of the Mounted Forces of the Army of Northern Virginia, 1861–1865* (Norman, OK: University of Oklahoma Press, 2012), 190–202; Edward G. Longacre, *Lincoln's Cavalrymen: A History of the Mounted Forces of the Army of the Potomac, 1861–1865* (Norman, OK: University of Oklahoma Press, 2012), 162–3.

24 Coddington, *The Gettysburg Campaign*, 70–1; Judson, *History of the Eighty-Third*, 63; Nash, *History of the Forty-Fourth*, 136; Judson, *History of the Eighty-Third*, 63; Spear, *Civil War Recollections*, 212; Ibid., 309; Crawford, *The 16th Michigan*, 326.

25 Nash, *History of the Forty-Fourth New York*, 136; Strong Vincent, "Report of Col. Strong Vincent, Eighty-third Pennsylvania Infantry, commanding Third Brigade," in *The War of the Rebellion: A Compilation of the Official Records of the Union and Confederate Armies* (Washington: Government Printing Office, 1889), Vol. 27, Part 1, 613–14.

26 Ibid.; Edward G. Longacre, *Lee's Cavalrymen: A History of the Mounted Forces of the Army of Northern Virginia, 1861–1865* (Norman, OK: University of Oklahoma Press, 2012), 201–2; Longacre, *Lincoln's Cavalrymen: A History of the Mounted Forces of the Army of the Potomac, 1861–1865* (Norman, OK: University of Oklahoma Press, 2012), 170–2.

27 Vincent, "Report ...", 614; Crawford, *The 16th Michigan*, 328–9; Judson, *History of the Eighty-Third*, 64.

28 David M. Gregg, "Reports of Brig. Gen. David McM. Gregg, U.S. Army, commanding Second Division, in *The War of the Rebellion: A Compilation of the Official Records of the Union and Confederate Armies* (Washington: Government Printing Office, 1889), Vol. 27, Part 1, 954; Vincent, "Report ...", 614.

29 Ibid.; L. A. Hendricks, "Mr. L. A. Hendricks's Letters," *New York Daily Herald* (New York, NY), June 26, 1863; John Robertson, *Michigan in the War* (Lansing, MI: W. S. George & Co. State Printers and Binders, 1882), 365.

30 Judson, *History of the Eighty-Third*, 64; Vincent, "Report ...", 615; Judson, *History of the Eighty-Third*, 64.

31 Larry Tagg, *The Generals of Gettysburg: The Leaders of America's Greatest Battle* (Cambridge, MA: Da Capo, 2003), 90; Nevins and Styple, *What Death More Glorious*, 64; Judson, *History of the Eighty-Third*, 64; Nash, *History of the Forty-Fourth New York*, 137.

32 Judson, *History of the Eighty-Third*, 65.

33 Joseph Hooker, Joseph Hooker to Major-General Halleck, June 27, 1863, in *The War of the Rebellion: A Compilation of the Official Records of the Union and Confederate Armies* (Washington: Government Printing Office, 1889), Vol. 27, Part 1, 60; Joseph Hooker, Joseph Hooker to Major-General Halleck, June 27, 1863–1 p.m., in *The War of the Rebellion: A Compilation of the Official Records of the Union and Confederate Armies* (Washington: Government Printing Office, 1889), Vol. 27, Part 1, 60.

34 Henry W. Halleck, Henry Halleck to Joseph Hooker, June 27, 1863–8 p.m. in *The War of the Rebellion: A Compilation of the Official Records of the Union and Confederate Armies* (Washington: Government Printing Office, 1889), Vol. 27, Part 1, 60; Wert, *Sword of Lincoln*, 266.
35 Ibid., 257; Coddington, *The Gettysburg Campaign*, 37; Ibid.
36 Wert, *Sword of* Lincoln, 266–7; General Orders No. 194, in *The War of the Rebellion: A Compilation of the Official Records of the Union and Confederate Armies* (Washington: Government Printing Office, 1889), Vol. 27, Part 3, 396; Henry W. Halleck, Henry Halleck to George G. Meade, June 27, 1863, in *The War of the Rebellion: A Compilation of the Official Records of the Union and Confederate Armies* (Washington: Government Printing Office, 1889), Vol. 27, Part 1, 61.
37 George G. Meade, George Meade to Mrs. George Meade, June 25, 1863, in *The Life and Letters of General Meade*, 1:388.
38 Judson, *History of the Eighty-Third*, 65; Nash, *History of the Forty-Fourth*, 140; George G. Meade, George Meade to Henry W. Halleck, June 28, 1863, in *The War of the Rebellion: A Compilation of the Official Records of the Union and Confederate Armies* (Washington: Government Printing Office, 1889), Vol. 27, Part 1, 61; Strong Vincent, Strong Vincent to Elizabeth Vincent, June 30, 1863, in *What Death More Glorious*, 65.

8. March to Mortality: July 1, 1863

1 Anonymous, "Yankee Doodle," in Kate van Winkle Keller, "What are the Real Words to 'Yankee Doodle?,'" Colonial Music Institute, Center for Digital History, Washington Library, George Washington's Mount Vernon, December, 2001.
2 Coddington, *The Gettysburg Campaign*, 232–3; John Buford, John Buford to John Reynolds, June 30, 1863, 10:30 p.m. in *The War of the Rebellion: A Compilation of the Official Records of the Union and Confederate Armies* (Washington: Government Printing Office, 1889), Vol. 27, Part 1, 923; John Buford, John Buford to Alfred Pleasonton, June 30, 1863–10:40 p.m., in *The War of the Rebellion: A Compilation of the Official Records of the Union and Confederate Armies* (Washington: Government Printing Office, 1889), Vol. 27, Part 1, 62.
3 Stephen W. Sears, *Gettysburg* (New York: Mariner, 2003), 162.
4 Ibid., 162–4; Coddington, *The Gettysburg Campaign*, 266.
5 Ibid., 267–9.
6 Ibid., 269–70; Sears, *Gettysburg*, 176–9; Rufus R. Dawes, "With the Sixth Wisconsin at Gettysburg," The Gettysburg Discussion Group, accessed November 13, 2020; J. David Petruzzi and Steven A. Stanley, *The Gettysburg Campaign in Numbers and Losses: Synopses, Orders of Battle, Strengths, Casualties, and Maps, June 9–July 14, 1863* (El Dorado Hills, CA: Savas Beatie, 2012), 101.
7 Coddington, *The Gettysburg Campaign*, 286–91.
8 Sears, *Gettysburg*, 212–17; Coddington, *The Gettysburg Campaign*, 291–7; Daniel Butterfield, Daniel Butterfield to Major-General Hancock, July 1, 1863–1:10 p.m. in *The War of the Rebellion: A Compilation of the Official Records of the Union and

Confederate Armies (Washington: Government Printing Office, 1889), Vol. 27, Part 3, 461.

9 Schellhammer, *The 83rd Pennsylvania*, 165–6; Judson, *The Eighty-Third*, 66; Nash, *History of the Forty-Fourth*, 141; Crawford, *The 16th Michigan*, 335.

10 Schellhammer, *The 83rd Pennsylvania*, 166.

11 Judson, *History of the Eighty-Third*, 66.

12 Norton, *Attack and Defense*, 285; Nash, *History of the Forty-Fourth*, 141.

9. The Lion of Round Top: July 2, 1863

1 Stephen Collins Foster, *Was My Brother in the Battle?* (New York: Horace Waters, 1862), M3.3.F7 W22 1862, The Library of Congress Celebrates the Songs of America, Library of Congress, Washington, D.C..

2 Judson, *History of the Eighty-Third*, 66; Nash, *History of the Forty-Fourth*, 141; Schellhammer, *The 83rd Pennsylvania*, 167; Nevins and Styple, *What Death More Glorious*, 68.

3 Coddington, *The Gettysburg Campaign*, 369–76; James Longstreet, "Lee's Right Wing at Gettysburg," in *Retreat from Gettysburg*, Battles and Leaders of the Civil War: Being for the Most Part Contributions by Union and Confederate Officers. eds. Robert U. Johnson and Clarence C. Buel (New York: Castle Books, 1956), 340; Karlton Smith, "How Not to Conduct a Reconnaissance: Capt. Samuel R. Johnston, July 2, 1863–Part 1," *From the Fields of Gettysburg: The Blog of Gettysburg National Military Park*, March 12, 2015, accessed November 13, 2020; Harry W. Pfanz, *Gettysburg–The Second Day* (Chapel Hill: The University of North Carolina Press, 1987) 106–112; Karlton D. Smith, "'To Consider Every Contingency:' Lt. Gen. James Longstreet, Capt. Samuel R. Johnston, and the factors that affected the reconnaissance and countermarch, July 2, 1863," (lecture, Gettysburg, PA, April 8, 2006), National Park Service History eLibrary, The Gettysburg Seminars; Longstreet, "Lee's Right," 340–1; Petruzzi and Stanley, *The Gettysburg Campaign*, 121–4.

4 Longstreet, "Lee's Right Wing at Gettysburg," 340; Pfanz, *Gettysburg–The Second Day*, 113–4; Longstreet, *From Manassas to Appomattox*, 365.

5 Pfanz, *Gettysburg–The Second Day*, 113–4; Ezra J. Warner, "John Bell Hood," in *Generals in Gray*, 142–3; Coddington, *The Gettysburg Campaign*, 376.

6 Pfanz, *Gettysburg–The Second Day*, 90–2; Huntington, *Searching for George Gordon Meade*, 161–2; Allen C. Guelzo, *Gettysburg: The Last Invasion* (New York: Alfred A. Knopf, 2013), 245–6.

7 Pfanz, *Gettysburg–The Second Day*, 93–7; Henry J. Hunt, "The Second Day at Gettysburg," in *Retreat from Gettysburg*, Battles and Leaders of the Civil War: Being for the Most Part Contributions by Union and Confederate Officers, eds. Robert U. Johnson and Clarence C. Buel (New York: Castle Books, 1956), 301–2.

8 Coddington, *The Gettysburg Campaign*, 353; Hiram Berdan, "Report of Col. Hiram Berdan, First U.S. Sharpshooters, commanding First and Second U.S. Sharpshooters," in *The War of the Rebellion: A Compilation of the Official Records of*

the Union and Confederate Armies (Washington: Government Printing Office, 1889), Vol. 27, Part 1, 514–16.

9 Coddington, *The Gettysburg Campaign,* 353; Pfanz, *Gettysburg–The Second Day,* 102–3; Sears, *Gettysburg*, 252.

10 Pfanz, *Gettysburg–The Second Day*, 119–21; Lafayette McLaws to Emily McLaws, July 7, 1863, in *The Civil War: The Third Year as Told by Those Who Lived It*, ed. Brooks D. Simpson (New York: The Library of America, 2013), 338; Pfanz, *Gettysburg–The Second Day*, 152.

11 John Bell Hood, *Advance and Retreat: Personal Experiences in the United States and Confederate States Armies* (Bloomington, IN: Indiana University Press, 1959), 57; Longstreet, *From Manassas to Appomattox,* 367; Hood, *Advance and Retreat,* 58–9.

12 Pfanz, *Gettysburg–The Second Day*, 150–2; Coddington, *The Gettysburg Campaign,* 386; Alexander, *Military Memoirs of a Confederate*, 393.

13 Sears, *Gettysburg*, 262–3.

14 Nevins and Styple, *What Death More Glorious*, 68; Bates, *History of Erie County*, 967.

15 Nelson Ames, *History of Battery G, First Regiment, New York Light Artillery* (Marshalltown, IA: Marshall Printing Company, 1900), 66; Hunt, "The Second Day at Gettysburg," 304–5; William Glenn Robertson, "The Peach Orchard Revisited: Daniel Sickles and the Third Corps on July 2, 1863," in *The Second Day at Gettysburg: Essays on Confederate and Union Leadership*, ed. Gary W. Gallagher (Kent, OH: Kent State University Press, 1993), 50; Pfanz, *Gettysburg–The Second Day,* 142–4; Gouverneur K. Warren, Gouverneur Warren to Captain Porter Farley, July 13, 1872, in *Attack and Defense of Little Round Top*, 309; Washington Roebling, *Wash Roebling's War: Being a Selection from the Unpublished Civil War Letters of Washington Augustus Roebling* (Newark, DE: The Spiral Press, 1961), 21.

16 Coddington, *The Gettysburg Campaign,* 388; Warren to Farley, July 13, 1872, in *Attack and Defense of Little Round Top,* 309; Pfanz, *Gettysburg–The Second Day,* 206; Ibid., 167.

17 Petruzzi and Stanley, *The Gettysburg Campaign*, 124; J. Gary Laine and Morris Penny, *Law's Alabama Brigade in the War Between the Union and the Confederacy* (Shippensburg, PA: White Mane Publishing, 1996), 82; Norton, *Attack and Defense of Little Round Top*, 263; United States Congress, *Report of the Joint Committee on the Conduct of the War at the Second Session, Thirty Eighth Congress* (Washington: Government Printing Office, 1865), 1:377; Norton, *Attack and Defense of Little Round Top*, 263; Chris Mackowski, Kristopher D. White, and Daniel T. Davis, *Don't Give an Inch: The Second Day at Gettysburg, July 2, 1863–From Little Round Top to Cemetery Ridge,* Emerging Civil War Series (El Dorado Hills, CA: Savas Beatie, 2016), 45; Pfanz, *Gettysburg–The Second Day*, 206; Bradley M. Gottfried, *Brigades of Gettysburg: The Union and Confederate Brigades at the Battle of Gettysburg* (New York: Skyhorse, 2012), 246.

18 Norton, *Attack and Defense of Little Round Top,* 264.

19 Charles King, Charles King to Oliver Norton, January 21, 1910, in *Army Letters*, 364.

20 Petruzzi and Stanley, *The Gettysburg Campaign*, 109; Régis de Trobriand, *Four Years with the Army of the Potomac,* trans. George K. Dauchy (Boston: Ticknor and Co., 1889), 497; Coddington, *The Gettysburg Campaign*, 414; Hood, *Advance and Retreat*, 59; Pfanz, *Gettysburg–The Second Day*, 334; Ibid., 173.

21 Laine and Penny, *Law's Alabama Brigade*, 87; William C. Oates, *The War Between the Union and the Confederacy and its Lost Opportunities; With a History of the 15th Alabama Regiment and the Forty-Eight Battles in which it was Engaged* (New York: Neale, 1905), 210; John W. Stevens, *Reminiscences of the Civil War: A Soldier in Hood's Texas Brigade, Army of Northern Virginia* (Hillsboro, TX: Hillsboro Mirror Print, 1902), 113; John Anderson, John Anderson to E. P. Anderson, in *Law's Alabama Brigade*, 87; Pfanz, *Gettysburg–The Second Day*, 193–4.

22 Oliver Norton, Oliver Norton to "Sister L.," July 21, 1863, in *Army Letters*, 167; Oliver Willcox Norton, *Strong Vincent and His Brigade at Gettysburg, July 2, 1863* (Chicago: Privately Printed, 1909), 7–8.

23 Ibid.; Norton, *Attack and Defense of Little Round Top*, 265; Joshua Lawrence Chamberlain, Joshua Chamberlain to George Herendeen, July 6, 1863, "Letter from Chamberlain–Gettysburg Battle Report" Letter. Chamberlain Correspondence. Maine State Archives. Augusta, ME; Pfanz, *Gettysburg – The Second Day*, 212.

24 Norval E. Welch, "Report of Lieut. Col. Norval E. Welch, Sixteenth Michigan Infantry," in *The War of the Rebellion: A Compilation of the Official Records of the Union and Confederate Armies* (Washington: Government Printing Office, 1889), Vol. 27, Part 1, 627–8; Freeman Conner, "Report of Lieut. Col. Freeman Conner, Forty-fourth New York Infantry," in *The War of the Rebellion: A Compilation of the Official Records of the Union and Confederate Armies* (Washington: Government Printing Office, 1889), Vol. 27, Part 1, 630–1; Orpheus S. Woodward, "Report of Capt. Orpheus S. Woodward, Eighty-third Pennsylvania Infantry," in *The War of the Rebellion: A Compilation of the Official Records of the Union and Confederate Armies* (Washington: Government Printing Office, 1889), Vol. 27, Part 1, 632; Nash, *History of the Forty-Fourth*, 144; Judson, *History of the Eighty-Third*, 67; Schellhammer, *The 83rd Pennsylvania*, 175; Thomas A. Desjardin, *Stand Firm Ye Boys from Maine: The 20th Maine and the Gettysburg Campaign* (Oxford: Oxford University Press, 2009), 44; Chamberlain to Herendeen, July 6, 1863; Nash, *History of the Forty-Fourth*, 144.

25 Oates, *The War Between the Union and the Confederacy,* 210; Homer Stoughton, "Report of Maj. Homer R. Stoughton, Second U.S. Sharpshooters," in *The War of the Rebellion: A Compilation of the Official Records of the Union and Confederate Armies* (Washington: Government Printing Office, 1889), Vol. 27, Part 1, 518–19; Oates, *The War Between the Union and the Confederacy,* 211; Pfanz, *Gettysburg–The Second Day*, 217.

26 Warren to Farley, July 13, 1872, in *Attack and Defense of Little Round Top*, 310; Pfanz, *Gettysburg–The Second Day*, 223; Guelzo, *Gettysburg*, 269–70; Gouverneur K. Warren, Gouverneur Warren to Captain Porter Farley, July 24, 1872, in *Attack and Defense of Little Round Top*, 311–12; Roebling, *Wash Roebling's War*, 22; A. P. Martin, "Little Round-Top: By A. P. Martin, Commanding Artillery Brigade, 5th Corps," *Fulton Democrat* (McConnelslburg, PA), September 20, 1900; Benjamin F. Rittenhouse, *The Battle of Gettysburg As Seen From Little Round Top: A Paper Read Before the District of Columbia Commandery of the Military Order of the Loyal Legion of the United States, May 4, 1887* (Washington: Judd & Detweiler, Printers, 1887), 5–6.
27 Pfanz, *Gettysburg–The Second Day*, 213–15; Judson, *History of the Eighty-Third*, 67; Crawford, *The 16th Michigan*, 349–50.
28 Glenn W. LaFantasie, *Twilight at Little Round Top: July 2, 1863–The Tide Turns at Gettysburg* (New York: Vintage, 2005), 115–29; Stevens, *Reminiscences*, 114; William A. Fletcher, *Rebel Private, Front and Rear: Experiences and Observations from the Early Fifties and Through the Civil War* (Beaumont, TX: The Greer Print, 1908), 74.
29 Judson, *History of the Eighty-Third*, 67.
30 Gouverneur Warren to Captain Porter Farley, July 13, 1872, in *Attack and Defense of Little Round Top*, 311; Ibid., 310; Pfanz, *Gettysburg–The Second Day*, 225.
31 Porter Farley, "Bloody Round Top: The Key to the Position at the Battle of Gettysburg," *The National Tribune*, May 3, 1883.
32 John P. Bane, "Report of Major John P. Bane, Fourth Texas Infantry," in *The War of the Rebellion: Being A Compilation of the Official Records of the Union and Confederate Armies* (Washington: Government Printing Office, 1889), Vol. 27, Part 2, 411; King Bryan, "Report of Lieut. Col. K. Bryan, Fifth Texas Infantry," in *The War of the Rebellion: Being A Compilation of the Official Records of the Union and Confederate Armies* (Washington: Government Printing Office, 1889), Vol. 27, Part 2, 412; Holman Melcher, Holman Melcher to Nathaniel Melcher, June 27, 1863, in *With a Flash of His Sword*, 35; Chamberlain to Herendeen, July 6, 1863.
33 Pfanz, *Gettysburg–The Second Day*, 169; Oates, *The War Between the Union and the Confederacy*, 214; Norton, *Attack and Defense of Little Round Top*, 259; Bane, "Report …", 411; Bryan, "Report …", 412; Lawrence Houston Scruggs, "Report of Lieut. Col. L. H. Scruggs, Fourth Alabama Infantry," in *The War of the Rebellion: Being a Compilation of the Official Records of the Union and Confederate Armies* (Washington: Government Printing Office, 1889), Vol. 27, Part 2, 391.
34 William H. Brown, "On Gettysburg Field: A View from Little Round Top During the Progress of the Battle," *The Philadelphia Weekly Times*, March 17, 1882; Welch, "Report …", 628; Conner, "Report …", 630; Oliver Norton, Oliver Norton to "Sister L.," July 21, 1863, in *Army Letters*, 167; R. M. Powell, "With Hood at Gettysburg," *The Philadelphia Weekly Times*, December 13, 1884; Stevens, *Reminiscences*, 114.
35 Judson, *History of the Eighty-Third*, 67; Philander Platt, "On Little Round Top: The Bitter, Obstinate, Victorious Struggle Made by Vincent's Brigade to Save Our

Left," *The National Tribune*, April 11, 1907; W. C. Ward, "Incidents and Personal Experiences on the Battlefield at Gettysburg," *Confederate Veteran* 8, No. 8 (August 1900), 347–8; Captain A. N. Husted, "Gettysburg in Perspective," in *A History of the Forty-Fourth Regiment, New York Volunteer Infantry, in the Civil War, 1861–1865*, ed. Eugene A. Nash (Chicago: R. R. Donnelly & Sons, 1911), 297–303; Judson, *History of the Eighty-Third*, 67.

36 Ellis Spear, "The Left at Gettysburg," *The National Tribune*, June 12, 1913; Chamberlain to Herendeen, July 6, 1863; Oates, *The War Between the Union and the Confederacy*, 214–17.

37 Chamberlain to Herendeen, July 6, 1863; Norton, *Attack and Defense of Little Round Top*, 268; John J. Pullen, *The Twentieth Maine: A Classic Story of Joshua Chamberlain and His Volunteer Regiment* (Mechanicsburg, PA: Stackpole, 2008), 123; Norton, *Attack and Defense of Little Round Top*, 269.

38 LaFantasie, *Twilight at Little Round Top*, 126; Welch, "Report …", 628; Norton, *Attack and Defense of Little Round Top*, 259; Oates, *The War Between the Union and the Confederacy*, 217; Scruggs, "Report …", 391; Oates, *The War Between the Union and the Confederacy*, 217–18.

39 Welch, "Report …", 628; Norton, *Attack and Defense of Little Round Top*, 271, parentheses in the original text; Norton, *Strong Vincent and His Brigade*, 9; Charles E. Sprague, Charles Sprague to Oliver Norton, January 16, 1910, in *Army Letters*, 363, parentheses in the original.

40 Ibid.; Nevins and Styple, *What Death More Glorious*, 54–5; LaFantasie, *Twilight on Little Round Top*, 144; Swan, "Strong Vincent," 78; John F. Vincent, John Vincent to D. McConaughy, Esq., November 30, 1863, in *What Death more Glorious*, 77; Boyd Vincent, *Our Family of Vincents*, 59; Judson, *History of the Eighty-Third*, 67.

41 Farley, "Bloody Round Top."

42 Pfanz, *Gettysburg–The Second Day*, 228; Farley, "Bloody Round Top."; Pfanz, *Gettysburg–The Second Day*, 229.

43 Oliver Norton, Oliver Norton to Bishop Boyd Vincent, August 3, 1914, in *Army Letters*, 386–7; James C. Rice, "Reports of Col. James C. Rice, Forty-fourth New York Infantry, commanding regiment and Third Brigade," in *The War of the Rebellion: Being a Compilation of the Official Records of the Union and Confederate Armies*, Vol. 27, Part 1, 617–18.

44 Laine and Penny, *Law's Alabama Brigade*, 101; James Sheffield, "Report of Col. James L. Sheffield, Forty-eighth Alabama Infantry," in *The War of the Rebellion: Being a Compilation of the Official Records of the Union and Confederate Armies*, Vol. 27, Part 2, 395–6; Bane, "Report …", 411; Bryan, "Report …", 412; Oates, *The War Between the Union and the Confederacy*, 218–21.

45 Coddington, *The Gettysburg Campaign*, 394; Chamberlain to Herendeen, July 6, 1863; Howard L. Prince, "Captain Howard L. Prince's Address" in *With a Flash of His Sword*, 115; Spear, *Civil War Recollections*, 314; Oates, *The War Between the Union and the Confederacy*, 219.

46 Chamberlain to Herendeen, July 6, 1863; Norton, *The Attack and Defense of Little Round Top*, 262; Crawford, *The 16th Michigan*, 352–4; Oates, *The War Between the Union and the Confederacy*, 219–20; Ibid., 222.
47 Pfanz, *Gettysburg–The Second Day*, 238; Ibid., 392–401; William C. Oates, William Oates to F. A. Dearborn, March 28, 1898, in Sears, *Gettysburg*, 297.
48 Gregory A. Coco, *A Vast Sea of Misery: A History and Guide to the Union and Confederate Field Hospitals at Gettysburg, July 1–November 20, 1863* (El Dorado Hills, CA: Savas Beatie, 2017), 68–70; Norton, *Attack and Defense of Little Round Top*, 244; Tillie Pierce Alleman, *At Gettysburg, or What a Girl Saw and Heard of the Battle: A True Narrative* (New York: W. Lake Borland, 1889); Norton, *Attack and Defense of Little Round Top*, 244–5.

10. The Road to Immortality: July 3 to July 7, 1863

1 Julia Ward Howe, *The Battle Hymn of the Republic* (Philadelphia: The Supervisory Committee for Recruiting Colored Regiments, 1863), 98101743, Rare Book and Special Collections Division, Library of Congress, Washington, D.C..
2 George G. Meade, George Meade to Henry W. Halleck, July 3, 1863, in *The War of the Rebellion: Being a Compilation of the Official Records of the Union and Confederate Armies*, Vol. 27, Part 1, 1041.
3 Nevins and Styple, *What Death More Glorious*, 80–1; Judson, *History of the Eighty-Third*, 71.
4 Ibid.; Nevins and Styple, *What Death More Glorious*, 78; Coco, *A Vast Sea of Misery*, 70–2.
5 Swan, "Strong Vincent," 80; Oliver Norton, Oliver Norton to Father, July 4, 1863, in *Army Letters*, 161.
6 Stonesifer, *Strong Vincent*, 8.
7 Judson, *History of the Eighty-Third*, 72; Swan, "Strong Vincent," 80.
8 Nevins and Styple, *What Death More Glorious*, 81; Swan, "Strong Vincent," 80; Judson, *History of the Eighty-Third*, 71–2.
9 Swan, "Strong Vincent," 80.
10 Ibid.; Judson, *History of the Eighty-Third*, 71; Ibid., 72.
11 Stonesifer, *Strong* Vincent, 8; Judson, *History of the Eighty-Third*, 72.

11. The Path to Being Forgotten: The Legacy of Strong Vincent

1 Jari Villanueva, "Lyrics or Words to Taps," The Taps Bugler: Jari Villanueva, Taps Historian and Professional Bugler, January 11, 2020, accessed November 14, 2020.
2 Judson, *History of the Eighty-Third*, 72; Oliver Norton, Oliver Norton to "Friends at Home," July 17, 1863, in *Army Letters*, 165; "Local Paragraphs," *The Erie Weekly Gazette* (Erie, PA), July 16, 1863.
3 "Our Wounded," *The Erie Weekly Gazette* (Erie, PA), July 9, 1863; "General Strong Vincent," *The Erie Weekly Gazette* (Erie, PA), July 16, 1863.
4 Ibid.

5 Ibid.

6 Ibid.

7 Ibid.

8 "The Late Gen. Vincent," *The Erie Observer* (Erie, PA), July 18, 1863.

9 L. C. B., "Don't Yield an Inch, Boys!," *The Erie Weekly Gazette*, July 23, 1863.

10 Boyd Vincent, *Our Family of Vincents*, 60; Nevins and Styple, *What Death More Glorious*, 86–7; Boyd Vincent, *Our Family of Vincents*, 60.

11 Gregory A. Coco, *A Strange and Blighted Land: Gettysburg–The Aftermath of a Battle* (El Dorado Hills, CA: Savas Beatie, 2017), 30–5.

12 Thomas Desjardin, *Joshua L. Chamberlain: A Life in Letters*, 202 n. 30; "The Camp on the Battle Field," *Harrisburg Daily Independent* (Harrisburg, PA), July 26, 1878; Oliver Norton, Oliver Norton to Boyd Vincent, August 3, 1914, in *Army Letters*, 386–7.

13 "A Brave Man in Moulded Clay," *The Boston Globe* (Boston, MA), July 31, 1888; "On Little Round Top," *The Evening Republican* (Meadville, PA), August 27, 1889; Boyd Vincent, *Our Family of Vincents*, 101–3.

14 Ellis Spear, Ellis Spear to Oliver Norton, July 5, 1913, in *Army Letters*, 380.

15 Ellis Spear, Ellis Spear to Oliver Norton, January 18, 1916, in *With a Flash of His Sword*, 297.

16 Norton, *Attack and Defense of Little Round Top,* 12; LaFantasie, "Joshua Chamberlain and the American Dream," 45–7.

17 Ellis Spear, Ellis Spear to Oliver Norton, February 1, 1916, in *With a Flash of His Sword*, 298–9; Ellis Spear, Ellis Spear to Oliver Norton, January 18, 1916, in *With a Flash of His Sword*, 298.

18 Fred S. Anderson, "Strong Vincent High School," in *A History of the School District of the City of Erie, PA., 1795–1970* (Erie, PA: The School District of the City of Erie, 1975), 109; *Program of Dedication: Strong Vincent High School, Erie, Pennsylvania, October 24, 1930.*

19 Joshua Lawrence Chamberlain, Joshua L. Chamberlain to Oliver W. Norton, January 15, 1910, in *Army Letters*, 363; Daniel Butterfield, Daniel Butterfield to Oliver Norton, February 19, 1901, in *Strong Vincent and His Brigade at Gettysburg* (Chicago: O. L. Deming, 1909), 55; Daniel Sickles, Daniel Sickles to Oliver Norton, November 21, 1901, in *Strong Vincent and His Brigade*, 55–6; Henry E. Tremain, Henry Tremain to Oliver Norton, November 23, 1901, in *Strong Vincent and His Brigade*, 56; James Longstreet, James Longstreet to Oliver Norton, December 6, 1901, in *Strong Vincent and His Brigade*, 57.

20 LaFantasie, "Joshua Chamberlain and the American Dream," 45–7; Ellis Spear, Ellis Spear to Oliver Norton, January 18, 1916, in *With a Flash of His Sword*, 298; Frank P. Varney, *General Grant and the Rewriting of History: How the Destruction of General William S. Rosecrans Influenced Our Understanding of the Civil War* (El Dorado Hills, CA: Savas Beatie, 2013), 269.

Appendix: The Origins of the "Chamberlain Myth"

1 Joshua Lawrence Chamberlain, *The Passing of the Armies: An Account of the Final Campaign of the Army of the Potomac, Based upon Personal Reminiscences of the Fifth Army Corps* (New York: G. P. Putnam's Sons, 1915), xi.
2 Varney, *General Grant and the Rewriting of History*, 269.
3 LaFantasie, "Joshua Chamberlain and the American Dream," 31; Alice Rains Trulock, *In the Hands of Providence: Joshua L. Chamberlain and the American Civil War* (Chapel Hill, NC: The University of North Carolina Press, 1992), 334, 363–5; Ibid., 373–4.
4 LaFantasie, "Joshua Chamberlain and the American Dream," 39–43.
5 Ellis Spear to Oliver Norton, January 18, 1916, in *With a Flash of His Sword*, 297.
6 Spear, *The Civil War Recollections of General Ellis Spear*, 3.
7 Desjardin, *These Honored Dead*, 130.
8 James Longstreet, "General James Longstreet's Account of the Campaign and Battle," *Southern Historical Society Papers* 5, no 1 (1878): 64.
9 William C. Oates, "Gettysburg—The Battle on the Right," *Southern Historical Society Papers* 6, no 1 (1878): 172–3; Ibid., 178; Petruzzi and Stanley, *The Gettysburg Campaign*, 124.
10 Oates, *The War Between the Union and the Confederacy*, 222.
11 Howard Prince, "Twentieth Maine Regiment" in *Maine at Gettysburg: Report of Maine Commissioners, Prepared by The Executive Committee,* ed. Charles Hamlin, Greenlief T. Stevens and George W. Verrill (Portland, ME: Lakeside Press, 1898), 255–6; Petruzzi and Stanley, *The Gettysburg Campaign*, 109; Oates, *The War Between the Union and the Confederacy*, 222.
12 Pullen quoted in Desjardin, *These Honored Dead*, 134.
13 Desjardin, *Stand Firm Ye Boys from Maine*, 127; Gerrish, *Army Life*, 108–11.
14 James Nichols, *Lincoln County News*, April 1882; Joshua Chamberlain to Theodore Gerrish, circa 1882 "*Letter from Chamberlain to Rev. Theodore Gerrish Regarding His Recollection of Gettysburg, circa 1882*" Letter. Maine State Archives, *Joshua L. Chamberlain Correspondence.*
15 Joshua Chamberlain to Lieutenant George Herendeen, July 6, 1863, in *Through Blood & Fire: Selected Civil War Papers of Major General Joshua Chamberlain*, ed. Mark Nesbitt (Mechanicsburg, PA: Stackpole Books, 1996), 87; Joshua Chamberlain to Fanny Chamberlain, July 18, 1863; in *Joshua L. Chamberlain: A Life in Letters*, 202; Joshua Chamberlain to James Barnes, July 6, 1863, in *Joshua Chamberlain: A Life in Letters*, 201; Ibid., 202 *n. 30.*
16 Joshua L. Chamberlain, "Report of Col. Joshua L. Chamberlain, Twentieth Maine Infantry," in *The War of the Rebellion: A Compilation of the Official Records of the Union and Confederate Armies* (Washington: Government Printing Office, 1889), Vol. 27, Part 1, 626; Desjardin, *These Honored Dead*, 139.
17 Ibid., 139–40.

18 Joshua Chamberlain to George Herendeen, July 6, 1863 *"Letter from Chamberlain–Gettysburg battle report"* Letter. From Maine State Archives, *Joshua L. Chamberlain Correspondence.*

19 LaFantasie, "Joshua Chamberlain and the American Dream," 42–3.

20 Ibid., 45–7.

21 Joshua Chamberlain to "Mrs. Eckstrom," May 28, 1913, Folger Library Special Collections, University of Maine, *Chamberlain Family Papers*; Joshua Chamberlain to Elliot Dill, June 12, 1913, Maine State Archives, *Records of the Adjutant General of Maine.*

22 John J. Pullen, *Joshua Chamberlain: A Hero's Life and Legacy* (Mechanicsburg, PA: Stackpole Books, 1999), 169.

23 Ibid., 170.

Index